Strategies for Struggling Learners

In the Era of CCSS & RTI

by
Jim Wright

DUDE PUBLISHING
A Division of
National Professional Resources, Inc.
www.NPRinc.com

Printed in the United States of America

ISBN 978-1-935609-91-9

PUBLISHING
A Division of:
National Professional Resources, Inc.
Corporate: Katonah, NY
Operations: Naples, FL

For information:
National Professional Resources, Inc.
1455 Rail Head Blvd., Suite 6
Naples, FL 34110
www.NPRinc.com
Toll Free: (800) 453-7461

Cover Design/Editorial Production: Andrea Cerone
Acquisitions Editor: Helene M. Hanson

Contents

Preface

The novelist John Steinbeck once said, "I have come to believe that a great teacher is a great artist and that there are as few as there are any other great artists. Teaching might even be the greatest of the arts since the medium is the human mind and spirit." Steinbeck's quote illustrates one side of an intense debate now unfolding in public education: Is teaching an art or science (Green, 2010). To state the point another way, are teachers born with mysterious qualities that make them gifted educators or is there an accessible science of teaching that anyone can learn?

Some will argue that this debate was resolved long ago in favor of teaching as a science. After all, there are over 1,100 teacher training programs in the United States that collectively have trained virtually all teachers presently employed as educators (Greenberg, McKee & Walsh, 2013). It's logical to assume that these graduate programs immerse aspiring teachers in a rigorous curriculum of research-derived practices of instruction and behavior management. However, evidence suggests that the great majority of educator training programs actually fail to train teachers in effective instructional methods (Greenberg, McKee, & Walsh, 2013) or behavior management (Greenberg, Putman, & Walsh, 2014). Further complicating our ability to judge training programs is the fact that there is little agreement among experts about how to measure the effectiveness of teachers. Traditional measures of professional quality, such as college coursework or teaching credentials, are found to be poor predictors of teacher effectiveness (McCaffrey, Lockwood, Koretz, & Hamilton, 2003).

The debate about whether teaching is an art or a science is more than an intellectual exercise: it comes with high stakes for practicing teachers. If one believes that teaching is an art, it follows that teachers who fail to rapidly produce strong academic gains must lack the requisite innate gifts of great teachers and should be quickly weeded out. If, however, one instead accepts that teaching is a replicable science, then underperforming but promising teachers can be given time and training to allow them to weave research-based methods of instruction and behavior management into their teaching routine.

This book embraces the view that teaching is a well-defined science, and that any teacher who carefully reviews and implements best practices in core instruction, academic intervention, behavior management, and classroom assessment can expect to see substantial gains in student performance. This view is inherently optimistic, because it assumes that teachers are not passive or helpless when presented with underperforming students--but rather, that they can respond actively to achieve positive outcomes. The conviction that there is a science to effective teaching also comes with a caution: changing one's professional practice is very hard work and requires a great deal of energy and commitment!

Because educators who regard teaching as a science possess a bias toward organized action, they have an obvious advantage when confronting several recent, looming developments in education: the Common Core State Standards (CCSS), Response To Intervention (RTI), new "value-added" models of teacher accountability, and a substantial downsizing of school resources.

- *Roll-out of the Common Core.* Academic expectations for students are increasing. In recent years, the great majority of states have adopted the Common Core State Standards in English Language Arts and Mathematics, creating uniform expectations for student learning across most of the country. For many states, these ambitious new standards highlight the starkly large number of students who lack the foundation skills required for academic success.

- *Implementation of RTI.* Many states have mandated that schools put into place a comprehensive, multi-tiered model to support at-risk students. This model, Response To Intervention, includes the expectation that teachers develop expertise in intervention-planning and formative assessment to allow them to serve as classroom "first responders" when students display emerging academic or behavioral problems (Wright, 2007).

- *Adoption of Value-Added Teacher Evaluation.* Coinciding with the introduction of the Common Core, there is a strong push among states to base teacher-effectiveness ratings on "value-added" assessment models that analyze student achievement data to discern the instructional impact ('added value') of individual teachers (McCaffrey, Lockwood, Koretz, & Hamilton, 2003). In many states, teachers whose students fail to show evidence of adequate academic growth across several successive years can lose their jobs.

- *Reductions in School Resources.* While the Common Core Standards and "value-added" teacher evaluations ramp up the pressure on educators to demonstrate effectiveness, there is yet another pernicious factor working against schools. Beginning with the Great Recession of 2007, school districts across the country were forced to make drastic budget cuts that resulted in reduced staffing levels and increased class size (Dillon, 2011). Although that recession has ended, many districts have not been able to fully restore those cuts and they continue to grapple with staffing shortfalls and larger classes (Rich, 2013). So even as the new standards raise expectations for student performance and teacher accountability, teachers are left with fewer resources in their schools to help struggling students close academic skill and performance gaps.

It is understandable that teachers may respond with dismay to this perfect storm of ambitious new academic standards, implementation of classroom interventions under Response to Intervention, increased teacher accountability for student performance, and cuts in resources to assist struggling learners. However, the teacher who attempts to solve any classroom problem by first asking, "What research-based idea(s) can help me fix that problem?" is more likely to be successful and in alignment with these new school initiatives than the one who sits passively on the sidelines. This book provides the guidance for engaged teachers who are ready to roll up their sleeves, become problem solvers, and discover classroom-based solutions.

What This Book Is—and What It Is Not

This book is designed as a convenient problem-solving manual that any teacher can use to quickly locate research-supported ideas for student instruction, academic and behavioral intervention, and assessment. The information contained is specifically tailored to match the needs of students with skills gaps and/or challenging behaviors that interfere with attaining success on the Common Core Standards. Substantial content included in this book first appeared on the author's website, Intervention Central (http://www.interventioncentral.org).

The formatting of the chapters reflects the practical focus of the book. Chapters 2 through 7 open with a brief overview of a topic, such as academic intervention or student assessment. The remainder of the chapter is made up of one or more "how-to" resources that link to the chapter's theme, but can also be used as stand-alone teacher resources. The structure of the book makes it equally useful to both the teacher who wishes to work sequentially through each chapter and the one who chooses to use the book as an instructional or behavior first-aid manual, accessing specific sections for answers to specific questions. The book also contains an extensive set of citations documenting the research literature consulted in preparing each of the chapters. These citations are included because many schools require that teachers be able to demonstrate that their instructional and intervention practices are research-based.

This book does *not* provide a systematic review of the Common Core State Standards for ELA or Math nor does it offer specific prescriptions for teaching each standard. While specific standards are referenced for the purpose of illustration at various points, this book is intended for use by teachers who wish to rapidly identify and fix impediments to student success with the Common Core.

Who Can Use This Book

Although primarily intended for use by teachers as a toolkit for revamping instruction and behavior management in the classroom, it has broader application for an entire school or district, or as a text for pre-service and in-service teacher-training/professional development.

- *Teachers* can use the information in this book to find research-based strategies for strengthening instruction, delivering academic interventions, and addressing behavior management issues for both general and special education students. Even teachers who find themselves in the unfortunate position of having to work in professional isolation—receiving little support from colleagues or administration—will discover ideas here that can substantially improve outcomes for their students.

- *Principals* can use this book as a guide to implementing effective school-wide instructional and behavior-management practices. A synchronized approach in which teachers throughout a school adopt a uniform set of best practices can greatly amplify positive student outcomes. Building administrators can also use this book as a road map for building teacher capacity to provide Tier 1 (classroom) interventions under RTI.

- *District administrators* can utilize this book as a standard toolkit to help teachers find strategies to assist students who are struggling with meeting the ambitious Common Core State Standards. This book also can also serve as the foundation for a district-wide definition of how RTI Tier 1 (classroom) interventions should be carried out.

- *Instructors in teacher-training programs* can assign this book as a course text for graduate students to consult as they work with struggling children in school settings. Encouraging educators-in-training to access this compendium of recommended practices addresses a common criticism of teacher-certification programs: that they often fail to teach a consistent set of empirically valid instructional and behavior management practices.

Schools are entering an unprecedented time in education, one in which teachers are held increasingly accountable for their skill in helping students with diverse needs to attain highly ambitious standards. This book is intended to give teachers the tools necessary to identify and overcome the many possible roadblocks to student success.

References

Dillon, S. (2011, March 6). Tight budgets mean squeeze in classrooms. *The New York Times,* p. A1. Retrieved from http://www.nytimes.com/2011/03/07/education/07classrooms.html

Green, E. (2010, March 2). Building a better teacher. *The New York Times.* Retrieved from http://www.nytimes.com/2010/03/07/magazine/07Teachers-t.html

Greenberg, J., McKee, A., & Walsh, K. (2013). *Teacher prep review: A review of the nation's teacher preparation programs.* National Council on Teacher Quality. Retrieved from http://www.nctq.org/dmsView/Teacher_Prep_Review_2013_Report

Greenberg, J., Putman, H., & Walsh, K. (2014). *Training our future teachers: Classroom management.* National Council on Teacher Quality. Retrieved from http://www.nctq.org/dmsView/Future_Teachers_Classroom_Management_NCTQ_Report

McCaffrey, D. F., Lockwood, J. R., Koretz, D. M., & Hamilton, L. S. (2003). *Evaluating value-added models for teacher accountability.* RAND Corporation: Santa Monica, CA. Retrieved from http://www.rand.org

Rich, M. (2013, December 21). Subtract teachers, add pupils: Math of today's jammed schools. *The New York Times,* p. A1. Retrieved from http://www.nytimes.com/2013/12/22/education/subtract-teachers-add-pupils-math-of-todays-jammed-schools.html

Wright, J. (2007). *RTI toolkit: A practical guide for schools.* Port Chester, NY: Dude Publishing, Inc.

Chapter 1

Finding the Right Tools to Help Struggling Learners in the Age of the Common Core

Teaching may well be the most important profession in America. On an average school day, 55 million elementary and secondary students attend our nation's public and private schools (Hussar & Bailey, 2013). Teachers in countless classrooms strive to engage these children and teach them the academic and social skills needed to attain their life goals and be successful citizens. Given the great responsibility and trust placed in educators, one can appreciate the comment of prominent business leader Lee Iacocca: "In a completely rational society, the best of us would be teachers and the rest of us would have to settle for something less."

The reality in American schools, though, is that teachers are not always successful in helping students acquire strong academic skills. The United States is among the top countries in the world in spending on education (OECD, 2012). Yet, statistics from the U.S. Department of Education in 2011 show that about half of students in grades 4 and 8 were less than proficient in reading and math, while more than three-quarters of 8th-grade students failed to reach proficiency in writing (National Center for Education Statistics, 2011a, 2011b, 2012). Furthermore, although national graduation rates have improved in recent years, more than 1 out of 5 students still fail to complete high school (Stillwell & Sable, 2013).

The persistence of academic underperformance in American schools despite high levels of educational spending has subjected public education to closer scrutiny. As one reaction, critics of school performance have focused on the quality of teacher training. Researchers have discovered that there is little if any correlation between teacher effectiveness and teacher certification (e.g., Kane, Rockoff, & Staiger, 2006)—a surprising finding that suggests that teacher training programs exert at best only a slight influence on the quality of teaching staff. According to Pianta (2011), the most likely explanation for the lack of effectiveness of many college teacher-preparation programs is simply that they fail to train educators in research-based classroom academic and behavioral strategies.

The good news, however, is that two important recent trends in the field of education show real promise in providing schools with a roadmap to more effectively educate struggling students. First, a majority of states have chosen to adopt the Common Core State Standards. This development has prompted school districts across the nation to replace the patchwork quilt of differing state educational standards with a uniform set of ambitious student reading and math goals. And, indeed, the Common Core offers signal advantages for schools. To begin with, its academic standards align closely with demanding international standards, particularly in mathematics (Schmidt, & Houang, 2012). And with the majority of states having fully adopted these standards at this writing, the Common Core has the potential to become a de facto national set of academic expectations, creating powerful economies of scale that should eventually allow participating states to pool training, assessment, and intervention resources and to make those resources available at minimal cost to any Common Core school. But there is an obvious limitation to the Common Core as well. Its developers explicitly state that the standards are not intended to provide guidance to the teacher on how to help students with particular at-risk profiles (e.g., English Language Learners, special-needs students) to succeed academically (National Governors Association, 2010a, 2010b).

A second national development transforming many of our nation's schools—and one that complements the Common Core—is Response To Intervention (RTI). RTI is a comprehensive model for systems-level change in which schools identify students at risk for academic or behavioral problems and uses that information to organize its scarce intervention resources into ascending levels of intervention support so that struggling students can be matched to the appropriate amount of intervention help (Burns & Gibbons, 2008). The greatest impact of RTI, however, is in the general-education classroom; a technology has emerged that provides teachers with a step-by-step guide to create and implement classroom behavioral and academic intervention plans. In fact, there is consensus throughout much of the research community that teachers who reliably follow these five problem-solving steps will have the tools most likely to benefit any at-risk student (Wright, 2007):

1. Describe the student problem in clear, explicit terms;
2. Match the student to research-based academic or behavioral intervention strategies that logically address the identified problem(s);
3. Set a specific outcome goal that defines student success;
4. Regularly track student progress during the intervention;
5. Adjust or change the intervention in response to the data collected.

These steps add up to a simple 'technology of intervention' that any teacher can learn. And because the elements of this individualized problem-solving approach have been validated through decades of research, they are almost certain to remain standard operating procedure for classroom interventions for the foreseeable future.

About This Book: Improving the Self-Organizing Classroom

Because the Common Core Standards prod schools to set ambitious academic goals and RTI provides a technology to remediate the skill deficits of at-risk students so that they can reach those standards, the primary focus of both initiatives is the general-education classroom. The typical classroom can be best understood as a complex, self-organizing system. The various solutions that a teacher selects to manage instruction, behaviors, personal connections with students, record-keeping, and the myriad additional challenges of a busy educational environment will themselves interact to create a dynamic 'system.' Well-chosen educational solutions will organize into a well-run classroom. However, a teacher who chooses methods of instruction or behavior management on a haphazard or ad hoc basis may discover too late that the larger classroom system arising out of those approaches is underperforming or even dysfunctional.

This book takes an optimistic view of classroom change, one consistent with the promise of both the Common Core and RTI. It embraces the belief that teaching is a science, one that can be taught and one that can be mastered by any educator willing to make the effort. The well-managed classroom whose students are academically engaged and well-behaved is not a fluke or rare occurrence—but is rather a predictable product of a teacher's adopting a set of basic research-based components of instruction and behavior management. As these components are put into place, they provide the teacher with increasing classroom order and control. The good news is that the results are synergistic: that is, the adoption of these academic and behavioral components as a single package can have a positive impact on student learning and conduct that far exceeds the sum of that package's parts. Here are several examples of how a teacher's adoption of research-based practices can have positive classroom ripple effects:

- Ms. Sampson, 6th-grade instructor, reviews the three components of the learn-unit (chapter 2): (1) academic opportunity to respond, (2) active student responding, (3) performance feedback. She realizes that the homework that she has routinely been assigning falls short of the expectations of the learn-unit: it is often 'busy work' that fails to engage, while the students frequently do not receive feedback once the homework is collected. So she revamps her homework, giving shorter and more engaging assignments, and providing students with immediate feedback through group correction and review on the day homework is turned in. Homework completion and quality improve (along with student motivation) as a result of the changes.

- Ms. Trifanov, a 3rd-grade teacher, begins the use the Color Wheel (chapter 4) to train students to follow different rule-sets for different activities: collaborative learning or free time, large-group instruction or seatwork, and transitions between activities. She finds with the Color Wheel that she has more teaching time. As her students rapidly learn the new system, they require fewer teacher behavior reminders and warnings, and transition quickly from one activity to another.

- Mr. Habon, a 5th-grade science teacher, creates a short list of instructional adjustments (chapter 3) that students can choose to take advantage of when completing independent seatwork: (1) decide the sequence of tasks to complete, (2) approach a peer for help as needed, (3) move to a low-distraction work area. He observes that rates of student academic engagement increase and that behavior problems decrease noticeably with the addition of these modest instructional adjustments.

This book is intended for the classroom teacher as a 'how-to' guide in the use of those components that research shows promote harmonious learning environments and improved student academic performance. The expectation is that, as teachers incorporate these components into their daily routine, their learning environments will 'self-organize' to be more conducive to learning. This book is also designed to be used in a wide variety of settings. For example, teachers will find the ideas presented here to be quite useful if they work in a school that has cut educational resources to the bone and has no process in place to identify and provide support to struggling students. Those teachers can simply close the classroom door and put these ideas into practice. Yet teachers can also benefit from this book if they are lucky enough to teach in a school that has organized its resources efficiently and built a referral process to find and help underperforming students. In either the strong- or weak-school scenario, the teacher is still the 'first responder' for students who are not successful, and this book provides the tools that any first-responder will need to find and fix academic and behavioral problems.

The book is organized into chapters that correspond to teacher challenges. The chapters can be thought of as comprising an interlocking system, with the content of each supporting ideas and strategies contained elsewhere in the book. A quick overview of the contents follows:

- **Chapter 2: Establishing Strong Core Instruction & Behavior Management—Foundations for Student Success.** The teacher's effective and efficient management of whole-group instruction and behaviors is the foundation for classroom success. This section reviews best practices for setting up a productive, well-managed instructional environment. Checklists are provided for the teacher to verify that the essential elements of instruction and behavior management are in place.

- **Chapter 3: Creating Academic Interventions That Promote Student Success in the Common Core.** When students begin to struggle with academics, the teacher requires ready access to the tools needed to match them to appropriate interventions and related supports. This section defines 'academic intervention' and related terms, provides guidelines for selecting 'instructional adjustments' (accommodations) for struggling learners, and offers advice on how to document use of interventions with individual students. Also provided are selected intervention ideas for reading, writing, mathematics, and spelling problems.

- **Chapter 4: Managing Behaviors to Promote Student Learning.** Students who display disruptive behaviors can quickly derail instruction. This section provides a brief refresher on 'big ideas' in effective behavior management and 'how to' advice on managing groups of students, using praise to motivate learners, setting up a classroom disciplinary continuum to increase teacher authority, and defusing tense situations with students who are emotionally upset.

- **Chapter 5: Collecting Data to Track Interventions —General Classroom Measures.** Teachers carry out 'on-the-spot' assessments of academic or behavioral targets to monitor whether particular students on intervention are making appropriate progress. This section provides a listing of common classroom assessments and corresponding student problems that they can monitor, a 3-part organizer for setting up classroom data collection ('baseline', 'goal', 'progress-monitoring'), and sample data collection forms.

- **Chapter 6: Collecting Data to Track Interventions— Curriculum-Based Measures.** Curriculum-based measurements (CBMs) are brief, timed measures of basic academic skills that teachers can use to track student reading, math, and writing interventions. This section gives an overview of CBM and provides research norms for 6 different types of CBM measures that instructors can use formatively to monitor student academic growth.

- **Chapter 7: Increasing Student Responsibility Through Self-Management.** As students advance through the grades, an increasing focus is placed on training them to be self-managing, self-advocating learners. This section offers teachers a structured format for conducting student (or student-parent) conferences that places student responsibility at the center of the process. Additionally, instructors will find here a format to train students to create and evaluate their own academic work plans.

- **Chapter 8: Using Techniques to Help Teachers to Succeed as Change-Agents.** A necessary prerequisite to improving students' academic skills or classroom behavior is that teachers first alter their own behavior to foster those positive student changes. After all, 'student intervention' is just another way of stating that the instructor will take an active role in teaching, intervening, observing, measuring, coaching, or otherwise engaging in professional behaviors intended to improve that student's status quo. This section provides research-supported strategies that educators can use to become their own 'behavioral engineers'—helping them to forge new professional habits that will lead to student improvements

References

Burns, M. K., & Gibbons, K. A. (2008). *Implementing response-to-intervention in elementary and secondary schools.* Routledge: New York.

Hussar, W.J., & Bailey, T.M. (2013). *Projections of education statistics to 2021* (NCES 2013-008). U.S. Department of Education, National Center for Education Statistics. Washington, DC: U.S. Government Printing Office.

Kane, T. J., Rockoff, J. E., & Staiger, D. O. (2006). *What does certification tell us about teacher effectiveness? Evidence from New York City.* Cambridge, MA: National Bureau of Economic Research. Retrieved from http://www.nber.org/papers/w12155

National Center for Education Statistics. (2011a). *The nation's report card: Mathematics 2011*(NCES 2012–458). Institute of Education Sciences, U.S. Department of Education, Washington, D.C.

National Center for Education Statistics. (2011b). *The nation's report card: Reading 2011*(NCES 2012–457). Institute of Education Sciences, U.S. Department of Education, Washington, D.C.

National Center for Education Statistics. (2012). *The nation's report card: Writing* 2011 (NCES 2012–470). Institute of Education Sciences, U.S. Department of Education, Washington, D.C.

National Governors Association Center for Best Practices & Council of Chief State School Officers. (2010a). *Common core state standards for English language arts and literacy in history/social studies, science, and technical subjects.* Washington, DC: Authors.

National Governors Association Center for Best Practices & Council of Chief State School Officers. (2010b). *Common core state standards for mathematics.* Washington, DC: Authors.

OECD-Organization for Economic Co-operation and Development. (2012). Education at a glace: OCED Indicators 2012: United States. Retrieved from Retrieved from http://www.oecd.org/

Pianta, R. C. (2011). *Teaching children well: New evidence-based approaches to teacher professional development.* Center for American Progress. Retrieved from http://www.american progress.org/

Schmidt, W. H., & Houang, R.T. (2012). Curricular coherence and the common core state standards for mathematics. *Educational Researcher,* 41, 294-308.

Stillwell, R., & Sable, J. (2013). *Public school graduates and dropouts from the common core of data: School year 2009–10: First look (provisional data)* (NCES 2013-09rev). U.S. Department of Education. Washington, DC: National Center for Education Statistics. Retrieved from http://nces. ed.gov/pubsearch

Wright, J. (2007). *RTI toolkit: A practical guide for schools.* Port Chester, NY: National Professional Resources, Inc.

Chapter 2

Core Instruction & Behavior Management: Foundations for Student Success

Classrooms are layered and dynamic settings. A typical elementary classroom, for example, has 20 or more students (Dillon, 2011) with variable academic skills and behaviors. At any given time, an exponentially large number of interactions are occurring in this instructional environment, as the teacher delivers instruction, students engage in academic work, students communicate with one another and the teacher, and so on. The shifting nature and sheer complexity of group instruction has prompted some researchers to characterize the setting as a 'classroom ecology' (Muyskens & Ysseldyke,1998). The teacher is charged with planning and delivering academic lessons in this ecological niche, as well as managing the often unpredictable behaviors of multiple students.

Recognizing that good instruction can take different forms, the developers of the Common Core State Standards have declined to endorse any specific approach to teaching. They state that, "the Standards define what all students are expected to know and be able to do, not how teachers should teach" (National Governors Association, 2010; p. 6). Nonetheless, current research suggests that specific direct-instruction and positive behavior-management techniques can be identified that form a paradigm of strong instruction and should be part of every teacher's repertoire (Burns, VanDerHeyden, & Boice, 2008; Simonsen, Fairbanks, Briesch, Myers, & Sugai, 2008).

Educators may have many ideas for measuring the 'health' of a classroom and its instructional and behavioral regimens. However, a direct and useful means to judge whether an educational setting is conducive to learning is simply to track *academic learning time* (ALT)—that time during instruction when students are "actively and productively engaged in learning" (Gettinger & Seibert, 2002, p. 774). Advantages of academic learning time as a measure of active learning are that it is easily observed (students can be seen engaged in assigned learning tasks) and it correlates highly with formal measures of student academic performance. Additionally, a benefit of ALT is that it is exquisitely sensitive to both instructional and behavior-management strategies. In other words, academic learning time is highest in those classrooms with highly organized and well-paced instruction, brief transitions between activities, and behavior management powered by positive, rather than punitive, techniques.

Roadmap to This Chapter

This chapter supplies teachers with resources for delivering direct instruction and using positive behavior-management techniques to promote active student engagement and increased academic learning time. Direct instruction (also known as explicit or supported instruction) is a framework for teaching large and small groups; it ensures a good instructional match between student and academic material, and uses modeling, demonstration, and supervised student practice. It also provides timely performance feedback (Burns, VanDerHeyden, & Boice, 2008; Rosenshine, 2008). Positive behavior management is characterized by pre-teaching of student behavioral expectations and use of proactive strategies to identify and defuse behavior problems before they derail instruction (Simonsen, Fairbanks, Briesch, Myers, & Sugai, 2008).

The remainder of this chapter lays out the direct-instruction and behavior-management elements that serve as the foundation of the well-run classroom. Included are these resources:

• *How To: Deliver Direct Instruction in General-Education Classrooms.* This checklist includes elements of direct instruction useful for increasing access to instruction, providing scaffolding support, giving timely performance feedback, and providing opportunities for review and practice.

- *How To: Structure Effective Instruction: The Learn Unit.* Good instruction has these 3 elements: (1) academic opportunity to respond, (2) active student responding, and (3) performance feedback. This resource describes the 3-step learn unit and supplies examples to illustrate.

- *How To: Choose the Right Amount of Daily Homework.* As students move into higher grades, teachers often give increasing amounts of homework. This resource provides information about how much daily homework to assign by grade level.

- *How To: Implement Critical Elements of Strong Core Classroom Behavior Management.* The teacher can use this quick checklist to verify that crucial behavior management components are in place to positively shape student behaviors.

References

Burns, M. K., VanDerHeyden, A. M., & Boice, C. H. (2008). Best practices in intensive academic interventions. In A. Thomas & J. Grimes (Eds.), *Best practices in school psychology V* (pp.1151-1162). Bethesda, MD: National Association of School Psychologists.

Dillon, S. (2011, March 6). Tight budgets mean squeeze in classrooms. *The New York Times.* Retrieved from http://www.nytimes.com.

Gettinger, M., & Seibert, J.K. (2002). *Best practices in increasing academic learning time. In A. Thomas (Ed.), Best practices in school psychology IV:* Volume I (4th ed., pp. 773-787). Bethesda, MD: National Association of School Psychologists.

Muyskens, P., & Ysseldyke, J. E. (1998). Student academic responding time as a function of classroom ecology and time of day. *Journal of Special Education,* 31, 411-424.

National Governors Association Center for Best Practices and Council of Chief State School Officers. (2010). *Common Core State Standards for English Language Arts & Literacy in History/Social Studies, Science, and Technical Subjects.* Retrieved from http://www.corestandards.org/

Rosenshine, B. (2008). *Five meanings of direct instruction.* Center on Innovation & Improvement. Retrieved from http://www.centerii.org

Simonsen, B., Fairbanks, S., Briesch, A., Myers, D., & Sugai, G. (2008). Evidence-based practices in classroom management: Considerations for research to practice. *Evaluation and Treatment of Children,* 31(3), 351-380.

How To: Deliver Direct Instruction in General-Education Classrooms

When teachers must present challenging academic material to struggling learners, they can make that material more accessible and promote faster learning by building assistance directly into instruction. Researchers use several terms to refer to this increased level of student instructional support: direct instruction, explicit instruction, supported instruction (Rosenshine, 2008).

The checklist below summarizes the essential elements of a direct-instruction approach. When preparing lesson plans, teachers can use this resource as a 'pre-flight' checklist to make sure that their lessons reach the widest range of diverse learners.

1. Increase Access to Instruction

Instructional Element	Notes
☐ **Instructional Match.** Lesson content is appropriately matched to students' abilities (Burns, VanDerHeyden, & Boice, 2008).	
☐ **Content Review at Lesson Start.** The lesson opens with a brief review of concepts or material that have previously been presented (Burns, VanDerHeyden, & Boice, 2008, Rosenshine, 2008).	
☐ **Preview of Lesson Goal(s).** At the start of instruction, the goals of the current day's lesson are shared (Rosenshine, 2008).	
☐ **Chunking of New Material.** The teacher breaks new material into small, manageable increments, 'chunks', or steps (Rosenshine, 2008).	

2. Provide 'Scaffolding' Support

Instructional Element	Notes
☐ **Detailed Explanations & Instructions.** Throughout the lesson, the teacher provides adequate explanations and detailed instructions for all concepts and materials being taught (Burns, VanDerHeyden, & Boice, 2008).	
☐ **Talk-Alouds/Think-Alouds.** When presenting cognitive strategies that cannot be observed directly, the teacher describes those strategies for students. Verbal explanations include 'talk-alouds' (e.g., the teacher describes and explains each step of a cognitive strategy) and 'think-alouds' (e.g., the teacher applies a cognitive strategy to a particular problem or task and verbalizes the steps in applying the strategy) (Burns, VanDerHeyden, & Boice, 2008, Rosenshine, 2008).	
☐ **Work Models.** The teacher makes exemplars of academic work (e.g., essays, completed math word problems) available to students for use as models (Rosenshine, 2008).	

Instructional Element	Notes
☐ **Active Engagement.** The teacher ensures that the lesson engages the student in 'active accurate responding' (Skinner, Pappas & Davis, 2005) often enough to capture student attention and to optimize learning.	
☐ **Collaborative Assignments.** Students have frequent opportunities to work collaboratively--in pairs or groups (Baker, Gersten, & Lee, 2002; Gettinger & Seibert, 2002).	
☐ **Checks for Understanding.** The instructor regularly checks for student understanding by posing frequent questions to the group (Rosenshine, 2008).	
☐ **Group Responding.** The teacher ensures full class participation and boosts levels of student attention by having all students respond in various ways (e.g., choral responding, response cards, white boards) to instructor questions (Rosenshine, 2008).	
☐ **High Rate of Student Success.** The teacher verifies that students are experiencing at least 80% success in the lesson content to shape their learning in the desired direction and to maintain student motivation and engagement (Gettinger & Seibert, 2002).	
☐ **Brisk Rate of Instruction.** The lesson moves at a brisk rate—sufficient to hold student attention (Carnine,1976; Gettinger & Seibert, 2002).	
☐ **Fix-Up Strategies.** Students are taught fix-up strategies (Rosenshine, 2008) for use during independent work (e.g., for defining unknown words in reading assignments, for solving challenging math word problems).	

3. Give Timely Performance Feedback

Instructional Element	Notes
☐ **Regular Feedback.** The teacher provides timely and regular performance feedback and corrections throughout the lesson as needed to guide student learning (Burns, VanDerHeyden, & Boice, 2008).	
☐ **Step-by-Step Checklists.** For multi-step cognitive strategies, the teacher creates checklists for students to use to self-monitor performance (Rosenshine, 2008).	

4. Provide Opportunities for Review & Practice	
Instructional Element	**Notes**
☐ **Spacing of Practice Throughout Lesson.** The lesson includes practice activities spaced throughout the lesson (e.g., through teacher demonstration; then group practice with teacher supervision and feedback; then independent, individual student practice) (Burns, VanDerHeyden, & Boice).	
☐ **Guided Practice.** When teaching challenging material, the teacher provides immediate corrective feedback to each student response. When the instructor anticipates the possibility of an incorrect response, that teacher forestalls student error through use of cues, prompts, or hints. The teacher also tracks student responding and ensures sufficient success during supervised lessons before having students practice the new skills or knowledge independently (Burns, VanDerHeyden, & Boice, 2008).	
☐ **Support for Independent Practice.** The teacher ensures that students have adequate support (e.g., clear and explicit instructions; teacher monitoring) to be successful during independent seatwork practice activities (Rosenshine, 2008).	
☐ **Distributed Practice.** The teacher reviews previously taught content one or more times over a period of several weeks or months (Pashler et al., 2007; Rosenshine & Stevens, 1995).	

References

Baker, S., Gersten, R., & Lee, D. (2002).A synthesis of empirical research on teaching mathematics to low-achieving students. *The Elementary School Journal,* 103(1), 51-73.

Burns, M. K., VanDerHeyden, A. M., & Boice, C. H. (2008). Best practices in intensive academic interventions. In A. Thomas & J. Grimes (Eds.), *Best practices in school psychology V* (pp.1151-1162). Bethesda, MD: National Association of School Psychologists.

Carnine, D.W. (1976). Effects of two teacher presentation rates on off-task behavior, answering correctly, and participation. *Journal of Applied Behavior Analysis,* 9, 199-206.

Gettinger, M., & Seibert, J.K. (2002). Best practices in increasing academic learning time. In A. Thomas (Ed.), *Best practices in school psychology IV: Volume I* (4th ed., pp. 773-787). Bethesda, MD: National Association of School Psychologists.

Pashler, H., Bain, P., Bottge, B., Graesser, A., Koedinger, K., McDaniel, M., and Metcalfe, J. (2007) *Organizing Instruction and Study to Improve Student Learning (NCER 2007-2004).* Washington, DC: National Center for Education Research, Institute of Education Sciences, U.S. Department of Education. Retrieved from http://ncer.ed.gov.

Rosenshine, B. (2008). *Five meanings of direct instruction.* Center on Innovation & Improvement. Retrieved from http://www.centerii.org

Rosenshine, B., & Stevens, R. (1995). Functions for teaching well-structured tasks. *Journal of Educational Research,* 88, 262–268.

Skinner, C. H., Pappas, D. N., & Davis, K. A. (2005). Enhancing academic engagement: Providing opportunities for responding and influencing students to choose to respond. *Psychology in the Schools,* 42, 389-403.

How To: Structure Effective Instruction—The Learn Unit

At the core of good instruction lies the "Learn Unit", a 3-step process in which the student is invited to engage in an academic task, deliver a response, and then receive immediate feedback about how he or she did on the task (Heward, 1996). An explanation of the elements of the 'Learn Unit' follow:

1. **Academic Opportunity to Respond.** The student is presented with a meaningful opportunity to respond to the academic task. A question posed by the teacher, a math word problem, and a spelling item on an educational computer 'Word Gobbler' game could all be considered academic opportunities to respond.

2. **Active Student Response.** The student answers the item, solves the problem presented, or completes the academic task. Answering the teacher's question, computing the answer to a math word problem (and showing all work), and typing in the correct spelling of an item when playing an educational computer game are all examples of active student response.

3. **Performance Feedback**. The student receives timely feedback about whether his or her response is correct—often with praise and encouragement. A teacher exclaiming 'Right! Good job!' when a student gives an response in class, a student using an answer key to check her answer to a math word problem, and a computer message that says 'Congratulations! You get 2 points for correctly spelling this word!" are all examples of corrective feedback.

The more frequently a student cycles through complete 'Learn Unit' trials, the faster that student is likely to make learning progress. If any one of these steps is missing, the quality of instruction will probably be compromised. Here are several examples of the Learn Unit in action:

Learn Unit: Classroom Examples

Academic Opportunity to Respond	Active Student Response	Performance Feedback
The teacher calls on the student and asks a question.	The student responds correctly.	The teacher says, "Correct!"
A peer shows the student a flash-card with a math-fact problem and asks the student to give the correct answer.	The student gives the correct answer.	The peer says, "Right. Good job."
A screen in an educational software program prompts the student to click the mouse on a European map to locate Finland.	The student clicks on France.	The computer delivers a verbal prompt: "Incorrect. Try again!"
Using the Cover-Copy-Compare spelling intervention, the student studies a correctly spelled word and then covers it with an index card.	The student copies the spelling word from memory.	The student uncovers the original spelling model and compares his word to it. He notes that he spelled the word correctly.

The Learn Unit demonstrates how flexible good instruction can be. The elements of the Learn Unit may be present in interactions between teacher and student, two students, a student and a volunteer tutor or parent, the student completing independent assignments, or even the student interacting with educational software. When designing group lessons or individual interventions, the Learn Unit can be used to verify that these instructional transactions include the 3 elements needed for optimal learning.

Reference

Heward, W.L. (1996). Three low-tech strategies for increasing the frequency of active student response during group instruction. In R. Gardner, D. M.Sainato, J. O. Cooper, T. E. Heron, W. L. Heward, J. W. Eshleman,& T. A. Grossi (Eds.), *Behavior analysis in education: Focus on measurably superior instruction* (pp.283-320). Pacific Grove, CA: Brooks/Cole.

How To: Choose the Right Amount of Daily Homework

Getting students to complete homework is a complex and ongoing challenge for teachers and parents. However, there is one key question that research can help answer: How much homework should be assigned per grade level? The table below, *How Much Homework Per Day is Optimal?*, provides recommendations from 3 sources on the lower and upper limits for daily homework time requirements.

Despite the differences in the recommendations from these sources, the table shows broad agreement about how much homework to assign at each grade. At grades 1-3, homework should be limited to an hour or less per day, while in grades 4-6, homework should not exceed 90 minutes. The upper limit in grades 7-8 is 2 hours and the limit in high school should be 2.5 hours.

Teachers can use the homework time recommendations included here as a point of comparison: in particular, schools should note that assigning homework that *exceeds* the upper limit of these time estimates is *not* likely to result in additional learning gains—and may even be counter-productive (Cooper, Robinson, & Patall, 2006).

It should also be remembered that the amount of homework assigned each day is not in itself a sign of high academic standards. Homework becomes a powerful tool to promote learning only when students grasp the purpose of each homework assignment, clearly understand homework directions, perceive that homework tasks are instructionally relevant, and receive timely performance feedback (e.g., teacher comments; grades) on submitted homework (Jenson, Sheridan, Olympia, & Andrews, 1994).

How Much Homework Per Day is Optimal?: What the Research Says...			
Grade	Source 1 (Barkley, 2008)	Source 2 (Cooper, Robinson, & Patall, 2006)	Source 3 (Jenson, 1994)
1	10 Minutes	---	10-45 Minutes
2	20 Minutes	---	10-45 Minutes
3	30 Minutes	---	10-45 Minutes
4	40 Minutes	---	45-90 Minutes
5	50 Minutes	---	45-90 Minutes
6	1 Hour	---	45-90 Minutes
7	1 Hour 10 Minutes	1 - 2 Hours	1 - 2 Hours
8	1 Hour 20 Minutes	1 - 2 Hours	1 - 2 Hours

References

Barkley, R. A. (2008). 80+ classroom accommodations for children or teens with ADHD. *The ADHD Report,* 16(4), 7-10.

Cooper, H., Robinson, J. C., & Patall, E A. (2006). Does homework improve academic achievement? A synthesis of research, 1987-2003. *Review of Educational Research,* 76(1), 1-62.

Jenson, W. R., Sheridan, S. M., Olympia, D., & Andrews, D. (1994). Homework and students with learning disabilities and behavior disorders: A practical, parent-based approach. *Journal of Learning Disabilities,* 27, 538-548.

How To: Implement Critical Elements of Strong Core Classroom Behavior Management

Students in classrooms are always engaged in behavior of some sort: listening to the teacher, completing independent work, talking to a friend, looking out the window. The constant unfolding of a student's behaviors can be thought of metaphorically as a 'behavior stream' (Schoenfeld & Farmer, 1970). The teacher's task is to channel this stream of student behaviors toward productive academic engagement—resulting in both an improved behavioral climate and better school outcomes. In the well-managed classroom, the teacher dedicates as much time as possible to instruction, arranges instructional activities to fully engage the student learner, and uses proactive strategies to manage behaviors (Simonsen, Fairbanks, Briesch, Myers, & Sugai, 2008).

Below is a checklist containing 6 elements that are critical to strong core classroom behavior management. Teachers can use this checklist proactively to ensure that these elements are in place. School administrators and consultants will find that the checklist serves as a helpful framework when they provide guidance to teachers on how to strengthen classroom behavior management.

Checklist: Critical Elements of Strong Core Classroom Behavior Management	
Behavior-Management Element	**Notes**
☐ **Components of Effective Instruction.** The teacher's lesson and instructional activities include these components (Burns, VanDerHeyden, & Boice, 2008): • *Instructional match.* Students are placed in work that provides them with an appropriate level of challenge (not too easy and not too difficult). • *Explicit instruction.* The teacher delivers instruction using modeling, demonstration, supervised student practice, etc. • *Active student engagement.* There are sufficient opportunities during the lesson for students to be actively engaged and 'show what they know'. • *Timely performance feedback.* Students receive feedback about their performance on independent seatwork, as well as whole-group and small-group activities.	
☐ **Explicit Teaching of Behavioral Expectations.** Students have been explicitly taught classroom behavioral expectations. Those positive behaviors are acknowledged and reinforced on an ongoing basis (Fairbanks, Sugai, Guardino, & Lathrop, 2007).	

Behavior-Management Element	Notes
☐ **Students Trained in Basic Class Routines.** The teacher has clearly established routines to deal with common class-room activities (Fairbanks, Sugai, Guardino, & Lathrop, 2007; Marzano, Marzano, & Pickering, 2003; Sprick, Borgmeier, & Nolet, 2002). These routines include but are not limited to: • Engaging students in meaningful academic activities at the start of class (e.g., using bell-ringer activities) • Assigning and collecting homework and classwork • Transitioning students efficiently between activities • Independent seatwork and cooperative learning groups • Students leaving and reentering the classroom • Dismissing students at the end of the period	
☐ **Positive Classroom Rules Posted.** The classroom has a set of 3-8 rules or behavioral expectations posted. When possible, those rules are stated in positive terms as 'goal' behaviors (e.g. 'Students participate in learning activities without distracting others from learning'). The rules are frequently reviewed (Simonsen, Fairbanks, Briesch, Myers, & Sugai, 2008).	
☐ **Effective Teacher Directives.** The teacher delivers clear directives to students that are: • Delivered calmly, • Brief, • Stated when possible as DO statements rather than as DON'T statements, • Presented in clear, simple language, and • Delivered one at a time and appropriately paced to avoid confusing or overloading students (Kern & Clemens, 2007; Walker & Walker, 1991). • Positive or neutral in tone, avoiding sarcasm or hostility and over-lengthy explanations that can distract or confuse students.	
☐ **Continuum of In-Class Consequences for Misbehavior.** The teacher has developed a continuum of classroom-based consequences for misbehavior (e.g., redirect the student; have a brief private conference with the student; remove classroom privileges; send the student to another classroom for a brief timeout) that are used before the teacher considers administrative removal of the student from the classroom (Sprick, Borgmeier, & Nolet, 2002). These strategies are used flexibly, matched to the behavioral situation and needs of the student (Marzano, Marzano, & Pickering, 2003).	

References

Burns, M. K., VanDerHeyden, A. M., & Boice, C. H. (2008). Best practices in intensive academic interventions. In A. Thomas & J. Grimes (Eds.), *Best practices in school psychology V* (pp.1151-1162). Bethesda, MD: National Association of School Psychologists.

Fairbanks, S., Sugai, G., Guardino, S., & Lathrop, M. (2007). Response to intervention: Examining classroom behavior support in second grade. *Exceptional Children, 73,* 288-310.

Kern, L. & Clemens, N. H. (2007). Antecedent strategies to promote appropriate classroom behavior. *Psychology in the Schools, 44,* 65-75.

Marzano, R. J., Marzano, J. S., & Pickering, D. J. (2003). *Classroom management that works: Research-based strategies for every teacher.* Alexandria, VA: Association for Supervision and Curriculum Development.

Schoenfeld, W. N., & Farmer, J. (1970). Reinforcement schedules and the "behavior stream." In W. N. Schoenfeld (Ed.), *The theory of reinforcement schedules* (pp. 215–245). New York: Appleton-Century-Crofts.

Simonsen, B., Fairbanks, S., Briesch, A., Myers, D., & Sugai, G. (2008). Evidence-based practices in classroom management: Considerations for research to practice. *Evaluation and Treatment of Children, 31*(3), 351-380.

Sprick, R. S., Borgmeier, C., & Nolet, V. (2002). Prevention and management of behavior problems in secondary schools. In M. A. Shinn, H. M. Walker & G. Stoner (Eds.), *Interventions for academic and behavior problems II: Preventive and remedial approaches* (pp.373-401). Bethesda, MD: National Association of School Psychologists.

Walker, H.M. & Walker, J.E. (1991). *Coping with noncompliance in the classroom: A positive approach for teachers.* Austin, TX:: Pro-Ed, Inc.

Chapter 3

Creating Academic Interventions That Promote Student Success in the Common Core

When a teacher observes that a student lacks academic skills needed to attain the Common Core Standards, that teacher must take on the role of intervention 'first responder.' This role implies having the tools and know-how to assemble for that student an academic intervention plan designed to repair areas of skill deficit or underperformance. Of course, educators have always attempted to provide struggling students in their classrooms with additional, individualized support: that is the paradigm of good teaching. Findings from research, however, have the potential to help teachers strengthen their effectiveness as interventionists for individual students even as they continue to deliver high-quality core instruction to the entire classroom.

This chapter provides teachers with a collection of resources to help them analyze the needs of underperforming students and to match them to effective academic intervention plans. Following are 7 'big ideas' about academic interventions that are addressed in greater depth through the chapter resources:

1. *Academic problems should be clearly defined.* Before selecting interventions to address a student academic problem, the teacher must be able to describe in clear and specific terms just what the student's problem is. In fact, the most important step in the entire process of

developing an intervention is being able to describe correctly and specifically the problem that must be fixed (Bergan, 1995).

2. *Academic problems should be linked to their probable cause.* Once an academic problem has been defined, the teacher should develop a hypothesis (educated guess) about the cause of that problem. For example, a student may do poorly on a reading comprehension task for a number of reasons: lacks the necessary comprehension skills; is accurate but not yet fluent in those skills; had once learned those skills but fails to retain them; can perform the skills but has limited endurance; possesses the skills but does not recognize situations when they should be used (Martens & Witt, 2004). Each of these hypotheses for the student's poor reading comprehension performance suggests different intervention ideas.

3. *Intervention strategies should be research-based.* When possible, the teacher should include in an intervention plan only those ideas supported by research. At present, there is no consensus on how to define 'research-based' interventions (Odom et al., 2005). However, a sensible rule of thumb to follow is that an intervention idea should be shown as effective in at least one study published in a reputable peer-reviewed research journal before it is used in school intervention plans.

4. *Intervention plans should help students to access instruction*—but not 'dumb down' instruction. When putting together classroom intervention plans, teachers can choose from a wide array of strategies to help the student achieve academic success. But teachers should take care not to cross the line and modify core instruction for struggling general-education students; that is, they should not hold underperforming students to a lesser academic standard than their classmates (Tindal & Fuchs, 1999). After all, it is illogical to expect that students who already evidence a significant academic gap can close that gap by being asked to do less than their peers.

5. *Interventions should be documented in writing.* When a teacher commits to developing an academic intervention to support a student, that teacher should always create a written plan to document the intervention prior to implementing it (Burns & Gibbons, 2008). Busy educators can be forgiven for viewing the requirement to write out intervention plans as meaningless paperwork. But there are actually compelling reasons for them to commit plans to paper before starting interventions. First, people have only a limited capacity to juggle details in their head. In a famous and ground-breaking article, for example, Miller (1956) cited a number of psychological studies demonstrating that the average person is able to actively maintain only about 7 discrete bits of information in working memory at one time—which explains why local phone numbers in the United States are 7 digits long. (These findings remain unchallenged.) A teacher who is running a whole classroom while trying to informally manage even 1 or 2 individual student interventions in her head must manage far more than 7 information-bits—and is thus likely to overlook important details about instruction or intervention simply because of cognitive overload. When that same teacher is able to rely on written intervention plans as a memory aid, however, she can manage the complexity with relative ease. A second reason that teachers should put intervention plans in writing is so that they can produce those plans when needed as proof that they are providing at-risk students with ongoing assistance. In this age of increased teacher accountability, the teacher who documents intervention efforts for marginal students is the one who will receive full credit for that intervention work.

6. *Interventions should be carried out with integrity.* If a student does not improve when given a classroom intervention, there are two possible explanations for this failure to respond: the intervention plan was well-selected, well-constructed and carefully implemented but the student simply failed to make progress; or some aspect of the plan was not carried out as designed, thus compromising the integrity of the intervention. Interventions can unravel for many reasons: e.g., change of school schedule, teacher or student illness, weather-related

school cancellations, a misunderstanding on the part of the interventionist about how to implement an intervention strategy, etc. The teacher should monitor the integrity of each classroom intervention closely, ensuring that the actual intervention conforms as closely as possible to the guidelines contained in the written intervention plan (Gansle & Noell, 2007) and taking steps when needed to bring the intervention back into alignment with good practices.

7. *Goal-setting and progress-monitoring should be a part of all academic interventions.* At their core, academic interventions are intended to improve student performance (Duhon, Mesmer, Atkins, Greguson, & Olinger, 2009). But teachers cannot know with certainty whether a student is actually benefiting from an intervention unless they set specific outcome goals up front and then collect data periodically throughout the intervention to verify that these goals are met (Wright 2007). NOTE: Progress-monitoring procedures and techniques are discussed at length in chapters 5 and 6.

Roadmap to This Chapter

The resources in this chapter provide teachers with the technical know-how to analyze student academic needs and to match them to effective academic interventions. Resources include:

- *How To: Define Academic Problems: The First Step in Effective Intervention Planning.* Correct identification of a student's academic problem(s) is the most important step in the problem-solving process. This resource gives teachers a simple framework for constructing academic problem-identification statements and for linking student problems to likely causes.

- *How To: Create a Written Record of Classroom Interventions.* Writing an academic intervention plan helps a teacher to better prepare for that intervention, keep its details fresh in mind, and be accountable in the role of interventionist. This resource is a streamlined 1-page form to use in documenting classroom interventions.

- *How To: Define Intervention-Related Terms: Core Instruction, Intervention, Instructional Adjustment (Accommodations), Modification.* This resource defines important terms that every interventionist should know when developing student intervention plans. In particular, an understanding of the definition of 'modification' can prevent a teacher from inadvertently holding a general-education student to a lesser academic standard than other students in the class.

- *How To: Use Accommodations With General-Education Students: Teacher Guidelines.* This resource discusses circumstances in which teachers might want to make accommodations available to general-education students. It draws an important distinction between access and target skills and points out that access skills can be the focus of accommodations without running the risk of 'dumbing down' instruction.

- *How To: Use the Instructional Hierarchy to Identify Effective Teaching and Intervention Targets.* This resource presents the Instructional Hierarchy, which is an invaluable tool for determining the stage of learning that a struggling student is currently in (acquisition, fluency, retention, endurance, generalization)—and giving the teacher the insight necessary to better match the student to effective interventions.

- *How To: Find Ideas for Academic Interventions: The 'Intervention Bank'.* This resource offers a starter set of research-based ideas for intervention in reading, spelling, math, and writing.

- *How To: Teach Student Writing Skills: Elements of Effective Writing Instruction & Intervention.* Teachers can use this resource of 9 effective writing-instruction strategies to strengthen writing instruction and build strong writing interventions.

The last two resources provide examples of specialized types of interventions that tap into 'student power':

- *How To: Promote Acquisition of Math Facts or Spelling Words Using Cover-Copy-Compare.* Students have the potential to play a role in managing their own interventions. In the intervention Cover-Copy-Compare, the student is trained to practice math facts or spelling words independently.

- *How To: Use Peers as Tutors: Math Computation with Constant Time Delay.* This resource demonstrates how students can work collaboratively to promote math-computation fluency skills, resulting in a more intensive practice experience than can be delivered in a large-group format.

References

Bergan, J. R. (1995). Evolution of a problem-solving model of consultation. *Journal of Educational and Psychological Consultation,* 6(2), 111-123.

Burns, M. K., & Gibbons, K. A. (2008). *Implementing response-to-intervention in elementary and secondary schools.* Routledge: New York.

Duhon, G. J., Mesmer, E. M., Atkins, M. E., Greguson, L. A., & Olinger, E. S. (2009). Quantifying intervention intensity: A systematic approach to evaluating student response to increasing intervention frequency. *Journal of Behavioral Education*, 18, 101-118.

Fuchs, D., & Deshler, D. D. (2007). What we need to know about responsiveness to intervention (and shouldn't be afraid to ask). *Learning Disabilities Research & Practice,* 22(2), 129-136.

Gansle, K. A., & Noell, G. H. (2007). The fundamental role of intervention implementation in assessing response to intervention. In S. R. Jimerson, M. K. Burns, & A. M. VanDerHeyden (Eds.), *Response to intervention: The science and practice of assessment and intervention* (pp. 244-251). New York: Springer Publishing.

Martens, B. K., & Witt, J. C. (2004). Competence, persistence, and success: The positive psychology of behavioral skill instruction. *Psychology in the Schools*, 41(1), 19-30.

Miller, G. A. (1956). The magical number seven, plus or minus two: Some limits on our capacity for processing information. *Psychological Review*, 63(2), 81–97.

Odom, S. L., Brantlinger, E., Gersten, R., Horner, R. H., Thompson, B., & Harris, K. R. (2005). Research in special education: Scientific methods and evidence-based practices. *Exceptional Children*, 71(2), 137-148.

Tindal, G., & Fuchs, L. (1999). *A summary of research on test changes: An empirical basis for defining accommodations.* Lexington, KY: Mid-South Regional Resource Center, University of Kentucky. Retrieved on January 25, 2013, from http://www.specialed.us/discoveridea/topdocs/msrrc/Tindal%26Fuchs.PDF

Wright, J. (2007). *RTI toolkit: A practical guide for schools.* Port Chester, NY: National Professional Resources, Inc.

How To: Define Academic Problems—
The First Step in Effective Intervention Planning

Students who struggle with academic deficits do not do so in isolation. Their difficulties are played out in the larger context of the school environment and curriculum—and represent a 'mismatch' between the characteristics of the student and the instructional demands of the classroom (Foorman & Torgesen, 2001). It may surprise educators to learn that the problem-identification step is the most critical for matching the student to an effective intervention (Bergan, 1995). Problem identification statements should be defined in clear and specific terms sufficient to pass 'the stranger test' (Howell, Hosp, & Kurns, 2008). That is, the student problem can be judged as adequately defined if a person with no background knowledge of the case and equipped only with the problem-identification statement can observe the student in the academic setting and know with confidence when the problem behavior is displayed and when it is not.

Here are recommendations for increasing teacher capacity to frame student skills in relation to curriculum requirements, describe student academic problems in specific terms, and generate a hypothesis about why the problem is occurring.

1. **Know the Common Core.** Academic abilities can best be described in terms of the specific curriculum skills or knowledge that students are required to demonstrate. The Common Core State Standards for English Language Arts and Mathematics are an excellent starting point. Teachers should have a firm grasp of the Common Core standards for ELA and Math at their instructional grade level. They should also know those standards extending to at least two grades below the current grade to allow them to better match students who are off-level academically to appropriate intervention strategies.

2. **Describe the academic problem in specific, skill-based terms with a meaningful instructional context** (Batsche et al., 2008; Upah, 2008). Write a clear, brief description of the academic skill or performance deficit that focuses on a specific skill or performance area. Include information about the conditions under which the academic problem is observed and typical or expected level of performance.

   - *Conditions.* Describe the environmental conditions or task demands in place when the academic problem is observed.

   - *Problem Description.* Describe the actual observable academic behavior with which the student has difficulty. If available, include specifics about student performance, such as rate of work, accuracy, or other relevant quantitative information.

   - *Typical or Expected Level of Performance.* Provide a typical or expected performance criterion for this skill or behavior. Typical or expected academic performance can be calculated using a variety of sources,

Academic Problems: Sample Definitions

Environmental Conditions or Task Demands	Problem Description	Typical or Expected Level of Performance
When completing a beginning-level algebra word problem...	...Ann is unable to translate that word problem into an equation with variables...	...while most peers in her class have mastered this skill.
During social studies large-group instruction...	...Franklin attends to instruction an average of 45% of the time...	... while peers in the same room attend to instruction an average of 85% of the time.
For science homework...	... Tye turns in assignments an average of 50% of the time...	... while the classroom median rate of homework turned in is 90%.
On weekly 30-minute in-class writing assignments...	... Angela produces compositions that average 145 words...	...while a sampling of peer compositions shows that the typical student writes an average of 254 words.

3. **Develop a hypothesis statement to explain the academic skill or performance problem.**
   The hypothesis states the assumed reason(s) or cause(s) for the student's academic problems. Once it has been developed, the hypothesis statement acts as a compass needle, pointing toward interventions that most logically address the student academic problems. Listed below are common reasons for academic problems. Note that more than one hypothesis may apply to a particular student (e.g., a student may have both a skill deficit and a motivation deficit).

Academic Problems: Possible Hypotheses & Recommendations

Hypothesis	Recommendation
• *Skill Deficit.* The student has not yet acquired the skill.	Provide direct, explicit instruction to acquire the skill. Reinforce the student for effort and accuracy.
• *Fluency Deficit.* The student has acquired the basic skill but is not yet proficient.	Provide opportunities for the student to practice the skill and give timely performance feedback. Reinforce the student for fluency as well as accuracy.
• *Retention Deficit.* The student can acquire the skill but has difficulty retaining it over an extended period.	Give the student frequent opportunities for practice to entrench a skill and help the student to retain it over time. Begin by scheduling more numerous practice episodes within a short time ('massed review') to promote initial fluency and then strengthen longer-term skill retention by scheduling additional periodic review ('distributed review') across longer spans of several weeks or more.
• *Endurance.* The student can do the skill but engages in it only for brief periods.	Consider these ideas to boost endurance: • In structuring lessons or independent work, gradually lengthen the period of time that the student spends in skills practice or use. • Have the student self-monitor active engagement in skill-building activities--setting daily, increasingly ambitious work goals and then tracking whether he or she successfully reaches those goals.
• *Generalization Deficit.* The student possesses the basic skill but fails to use it across appropriate situations or settings.	Train the student to identify the relevant characteristics of situations or settings when the skill should be used. Provide incentives for the student to use the skill in the appropriate settings.
• *Motivation (Performance) Deficit.* The student is capable of performing the skill and can identify when use of the skill is appropriate—but nonetheless is not motivated to use the skill.	Use various strategies to engage the student in the skill (e.g., select high-interest learning activities; offer incentives to the student for successful use of the skill, etc.).

References

Batsche, G. M., Castillo, J. M., Dixon, D. N., & Forde, S. (2008). Best practices in designing, implementing, and evaluating quality interventions. In A. Thomas & J. Grimes (Eds.), *Best practices in school psychology V* (pp. 177-193). Bethesda, MD: National Association of School Psychologists.

Bergan, J. R. (1995). Evolution of a problem-solving model of consultation. *Journal of Educational and Psychological Consultation,* 6(2), 111-123.

Christ, T. (2008). Best practices in problem analysis. In A. Thomas & J. Grimes (Eds.), *Best practices in school psychology V* (pp. 159-176). Bethesda, MD: National Association of School Psychologists.

Fennell, F., Faulkner, L. R., Ma, L., Schmid, W., Stotsky, S., Wu, H., & Flawn, T. (2008). *Foundations for success: The final report of the National Mathematics Advisory Panel: Chapter 3: Report of the task group on conceptual knowledge and skills.* U.S., Department of Education: Washington, D.C. Retrieved from http://www.ed.gov/about/bdscomm/list/mathpanel/reports.html

Foorman, B. R., & Torgesen, J. (2001). Critical elements of classroom and small-group instruction promote reading success in all children. *Learning Disabilities Research & Practice,* 16, 203-212.

Howell, K. W., Hosp, J. L., & Kurns, S. (2008). Best practices in curriculum-based evaluation. In A. Thomas & J. Grimes (Eds.), *Best practices in school psychology V* (pp.349-362). Bethesda, MD: National Association of School Psychologists.

Upah, K. R. F. (2008). Best practices in designing, implementing, and evaluating quality interventions. In A. Thomas & J. Grimes (Eds.), *Best practices in school psychology V* (pp. 209-223). Bethesda, MD: National Association of School Psychologists.

Academic Problems: Sample Definitions		
Environmental Conditions or Task Demands	Problem Description	Typical or Expected Level of Performance

How To: Create a Written Record of Classroom Interventions

When general-education students begin to struggle with academic or behavioral issues, the classroom teacher will typically select and implement one or more evidence-based intervention strategies to assist those students. But a strong intervention plan needs more than just well-chosen interventions. It also requires 4 additional components (Witt, VanDerHeyden, & Gilbertson, 2004): (1) student concerns should be clearly and specifically defined; (2) one or more methods of formative assessment should be used to track the effectiveness of the intervention; (3) baseline student data should be collected prior to the intervention; and (4) a goal for student improvement should be calculated before the start of the intervention to judge whether that intervention is ultimately successful. If a single one of these essential 4 components is missing, the intervention is to be judged as fatally flawed (Witt, VanDerHeyden, & Gilbertson, 2004) and as not meeting minimum Response to Intervention standards.

Teachers need a standard format to use in documenting their classroom intervention plans. The *Classroom Intervention Planning Sheet* that appears later in this article is designed to include all of the essential documentation elements of an effective intervention plan. The form includes space to document:

- *Case information.* In this first section of the form, the teacher notes general information, such as the name of the target student, the adult(s) responsible for carrying out the intervention, the date the intervention plan is being created, the expected start and end dates for the intervention plan, and the total number of instructional weeks that the intervention will be in place. Most importantly, this section includes a description of the student problem; research shows that the most significant step in selecting an effective classroom intervention is to correctly identify the target student concern(s) in clear, specific, measureable terms (Bergan, 1995).
- *Intervention.* The teacher describes the evidence-based intervention(s) that will be used to address the identified student concern(s). As a shortcut, the instructor can simply write the intervention name in this section and attach a more detailed intervention script/description to the intervention plan.
- *Materials.* The teacher lists any materials (e.g., flashcards, wordlists, worksheets) or other resources (e.g., Internet-connected computer) necessary for the intervention.
- *Training.* If adults and/or the target student require any training prior to the intervention, the teacher records those training needs in this section of the form.
- *Progress-Monitoring.* The teacher selects a method to monitor student progress during the intervention. For the method selected, the instructor records what type of data is to be used, collects and enters student baseline (starting-point) information, calculates an intervention outcome goal, and notes how frequently he or she plans to monitor the intervention.

A completed example of the *Classroom Intervention Planning Sheet* that includes a math computation intervention can be found later in this article.

While a simple intervention documentation form is a helpful planning tool, schools should remember that teachers will need other resources and types of assistance as well to be successful in selecting and using classroom interventions. For example, teachers should have access to an 'intervention menu' that contains evidence-based strategies to address the most common academic and behavioral concerns and should be able to get coaching support as they learn how to implement new classroom intervention ideas.

References
Bergan, J. R. (1995). Evolution of a problem-solving model of consultation. *Journal of Educational and Psychological Consultation, 6(2),* 111-123.

Witt, J. C., VanDerHeyden, A. M., & Gilbertson, D. (2004). Troubleshooting behavioral interventions. A systematic process for finding and eliminating problems. *School Psychology Review, 33,* 363-383.

Classroom Intervention Planning Sheet

This worksheet is designed to help teachers to quickly create classroom plans for academic and behavioral interventions. (For a tutorial on how to fill out this sheet, review the accompanying directions.)

Case Information

What to Write: Record the important case information, including student, person delivering the intervention, date of plan, start and end dates for the intervention plan, and the total number of instructional weeks that the intervention will run.

Student:		Interventionist(s):		Date Intervention Plan Was Written:	
Date Intervention is to Start:		Date Intervention is to End:		Total Number of Intervention Weeks:	
Description of the Student Problem:					

Intervention

What to Write: Write a brief description of the intervention(s) to be used with this student. TIP: If you have a script for this intervention, you can just write its name here and attach the script to this sheet.

Materials

What to Write: Jot down materials (e.g., flashcards) or resources (e.g., Internet-connected computer) needed to carry out this intervention.

Training

What to Write: Note what training--if any--is needed to prepare adult(s) and/or the student to carry out the intervention.

Progress-Monitoring

What to Write: Select a method to monitor student progress on this intervention. For the method selected, record what type of data is to be used, enter student baseline (starting-point) information, calculate an intervention outcome goal, and note how frequently you plan to monitor the intervention. Tip: Several ideas for classroom data collection appear on the right side of this table.

Type of Data Used to Monitor:		Ideas for Intervention Progress-Monitoring
Baseline	Outcome Goal	• Existing data: grades, homework logs, etc. • Cumulative mastery log • Rubric • Curriculum-based measurement • Behavior report card • Behavior checklist
How often will data be collected? (e.g., daily, every other day, weekly):		

Classroom Intervention Planning Sheet: Math Computation Example

This worksheet is designed to help teachers to quickly create classroom plans for academic and behavioral interventions. (For a tutorial on how to fill out this sheet, review the accompanying directions.)

Case Information

What to Write: Record the important case information, including student, person delivering the intervention, date of plan, start and end dates for the intervention plan, and the total number of instructional weeks that the intervention will run.

Student:	John Samuelson-Gr 4	Interventionist(s):	Mrs. Kennedy, classroom teacher	Date Intervention Plan Was Written:	10 October 2012
Date Intervention is to Start:	M 8 Oct 2012	Date Intervention is to End:	F 16 Nov 2012	Total Number of Intervention Weeks:	6 weeks

Description of the Student Problem:	Slow math computation speed (computes multiplication facts at 12 correct digits in 2 minutes, when typical gr 4 peers compute at least 24 correct digits).

Intervention

What to Write: Write a brief description of the intervention(s) to be used with this student. TIP: If you have a script for this intervention, you can just write its name here and attach the script to this sheet.

Math Computation Time Drill.(Rhymer et al., 2002)
Explicit time-drills are a method to boost students' rate of responding on arithmetic-fact worksheets: (1) The teacher hands out the worksheet. Students are instructed that they will have 3 minutes to work on problems on the sheet. (2) The teacher starts the stop watch and tells the students to start work. (3) At the end of the first minute in the 3-minute span, the teacher 'calls time', stops the stopwatch, and tells the students to underline the last number written and to put their pencils in the air. Then students are told to resume work and the teacher restarts the stopwatch. (4) This process is repeated at the end of minutes 2 and 3. (5) At the conclusion of the 3 minutes, the teacher collects the student worksheets.

Materials	Training
What to Write: Jot down materials (e.g., flashcards) or resources (e.g., Internet-connected computer) needed to carry out this intervention.	**What to Write:** Note what training--if any--is needed to prepare adult(s) and/or the student to carry out the intervention.
Use math worksheet generator on www.interventioncentral.org to create all time-drill and assessment materials.	*Meet with the student at least once before the intervention to familiarize with the time-drill technique and timed math computation assessments.*

Progress-Monitoring

What to Write: Select a method to monitor student progress on this intervention. For the method selected, record what type of data is to be used, enter student baseline (starting-point) information, calculate an intervention outcome goal, and note how frequently you plan to monitor the intervention. Tip: Several ideas for classroom data collection appear on the right side of this table.

Type of Data Used to Monitor: *Curriculum-based measurement: math computation assessments: 2 minute single-skill probes*

Ideas for Intervention Progress-Monitoring
- Existing data: grades, homework logs, etc.
- Cumulative mastery log
- Rubric
- Curriculum-based measurement
- Behavior report card
- Behavior checklist

Baseline	Outcome Goal
12 correct digits per 2 minute probe	*24 correct digits per 2 minute probe*

How often will data be collected? (e.g., daily, every other day, weekly):
WEEKLY

How To: Define Intervention-Related Terms—
Core Instruction, Intervention, Instructional Adjustment, Modification

Educators who serve as interventionists should be able to define and distinguish among the terms core instruction, intervention, instructional adjustment, and modification. In particular, interventionists should avoid using modifications as part of an intervention plan to support a general education student in core instruction—as they can be predicted to undermine the student's academic performance. Here are definitions for these key terms. (Tindal & Fuchs, 1999; Wright, 2007).

Intervention-Related Terms & Definitions

☐ **Core Instruction**. Those instructional strategies that are used routinely with all students in a general-education setting are considered 'core instruction'. High-quality instruction is essential and forms the foundation of classroom academic support. NOTE: While it is important to verify that a struggling student receives good core instructional practices, those routine practices do not 'count' as individual student interventions.

☐ **Intervention**. An academic *intervention* is a strategy used to teach a new skill, build fluency in a skill, or encourage a child to apply an existing skill to new situations or settings. An intervention can be thought of as "a set of actions that, when taken, have demonstrated ability to change a fixed educational trajectory" (Methe & Riley-Tillman, 2008; p. 37). As an example of an academic intervention, the teacher may select question generation (Davey & McBride,1986; Rosenshine, Meister & Chapman, 1996), a strategy in which the student is taught to locate or generate main idea sentences for each paragraph in a passage and record those 'gist' sentences for later review.

☐ **Instructional Adjustment (Accommodation)**. An *instructional adjustment* (also known as an 'accommodation') is intended to help the student to fully access and participate in the general-education curriculum without changing the instructional content and without reducing the student's rate of learning (Skinner, Pappas & Davis, 2005). An instructional adjustment is intended to remove barriers to learning while still expecting that students will master the same instructional content as their typical peers. An instructional adjustment for students who are slow readers, for example, may include having them supplement their silent reading of a novel by listening to the book on tape. An instructional adjustment for unmotivated students may include breaking larger assignments into smaller 'chunks' and providing students with performance feedback and praise for each completed 'chunk' of assigned work (Skinner, Pappas & Davis, 2005).

☐ **Modification**. A modification changes the expectations of what a student is expected to know or do—typically by lowering the academic standards against which the student is to be evaluated. Examples of modifications are giving a student 5 math computation problems for practice instead of the 20 problems assigned to the rest of the class or letting the student consult course notes during a test when peers are not permitted to do so. Instructional modifications are essential elements on the Individualized Education Plans (IEPs) or Section 504 Plans of many students with special needs. Modifications are generally not included on a general-education student's classroom intervention plan, however, because the assumption is that the student can be successful in the curriculum with appropriate interventions and instructional adjustments alone. In fact, modifying the work of struggling general education students is likely to have a negative effect that works against the goals of intervention. Reducing academic expectations will result in these students falling further behind rather than closing the performance gap with peers.

References

Davey, B., & McBride, S. (1986). Effects of question-generation training on reading comprehension. *Journal of Educational Psychology,* 78, 256-262.

Methe, S. A., & Riley-Tillman, T. C. (2008). An informed approach to selecting and designing early mathematics interventions. *School Psychology Forum: Research into Practice,* 2, 29-41.

Rosenshine, B., Meister, C., & Chapman, S. (1996). Teaching students to generate questions: A review of the intervention studies. *Review of Educational Research,* 66, 181-221.

Skinner, C. H., Pappas, D. N., & Davis, K. A. (2005). Enhancing academic engagement: Providing opportunities for responding and influencing students to choose to respond. *Psychology in the Schools,* 42, 389-403.

Tindal, G., & Fuchs, L. (1999). *A summary of research on test changes: An empirical basis for defining accommodations.* Lexington, KY: Mid-South Regional Resource Center, University of Kentucky. Retrieved on January 25, 2013, from http://www.specialed.us/discoveridea/topdocs/msrrc/Tindal%26Fuchs.PDF.

Wright, J. (2007). *The RTI toolkit: A practical guide for schools.* Port Chester, NY: National Professional Resources, Inc.

How To: Use Accommodations With General-Education Students—Teacher Guidelines

Classrooms in most schools look pretty much alike, with students sitting at rows of desks attending (more or less) to teacher instruction. But a teacher facing any class knows that behind that group of attentive student faces lies a kaleidoscope of differences in academic, social, self-management, and language skills. For example, recent national test results indicate that well over half of elementary and middle-school students have not yet attained proficiency in mathematics (NAEP, 20011a) or reading (NAEP 2011b). Furthermore, 1 in 10 students now attending American schools is an English Language Learner (Institute of Education Sciences, 2012) who must grapple with the complexities of language acquisition in addition to the demands of academic coursework.

Teachers can increase the chances for academic success by weaving into their instructional routine an appropriate array of classwide curricular accommodations made available to any general-education student who needs them (Kern, Bambara, & Fogt, 2002). However, teachers also know that they must strike an appropriate balance: while accommodations have the potential to help struggling learners to more fully engage in demanding academics, they should not compromise learning by holding a general-education student who accesses them to a lesser performance standard than the rest of the class. After all, students with academic deficits must actually accelerate learning to close the skill-gap with peers, so allowing them to do less is simply not a realistic option.

Read on for guidelines on how to select classroom accommodations to promote school success, verify whether a student actually *needs* a particular accommodation, and judge when accommodations should be used in instruction even if not allowed on state tests.

Identifying Appropriate Accommodations: Access vs. Target Skills. As an aid in determining whether a particular accommodation both supports individual student differences and sustains a demanding academic environment, teachers should distinguish between target and access skills (Tindal, Daesik, & Ketterlin, 2008). Target skills are those academic skills that the teacher is actively trying to assess or to teach. Target skills are therefore 'non-negotiable'; the teacher must ensure that these skills are not compromised in the instruction or assessment of any general-education student. For example, a 4th-grade teacher sets as a target skill for his class the development of computational fluency in basic multiplication facts. To work toward this goal, the teacher has his class complete a worksheet of 20 computation problems under timed conditions. This teacher would not allow a typical student who struggles with computation to do fewer than the assigned 20 problems, as this change would undermine the target skill of computational fluency that is the purpose of the assignment.

In contrast, access skills are those needed for the student to take part in a class assessment or instructional activity but are not themselves the target of current assessment or instruction. Access skills, therefore, *can* be the focus of accommodations, as altering them may remove a barrier to student participation but will not compromise the academic rigor of classroom activities. For example, a 7th-grade teacher assigns a 5-paragraph essay as an in-class writing assignment. She notes that one student finds the access skill of handwriting to be difficult and aversive, so she instead allows that student the accommodation of writing his essay on a classroom desktop computer. While the access skill (method of text production) is altered, the teacher preserves the integrity of those elements of the assignment that directly address the target skill (i.e., the student must still produce a full 5-paragraph essay).

Matching Accommodations to Students: Look for the 'Differential Boost.' The first principle in using accommodations in general-education classrooms, then, is that they should address access rather than target academic skills. However, teachers may also wish to identify whether an individual actually benefits from a particular accommodation strategy. A useful tool to investigate this question is the 'differential boost' test (Tindal & Fuchs, 1999). The teacher examines a student's performance both with and without the accommodation and asks these 2 questions: (1) Does the student perform significantly better with the accommodation than without?, and (2) Does the accommodation boost that particular student's performance substantially *beyond* what could be expected if it were given to all students in the class? If the answer to both questions is YES, there is clear evidence that this student receives a 'differential boost' from the accommodation and that this benefit can be explained as a unique rather than universal response. With such evidence in hand, the teacher should feel confident that the accommodation is an appropriate match for the student. Of course, if a teacher observes that most or all of a class seems to benefit from a particular accommodation idea, the best course is probably to revise the assignment or assessment activity to incorporate the accommodation!

For example, a teacher may routinely allocate 20 minutes for her class to complete an in-class writing assignment and finds that all but one of her students are able to complete the assignment adequately within that time. She therefore allows this one student 10 minutes of additional time for the assignment and discovers that his work is markedly better with this accommodation. The evidence shows that, in contrast to peers, the student gains a clear 'differential boost' from the accommodation of extended time because (1) his writing product is substantially improved when using it, while (2) few if any other students appear to need it.

Classroom Accommodations and State Tests: To Allow or Not to Allow? Teachers may sometimes be reluctant to allow a student to access classroom accommodations if the student cannot use those same accommodations on high-stakes state assessments (TIndal & Fuchs, 1999). This view is understandable; teachers do not want students to become dependent on accommodations only to have those accommodations yanked away at precisely the moment when the student needs them most. While the teacher must be the ultimate judge, however, there are 3 good reasons to consider allowing a general-education student to access accommodations in the classroom that will be off-limits during state testing.

1. *Accommodations can uncover 'academic blockers.'* The teacher who is able to identify which student access skills may require instructional accommodations is also in a good position to provide interventions proactively to strengthen those deficient access skills. For example, an instructor might note that a student does poorly on math word problems because that student has limited reading decoding skills. While the teacher may match the student to a peer who reads the word problems aloud (texts read) as a classroom accommodation, the teacher and school can also focus on improving that student's decoding skills so that she can complete similar math problems independently when taking the next state examinations.

2. *Accommodations can promote content knowledge.* Students who receive in-class accommodations are likely to increase their skills and knowledge in the course or subject content substantially beyond the level to be expected without such supports. It stands to reason that individuals whose academic skills have been strengthened through the right mix of classroom accommodations will come to the state tests with greater mastery of the content on which they are to be tested.

3. *Accommodations can build self-confidence.* When students receive classroom accommodations, they are empowered to better understand their unique pattern of learning strengths and weaknesses and the strategies that work best for them. Self-knowledge can build self-confidence. And not only are such students primed to advocate for their own educational needs; they are also well-placed to develop compensatory strategies to manage difficult, high-stakes academic situations where support is minimal—such as on state tests.

References

Institute of Education Sciences. (2012). *English Language Learners in public schools (indicator 8).* Washington, DC: National Center for Education Statistics, U.S. Department of Education. Retrieved on January 24, 2013, from http://nces.ed.gov/programs/coe/indicator_ell.asp.

Kern, L., Bambara, L., & Fogt, J. (2002). Class-wide curricular modifications to improve the behavior of students with emotional or behavioral disorders. *Behavioral Disorders, 27,* 317-326.

National Assessment of Educational Progress (NAEP). (2011a). *The nation's report card: Mathematics 2011.* Retrieved from http://nces.ed.gov/nationsreportcard/pubs/main2011/2012458.asp.

National Assessment of Educational Progress (NAEP). (2011b). *The nation's report card: Reading 2011.* Retrieved from http://nces.ed.gov/nationsreportcard/pubs/main2011/2012457.asp.

Tindal, G., Daesik, L., & Ketterlin, L. (2008). *The reliability of teacher decision-making in recommending accommodations for large-scale tests: Technical report # 08-01.* Eugene, OR: Behavioral Research and Teaching, University of Oregon.

Tindal, G., & Fuchs, L. (1999). *A summary of research on test changes: An empirical basis for defining accommodations.* Lexington, KY: Mid-South Regional Resource Center, University of Kentucky. Retrieved on January 25, 2013, from http://www.specialed.us/discoveridea/topdocs/msrrc/Tindal%26Fuchs.PDF.

How To: Use the Instructional Hierarchy to Identify Effective Teaching and Intervention Targets

Teachers recognize that learning is a continual process of growth and improvement. The student who grapples with the rudiments of a skill such as reading appears very different from the more advanced student who is a proficient and self-motivated reader. Intuitively, then, educators understand that students advance through predictable stages of learning as they move from novice to expert in a particular skill.

The Common Core Standards, too, acknowledge advancing levels of learning, as can be seen in their wording. For example, a 6th-grade Common Core Standard for Mathematics on the Number System (CCSM.6.NS.2) states that the student will "fluently divide multi-digit numbers using the standard algorithm." (National Governors Association Center for Best Practices et al., 2010; p. 42). This standard assumes that the successful student is both (1) accurate and (2) proficient (i.e., fluent) in multi-digit division--and implies as well that the student (3) will retain the skill over time, (4) will have the endurance to complete grade-appropriate tasks that include the skill, and (5) can flexibly apply or generalize the skill to those situations and settings in which multi-digit division will be useful.

The Instructional Hierarchy-IH (Haring et al., 1978) is a helpful framework to analyze stages of student learning. The Instructional Hierarchy breaks learning process into several levels, shifting from skill acquisition through skill mastery toward full integration of the skill into the student's academic repertoire. As presented here, the Instructional Hierarchy consists of 5 levels (Haring et al., 1978; Martens & Witt, 2004): Acquisition, fluency, retention, endurance, and generalization. Although initially formulated several decades ago, the Instructional Hierarchy is widely used as a model of learning in contemporary research into effective instruction and academic intervention (e.g., Ardoin & Daly, 2007).

By linking a particular student's target skill to the corresponding IH learning stage, the teacher can gain insight into what instructional supports and strategies will help that student to attain academic success. This linkage of learner to learning stage increases both teacher confidence and the probability for a positive student outcome. The table below (adapted from Haring et al., 1978 and Martens & Witt, 2004) gives instructors a brief description of each learning stage in the IH, along with suggested instructional strategies and a sample intervention idea:

1. Acquisition

Goal. At the beginning of the acquisition stage, the student has just begun to acquire the target skill. The objective is for the student to learn how to complete the skill accurately and repeatedly--without requiring the help of another.

Instructional Strategies. When just beginning a new skill, the student learns effectively through learning trials, in which the teacher: (1) *models* how to perform the skill, (2) *prompts* the student to perform the skill; and (3) *provides immediate performance feedback* to shape the student's learning in the desired direction. The teacher can maintain student motivation by providing frequent 'labeled praise' (that is, praise that specifically describes the student's positive academic behaviors and effort) and encouragement. As the student becomes accurate and more independent in the skill, the teacher can gradually fade prompting support.

Sample Intervention Idea. *Cover-copy-compare* is a student-delivered intervention that promotes acquisition of math-facts or spelling words (Skinner, McLaughlin, & Logan, 1997). The student is given a blank index card and a worksheet with spelling words or math-facts (with answers) appearing in the left column. One at a time, the student studies each original model (spelling word or math fact), covers the model with index card, from memory copies the model (spelling word or math-fact equation and answer) into the right column of the worksheet, then uncovers the model to confirm that the student work is correct. NOTE: This intervention is most appropriate for use as the student has acquired some accuracy and independence in the target skill.

2. Fluency

Goal. The student who advances into the fluency stage can complete the target skill with accuracy but works relatively slowly. The objective is for the student to maintain accuracy while increasing speed of responding (fluency).

Instructional Strategies. The student who has acquired the skill but must become more proficient benefits from (1) brief, frequent opportunities to practice the skill coupled with (2) instructional feedback about increasing speed of performance (Martens & Witt, 2004). To facilitate fluency-building, the teacher structures group learning activities to give the student plenty of opportunities for active (observable) responding. The student is also given multiple opportunities for drill (direct repetition of the target skill) and practice (combining the target skill with other skills to solve problems or accomplish tasks). The student receives feedback on the fluency and accuracy of the academic performance, as well as praise and encouragement tied to increased fluency.

Sample Intervention Idea. An example of a group strategy to promote fluency in math-facts is *explicit time drill* (Rhymer et al., 2002). The teacher hands out a math-fact worksheet. Students are told that they will have 3 minutes to work on problems on the sheet. The teacher starts the stop watch and tells the students to start work. At the end of the first minute in the 3-minute span, the teacher 'calls time', stops the stopwatch, and tells the students to underline the last number written and to put their pencils in the air. Then students are told to resume work and the teacher restarts the stopwatch. This process is repeated at the end of minutes 2 and 3. At the conclusion of the 3 minutes, the teacher collects the student worksheets.

3. Retention

Goal. At the start of the retention stage, the student is reasonably fluent but is at risk of losing proficiency in the target skill through lapses in use. At this point, the objective is to 'overlearn' the skill to insure its retention even after long periods of disuse.

Instructional Strategies. Frequent opportunities for practice can be an effective method to entrench a skill and help the student to retain it over time (Martens & Witt, 2004). The teacher can schedule numerous practice episodes within a short time ('massed review') to promote initial fluency and then reinforce longer-term retention of the skill by scheduling additional periodic review ('distributed review') across longer spans of several weeks or even months (Pashler et al., 2007).

Sample Intervention Idea. An illustration of an intervention to promote retention is *repeated reading* (Lo, Cooke, & Starling, 2011). This intervention targets reading fluency: The student is given a passage and first 'rehearses' that passage by following along silently as the tutor reads it aloud. Then the student reads the same passage aloud several times in a row, with the tutor giving performance feedback after each re-reading. If a teacher uses a fluency-building strategy such as repeated reading but sets an ambitious outcome goal that is *above* the minimum benchmark for success, the resulting 'overlearning' can support long-term retention of the skill. For example, a 4th-grade teacher uses repeated reading with a student during a mid-year intervention and tracks the student's reading fluency using timed 1-minute curriculum-based measurement oral reading fluency passages. Benchmark norms (Hasbrouck & Tindal, 2005) suggest that the student will cross over into the 'low-risk' range for reading fluency if he can read at least 87 words per minute according to the mid-year benchmark norms for grade 4. The teacher decides instead to overshoot, setting the outcome goal to a higher 95 words per minute ('overlearning') to give the student an additional margin of reading fluency to promote long-term skill retention.

4. Endurance

Goal. At the onset of the endurance stage, the student has become fluent in the target skill but will engage in it only reluctantly or for brief periods. The goal is to have the student persist in the skill for the longer intervals of time required in the classroom setting or expected for the student's age group. (Martens & Witt, 2004)

Instructional Strategies. Several instructional ideas can promote increased student endurance. In structuring lessons or independent work, for example, the teacher can gradually lengthen the period of time that the student spends in skills practice or use. The student can also be enlisted to self-monitor active engagement in skill-building activities--setting daily, increasingly ambitious work goals and then tracking whether he or she successfully reaches those goals. NOTE: If a student appears to lack 'endurance', the teacher should also verify that the fundamentals of good instruction are in place: for example, that the student can do the assigned work (instructional match), adequately understands directions, is receiving timely performance feedback, etc.

Sample Intervention Idea. An idea to increase student endurance provides breaks between gradually lengthening work intervals (*'fixed-time escape'*: adapted from Waller & Higbee, 2010). This strategy can be used with groups or individual students. The teacher first selects a target activity for endurance-building (e.g., independent reading). The teacher then sets the length of work periods by estimating the typical length of time that the student or group will currently engage in the activity (e.g., 5 minutes) before becoming off-task or disruptive. The teacher also decides on a length for brief 'escape' breaks (e.g., 2 minutes)--times when students can stop work and instead take part in preferred activities.

At the start of the intervention, the teacher directs the student or group to begin the target work activity. At the end of the work interval (e.g., 5 minutes), the teacher announces that the student or group can take a short break (e.g., 2 minutes). When that break is over, students are directed to again begin work. This sequence (work interval, escape interval) repeats until the scheduled work period is over. As students are able successfully to remain engaged during work periods, the teacher can gradually extend the length of these work periods by small increments, while reducing and then fading escape breaks, until work periods reach the desired length.

5. Generalization

Goal. At the beginning of the generalization stage, the student is accurate and fluent in using the target skill but does not always employ the skill where or when needed. The goal of this phase is to motivate the student to apply the skill in the widest possible range of appropriate settings and situations.

Instructional Strategies. The teacher can promote generalization of skills by first identifying the types of situations in which the student should apply the target skill and then programming instructional tasks that replicate or mimic these situations. So the teacher may create lessons in which students can generalize the target skills by interacting with a range of people, working with varied materials, and/or visiting different settings. The teacher can also use explicit prompts to remind students to apply skills in specific situations.

Sample Intervention Idea. For a student who does not always generalize the skill of carefully checking math assignments before turning them in, the teacher can work with that student to create a math *self-correction checklist* (Uberti, Mastropieri, & Scruggs, 2004). Teacher and student meet to create a checklist of that student's most common sources of errors on math assignments. The student is then expected to use the checklist to review math work before submitting to the teacher. This intervention strategy can be adopted to other disciplines (e.g., writing assignments) as well. And completed checklists can be collected with assignments to verify student use.

References

Ardoin, S. P., & Daly III, E. J. (2007). Close encounters of the instructional kind-how the instructional hierarchy is shaping instructional research 30 years later. *Journal of Behavioral Education, 16,* 1-6.

Haring, N.G., Lovitt, T.C., Eaton, M.D., & Hansen, C.L. (1978). The *fourth R: Research in the classroom.* Columbus, OH: Merrill.

Hasbrouck, J., & Tindal, G. (2005). *Oral reading fluency: 90 years of measurement.* Eugene, OR: Behavioral Research & Teaching/University of Oregon. Retrieved from http://brt.uoregon.edu

Lo, Y., Cooke, N. L. & Starling, A. L. P. (2011). Using a repeated reading program to improve generalization of oral reading fluency. *Education and Treatment of Children, 34*(1), 115-140.

Martens, B. K., & Witt, J. C. (2004). Competence, persistence, and success: The positive psychology of behavioral skill instruction. *Psychology in the Schools, 41*(1), 19-30.

National Governors Association Center for Best Practices & Council of Chief State School Officers. (2010). *Common core state standards for mathematics.* Washington, DC: Authors.

Pashler, H., Bain, P., Bottge, B., Graesser, A., Koedinger, K., McDaniel, M., and Metcalfe, J. (2007). *Organizing instruction and study to improve student learning* (NCER 2007-2004). Washington, DC: National Center for Education Research, Institute of Education Sciences, U.S. Department of Education. Retrieved from http://ncer.ed.gov.

Rhymer, K. N., Skinner, C. H., Jackson, S., McNeill, S., Smith, T., & Jackson, B. (2002). The 1-minute explicit timing intervention: The influence of mathematics problem difficulty. *Journal of Instructional Psychology, 29*(4), 305-311.

Skinner, C. H., McLaughlin, T. F., & Logan, P. (1997). Cover, copy, and compare: A self-managed academic intervention effective across skills, students, and settings. *Journal of Behavioral Education, 7,* 295-306.

Uberti, H. Z., Mastropieri, M. A., & Scruggs, T. E. (2004). Check it off: Individualizing a math algorithm for students with disabilities via self-monitoring checklists. *Intervention in School and Clinic, 39*(5), 269-275.

Waller, R. D., & Higbee, T. S. (2010). The effects of fixed-time escape on inappropriate and appropriate classroom behavior. *Journal of Applied Behavior Analysis, 43,* 149-153.

How To: Find Ideas for Academic Interventions—
The 'Intervention Bank'

This guide contains a range of classroom intervention ideas in reading, math, spelling, and writing that teachers can use in building their own student intervention plans. Each idea has at least one research citation to support it. While this intervention listing is not exhaustive, it can be a useful starting point for teachers to create their own 'intervention bank'.

ACADEMIC INTERVENTION SAMPLER: Reading Fluency

Academic Intervention Strategies	Research Citations
❏ READING FLUENCY: ASSISTED CLOZE. Fluency is the goal of this reading intervention. Sessions last 10-15 minutes. The teacher selects a passage at the student's instructional level. The teacher reads aloud from the passage while the student follows along silently and tracks the place in the text with a finger. Intermittently, the teacher pauses and the student is expected to read aloud the next word in passage. Then the teacher continues reading. The process continues until the entire passage has been read. Then the student is directed to read the text aloud while the teacher follows along silently. Whenever the student commits a reading error or hesitates for 3 seconds or longer (whether during the assisted cloze or independent reading phase), the teacher stops the student, points to and says the error word, has the student read the word aloud correctly, has the student read the surrounding phrase that includes the error word, and then continues the current reading activity. Optionally, the teacher may then have the student read the passage again (repeated reading) up to two more times as the teacher continues to silently monitor and correct any errors or hesitations.	Ellis, W. A. (2009). The impact of C-PEP (choral reading, partner reading, echo reading, and performance of text) on third grade fluency and comprehension development. Unpublished doctoral dissertation, University of Memphis. Homan, S. P., Klesius, J. P, & Hite, C. (1993). Effects of repeated readings and nonrepetive strategies on students' fluency and comprehension. Journal of Educational Research, 87(2), 94-99.
❏ READING FLUENCY: CHORAL READING. This simple strategy to build reading fluency can be used with individuals and groups of students. Sessions last 10-15 minutes. The teacher selects an engaging text at students' instructional or independent level. During choral reading sessions, the teacher or other fluent reader takes the role of 'lead reader', reading the passage aloud, while students also read aloud. Students are encouraged to read with expression.	Moskal, M. K., & Blachowicz, C. (2006). Partnering for fluency. New York: Guilford Press.
❏ READING FLUENCY: DUET READING. This strategy targets reading fluency. Sessions last for 10-15 minutes. The teacher selects an engaging text at the student's instructional or independent level. During duet reading, the teacher and student alternate reading aloud from the passage one word at a time, while the teacher tracks the place in the passage with an index finger. As the student grows more accomplished, the teacher can change the reading ratio to shift more responsibility to the student: for example, with the teacher reading one word aloud	Gallagher, T. M. (2008). The effects of a modified duet reading strategy on oral reading fluency. Unpublished doctoral dissertation, University of Wisconsin-Madison.

and then the student reading three words aloud in succession. As the student becomes more familiar with duet reading, the teacher can also direct the student to track the place in the text. Whenever the student commits a reading error or hesitates for 3 seconds or longer, the teacher stops the student, points to and says the error word, has the student read the word aloud correctly, has the student read the surrounding phrase that includes the error word, and then continues the reading activity.	
❏ READING FLUENCY: ECHO READING. In this strategy to boost student reading fluency, the teacher selects a text at the student's instructional level. The teacher reads aloud a short section (e.g., one-two sentences at a time) while the student follows along silently. The student then reads the same short section aloud--and the read-aloud activity continues, alternating between teacher and student, until the passage has been completed. Whenever the student commits a reading error or hesitates for 3 seconds or longer, the teacher stops the student, points to and says the error word, has the student read the word aloud correctly, has the student read the surrounding phrase that includes the error word, and then continues the reading activity.	Ellis, W. A. (2009). The impact of C-PEP (choral reading, partner reading, echo reading, and performance of text) on third grade fluency and comprehension development. Unpublished doctoral dissertation, University of Memphis. Homan, S. P., Klesius, J. P, & Hite, C. (1993). Effects of repeated readings and nonrepetive strategies on students' fluency and comprehension. Journal of Educational Research, 87(2), 94-99.
❏ READING FLUENCY: LISTENING PASSAGE PREVIEW. This intervention targets student reading fluency in sessions of 10-15 minutes. The teacher selects a passage at the student's instructional level. The student is directed to follow along silently and track the place in the text with a finger while the teacher reads the passage aloud. Then the student is prompted to read the passage aloud as the teacher follows along silently. Whenever the student commits a reading error or hesitates for 3 seconds or longer, the teacher stops the student, points to and says the error word, has the student read the word aloud correctly, has the student read the surrounding phrase that includes the error word, and then directs the student to continue reading. Optionally, the teacher may then have the student read the passage again (repeated reading) up to two more times as the teacher continues to silently monitor and correct any errors or hesitations.	Guzel-Ozmen, R. (2011). Evaluating the effectiveness of combined reading interventions on improving oral reading fluency of students with reading disabilities. Electronic Journal of Research in Educational Psychology, 9(3), 1063-1086. Hofstadter-Duke, K. L., & Daly, E. J. (2011). Improving oral reading fluency with a peer-mediated intervention. Journal of Applied Behavior

	Analysis, 44(3), 641-646.
❏ READING FLUENCY: PAIRED READING. This reading fluency intervention prompts the student to read independently with prompt corrective feedback. Each session lasts 10-15 minutes. The teacher selects an engaging passage at the student's instructional level. The student is told that the teacher and student will begin the session reading aloud in unison. The student is also told that, whenever the student chooses, he/she can give a silent signal (e.g., lightly tapping the teacher's wrist); at this signal, the teacher will stop reading aloud and instead follow along silently while the student continues to read aloud. In addition, the student is told that, if he/she hesitates for 3 seconds or longer or misreads a word when reading aloud independently, the teacher will correct the student and then resume reading in unison. The session then begins with teacher and student reading aloud together. Whenever the student commits a reading error or hesitates for 3 seconds or longer (during either unison or independent reading), the teacher stops the student, points to and says the error word, has the student read the word aloud correctly, has the student read the surrounding phrase that includes the error word, and resumes reading in unison. The teacher also praises the student for using the silent signal to read aloud independently and occasionally praises other aspects of the student's reading performance or effort.	Fiala, C. L., & Sheridan, S. M. (2003). Parent involvement and reading: Using curriculum-based measurement to assess the effects of paired reading. Psychology in the Schools, 40(6), 613-626.
❏ READING FLUENCY: REPEATED READING. During 15-20 minute sessions, the student practices difficult words in isolation, reads the same passage several times to boost fluency, and tries to beat a previous fluency score. (1) PREPARATION: Before each session, the teacher selects a text within the student's instructional range long enough occupy the student for more than a minute of reading aloud and makes teacher and student copies. The teacher locates five challenge words in the passage to practice. (2) GOAL-SETTING: The teacher shows the student the performance graph with his/her most recent repeated-reading score and encourages the student to beat that score; (3) PREVIEW CHALLENGING WORDS: The teacher introduces each of the passage challenge words: "This word is ___. What is this word?"; (4) INITIAL READ: The student is directed to read the passage aloud, to do his/her best reading, to start at the beginning of the passage [which the teacher points out] and to read until told to stop. Also, the student is told that--if stuck on a word--the teacher will supply it. While the student reads aloud, the teacher marks reading errors. At the end of one minute, the teacher says "Stop", marks the student's end-point in the text with a bracket, totals the number of words correctly read, plots that score on the student graph, and labels that graph data-point "1st reading". (5) FEEDBACK AND ERROR CORRECTION: The teacher shows the student his/her graphed performance. The teacher then reviews student errors. Pointing to each error word, the teacher says, "This word is ___. What is this word?" and has the student repeat the correct word three times before moving to the next. (6) MODELING: The teacher directs the student to read aloud in unison with the teacher while using a finger to track the place in the text. The teacher takes the lead, reading the entire passage aloud at a pace slightly faster than that of the student. (6) REPEAT STUDENT READS. The teacher has the student repeat steps 4 and 5 twice more, until the student has read the passage independently at least 3 times. If the student's fluency score on the final read exceeds that of the previous session, the teacher provides praise and perhaps incentives (e.g., sticker, points toward rewards).	Begeny, J C., Krouse, H. E., Ross, S. G., & Mitchell, R. C. (2009). Increasing elementary-aged students' reading fluency with small-group interventions: A comparison of repeated reading, listening passage preview, and listening only strategies. Journal of Behavioral Education, 18, 211-228.

Lo, Y., Cooke, N. L. & Starling, A. L. P. (2011). Using a repeated reading program to improve generalization of oral reading fluency. Education and Treatment of Children, 34(1), 115-140. |

Academic Intervention Strategies	Research Citations
❏ READING COMPREHENSION: ACTIVATE PRIOR KNOWLEDGE AND DEVELOP QUESTIONS. In this two-part strategy, students first engage in an activity to activate their prior knowledge of a topic, then preview an informational passage on the same topic to generate questions. ACTIVATING PRIOR KNOWLEDGE: The teacher prepares a short series (e.g., 3-5) of general questions or prompts about the topic to be covered in the informational passage assigned for the day's reading (e.g., "Today we are going to read about animals that live in and around the seashore. Describe animals that live around a beach."). Students are given a brief period (10-20 minutes) to write answers to these general questions based on their prior knowledge of, and experience with, the topic. DEVELOPING QUESTIONS: Students are next given a short amount of time (e.g. 3-5 minutes) to preview the informational passage assigned for that day's reading and glance over titles, figures, pictures, graphs, and other text structures appearing in the selection. Students then put the text aside and are told to write questions about the topic that they hope to have answered when they read the text. The teacher can collect these prior activation/question generation sheets as evidence of student use of this strategy.	Taboada, A., & Guthrie, J. T. (2006). Contributions of student questioning and prior knowledge to construction of knowledge from reading information text. Journal of Literacy Research, 38(1), 1-35.
❏ READING COMPREHENSION: CLASSWIDE INSTRUCTION: DEVELOP A BANK OF MULTIPLE PASSAGES FOR CHALLENGING CONCEPTS. Having several passages of differing reading levels can be a useful way to help more students grasp challenging content. The teacher notes which course concepts, cognitive strategies, or other information will likely present the greatest challenge to students. For these 'challenge' topics, the teacher selects alternative readings that present the same general information and review the same key vocabulary as the course text but that are more accessible to struggling readers (e.g., with selections written at an easier reading level or that use graphics to visually illustrate concepts). These alternative selections are organized into a bank. Students are encouraged to engage in wide reading by choosing selections from the bank as a means to better understand difficult material.	Kamil, M. L., Borman, G. D., Dole, J., Kral, C. C., Salinger, T., & Torgesen, J. (2008). Improving adolescent literacy: Effective classroom and intervention practices: A practice guide (NCEE #2008-4027). Washington, DC: National Center for Education Evaluation and Regional Assistance, Institute of Education Sciences, U.S. Department of Education. Retrieved from http://ies.ed.gov/ncee/wwc
❏ READING COMPREHENSION: CLASSWIDE INSTRUCTION: PROVIDE MAIN-IDEA PRACTICE THROUGH PARTNER RETELL. This brief paired activity can be during lectures to facilitate promote students' ability to summarize passage main ideas. Students are paired off in class and are assigned a short information passage, which either one student reads aloud to the other or is read silently by each student. Next,	Carnine, L., & Carnine, D. (2004). The interaction of reading skills and science content knowledge when

one student is assigned the role of 'reteller' and the other appointed as 'listener'. During a 1-2 minute discussion period, the reteller recounts the main idea to the listener, who can comment or ask questions. The teacher then pulls the class together and, with student input, summarizes the passage main idea and writes it on the board.. Then the student pairs resume their work, with the reteller locating two key details from the reading that support the main idea and sharing these with the listener. At the end of the activity, the teacher does a spot check -- randomly calling on one or more students in the listener role and asking them to recap what information was shared by the reteller.	teaching struggling secondary students. Reading & Writing Quarterly, 20, 203-218.
❏ READING COMPREHENSION: LINK PRONOUNS TO REFERENTS. The student reinforces understanding of abstract text by replacing pronouns with their referent nouns during independent reading. (1) PREPARING THE TEXT. On a photocopy of the text, the student circles each pronoun, identifies that pronoun's referent (i.e., the noun that it refers to), and writes next to the pronoun the name of its referent. For example, the student may add the referent to a pronoun in this sentence from a biology text: "The Cambrian Period is the first geological age that has large numbers of multi-celled organisms associated with it. [Cambrian Period]". (2) WHEN READING, SUBSTUTE REFERENTS FOR PRONOUNS. In each subsequent reading of the text, the student substitutes the referent for each pronoun.	Hedin, L. R., & Conderman, G. (2010). Teaching students to comprehend informational text through rereading. The Reading Teacher, 63(7), 556–565.
❏ READING COMPREHENSION: QUESTION GENERATION. This strategy incorporates paragraph main ideas and note-cards to promote retention of textual information: (1) LOCATE MAIN IDEAs. For each paragraph in an assigned reading, the student either (a) highlights the main idea sentence or (b) highlights key details and uses them to write a 'gist' sentence. (2) WRITE MAIN IDEAS ON NOTE-CARDS. The student then writes the main idea of that paragraph on an index card. Cards are sequentially numbered to correspond with paragraphs in the passage. (3) GENERATE REVIEW QUESTIONS. On the other side of the card, the student writes a question whose answer is that paragraph's main idea sentence. This stack of 'main idea' cards becomes a useful tool to review assigned readings.	Davey, B., & McBride, S. (1986). Effects of question-generation training on reading comprehension. Journal of Educational Psychology, 78, 256-262. Rosenshine, B., Meister, C., & Chapman, S. (1996). Teaching students to generate questions: A review of the intervention studies. Review of Educational Research, 66, 181-221.
❏ READING COMPREHENSION: READING ACTIVELY THROUGH TEXT ANNOTATION. Students are likely to increase their retention of information when they interact actively with their reading by jotting comments in the margin of the text. Using photocopies, the student is taught to engage in an ongoing 'conversation' with the writer by recording a running series of brief comments in the margins of the text. The student may write annotations to record opinions about points raised by the writer, questions triggered by the reading, or unknown vocabulary words. The teacher can set specific student annotation goals (e.g., directing the student to complete and turn in a reading with a minimum of six annotations in the margins).	Harris, J. (1990). Text annotation and underlining as metacognitive strategies to improve comprehension and retention of expository text. Paper presented at the Annual Meeting of the National Reading Conference (Miami).

	Sarkisian V., Toscano, M., Tomkins-Tinch, K., & Casey, K. (2003). Reading strategies and critical thinking. Retrieved from http://www.academic.marist.edu/alcuin/ssk/stratthink.html
❏ READING COMPREHENSION: READING-REFLECTION PAUSES: This strategy is useful both for students who need to monitor their understanding as well as those who benefit from brief breaks when engaging in intensive reading as a means to build up endurance as attentive readers. The student decides on a reading interval (e.g., every four sentences; every 3 minutes; at the end of each paragraph). At the end of each interval, the student pauses briefly to recall the main points of the reading. If the student has questions or is uncertain about the content, the student rereads part or all of the section just read.	Hedin, L. R., & Conderman, G. (2010). Teaching students to comprehend informational text through rereading. The Reading Teacher, 63(7), 556–565.
❏ READING COMPREHENSION: RECIPROCAL TEACHING. This cooperative-learning activity builds independent reading-comprehension skills while motivating students through regular (e.g., daily) peer interactions. Students meet in pairs, with reciprocal teaching sessions lasting 30-40 minutes. In advance of each session, students are given a challenging passage. Alternating roles at each session, one of the students assumes the 'teacher' role, taking the lead in guiding discussion through these six steps of the reciprocal tutoring model: The students (1) look over the passage and predict what it will cover; (2) discuss what they currently know ('prior knowledge') about the passage topic; (3) review the passage for words or phrases that are unclear and attempt to clarify their meaning; (4) review each paragraph in the passage and highlight its main idea; (5) review each paragraph again to summarize (either orally or in writing) its main idea and important details; and (6) develop questions about the passage and answer those questions from the text or their own knowledge and experience. Students practice these steps under teacher guidance until fluent. They also have the reciprocal teaching steps posted to refer to as needed.	Klingner, J. K., & Vaughn, S. (1996). Reciprocal teaching of reading comprehension strategies for students with learning disabilities who use English as a second language. The Elementary School Journal, 96, 275-293.
❏ READING COMPREHENSION: RESTRUCTURING PARAGRAPHS TO PUT MAIN IDEA FIRST. This intervention draws attention to the main-idea sentence during independent reading. The student highlights or creates a main idea sentence for each paragraph in the assigned reading. When rereading each paragraph of the selection, the student (1) reads the main idea sentence or student-generated 'gist' sentence first (irrespective of where that sentence actually falls in the paragraph); (2) reads the remainder of the paragraph, and (3) reflects on how the main idea relates to the paragraph content.	Hedin, L. R., & Conderman, G. (2010). Teaching students to comprehend informational text through rereading. The Reading Teacher, 63(7), 556–565.
❏ READING COMPREHENSION: RETAIN STORY DETAILS WITH TEXT PREVIEWING. To help students to better comprehend and retain details from an assigned story, the teacher prepares a written text preview script to be shared with students before they read the story. The strategy can be used with an individual or group of students. SCRIPT: The script opens with several statements and questions	Burns, M. K., Hodgson, J., Parker, D. C., & Fremont, K. (2011). Comparison of the effectiveness and

chosen to interest students in a discussion about the story topic or theme (e.g., "Today we are going to read about a boy who gets lost in the wilderness and must find his way home. Has anyone in this class ever been lost?"). The preview next includes a plot-summary up to the story climax--but does not give away the ending. As part of the summary, the preview describes the setting of the narrative and introduces the main characters. The preview also selects three to four difficult words appearing in the story and defines them. PRESENTATION: The teacher uses the preview script as a framework for introducing the story. Optionally, students also receive a handout listing main characters and their descriptions and the difficult vocabulary terms and definitions.	efficiency of text previewing and preteaching keywords as small-group reading comprehension strategies with middle-school students. Literacy Research and Instruction, 50, 241-252. Graves, M. F., Cooke, C. L., & Laberge, M. J. (1983). Effects of previewing difficult short stories on low ability junior high school students' comprehension, recall, and attitudes. Reading Research Quarterly,18(3), 262-276.
❏ READING COMPREHENSION: RETAIN TEXT INFORMATION WITH PARAPHRASING (RAP). Students who fail to retain important details from their reading can be taught a self-directed paraphrasing strategy. The student is trained to use a 3-step cognitive strategy when reading each paragraph of an information-text passage: (1) READ the paragraph; (2) ASK oneself what the main idea of the paragraph is and what two key details support that main idea; (3) PARAPHRASE the main idea and two supporting details into one's own words. This 3-step strategy is easily memorized using the acronym RAP (read-ask-paraphrase). OPTIONAL BUT RECOMMENDED: Create an organizer sheet with spaces for the student to record the main idea and supporting details of multiple paragraphs to be used with the RAP strategy. RAP organizer forms can provide structure to the student and yield work products that the teacher can collect to verify that the student is using the strategy.	Hagaman, J. L., Casey, K. J., & Reid, R. (2010). The effects of the paraphrasing strategy on the reading comprehension of young students. Remedial and Special Education, 33, 110-123. Klingner, J. K., & Vaughn, S. (1996). Reciprocal teaching of reading comprehension strategies for students with learning disabilities who use English as a second language. The Elementary School Journal, 96, 275-293.
❏ READING COMPREHENSION: RETAIN TEXT INFORMATION WITH SELF-QUESTIONING FROM TEXT TITLES. To better retain information from textbooks and other informational text, the student is taught to use a four-step self-questioning strategy and related 'fix-up' skills during independent reading. SELF-QUESTIONING STRATEGY: The teacher creates a strategy sheet as a student resource for this intervention. The sheet contains several simple steps in	Berkeley, S., Marshak, L., Mastropieri, M. A., & Scruggs, T. E. (2011). Improving student comprehension of social studies text: A

checklist format that the student applies to independent reading of an informational passage: (1) Preview the titles and sub-titles in the passage; (2) Rewrite each title as a question: e.g., The title "Causes of the American Civil War" might convert to the question "What were the main causes of the Civil War?"; (3) Read the passage; (4) Review the self-generated questions and--based on the reading--attempt to answer them. FIX-UP STRATEGIES: The strategy sheet also directs the student to apply simple fix-up strategies if unable to answer a self-generated question: (1) Re-read that section of the passage; (2) Verify that you know all vocabulary terms in the passage--and look up the meaning of any unknown words; (3) examine the passage for other 'text structures' such as tables, graphs, maps, or captioned pictures that may help to answer the question; (4) write down remaining unanswered questions to review with the teacher or tutor. To monitor use of this strategy, the teacher may direct the student to write down self-generated questions from reading assignments for the teacher's review.	self-questioning strategy for inclusive middle school classes. Remedial and Special Education 32, 105-113.
❏ READING COMPREHENSION: SUMMARIZE READINGS. The act of summarizing longer readings can promote understanding and retention of content while the summarized text itself can be a useful study tool. The student is taught to condense assigned readings into condensed summaries--consisting of main ideas and essential details and stripped of superfluous content.	Boardman, A. G., Roberts, G., Vaughn, S., Wexler, J., Murray, C. S., & Kosanovich, M. (2008). Effective instruction for adolescent struggling readers: A practice brief. Portsmouth, NH: RMC Research Corporation, Center on Instruction.
❏ READING COMPREHENSION: TEXT ENHANCEMENTS. Text enhancements can be used to tag important vocabulary terms, key ideas, or other reading content. If working with photocopied material, the student can use a highlighter to note key ideas or vocabulary. Another enhancement strategy is the 'lasso and rope' technique—using a pen or pencil to circle a vocabulary term and then drawing a line that connects that term to its underlined definition. If working from a textbook, the student can cut sticky notes into strips. These strips can be inserted in the book as pointers to text of interest. They can also be used as temporary labels—e.g., for writing a vocabulary term and its definition.	Hedin, L. R., & Conderman, G. (2010). Teaching students to comprehend informational text through rereading. The Reading Teacher, 63(7), 556–565.
❏ READING COMPREHENSION: VERBAL PROMPT WITH INCENTIVE. To boost student comprehension of a passage, use a verbal prompt before the reading paired with an incentive. Before the student begins reading a story or informational-text passage, the teacher says: "Read this story/passage out loud. Try to remember as much as you can about the story/passage. Then I will have you retell the main points of the story/passage. If you remember enough of the reading, you will get a sticker [or other prize or incentive]." If the student needs a reminder during the reading, the teacher says: "Work on remembering as much of the reading as you can." At the end of the reading, the student is told to recount the main points of the passage and is awarded the promised incentive at the discretion of the teacher.	O'Shea, L. J., Sindelar, P. T., & O'Shea, D. J. (1985). The effects of repeated reading and attentional cues on reading fluency and comprehension. Journal of Literacy Research, 17(2), 129-142.

Academic Intervention Strategies	Research Citations
❑ WRITING: PRODUCTION: DRAWING AS A PRE-WRITING ACTIVITY. The teacher presents the student with a motivating writing topic and allocates a sufficient time (e.g., 30 minutes) for the student to produce a composition. During the writing period, the student is directed to first draw a picture about the topic and then to write a composition on the same topic.	Norris, E., Mokhtari, K., & Reichard, C. (1998). Children's use of drawing as a pre-writing strategy. Journal of Research in Reading, 21(1), 69-74.
❑ WRITING: PRODUCTION: REGULAR WRITING WITH PROMPTS. The student engages in 20-minute writing sessions. Before each writing session the student briefly reviews the following prompts for writing mechanics--with an instructor or in peer pairs or groups--and has them available as a written checklist: (1) Use complete sentences. Each sentence should 'sound complete' and contain at least one subject and one verb. (2) Indent and punctuate. The first sentence of each new paragraph is indented. Each sentence in the passage has appropriate end-punctuation (period, question mark, exclamation point). Quotation marks are used to denote the exact words spoken by someone. (3) Capitalize. The initial letters of these words are capitalized: the first word in a sentence; the names of proper nouns. At the end of the session, the student uses the mechanics checklist to revise the writing sample before turning it in.	Harriman, N. E., & Gajar, A.H. (1986). The effects of repeated writing and repeated revision strategies on composing fluency of learning disabled adolescents (Report No. ED290312). Educational Resources Information Center.
❑ WRITING: PRODUCTION: TIME-DRILLS AND GRAPHING. This intervention uses 5-minute writing drills with visual feedback (graphing) to improve the writing fluency of groups or the entire class. WRITING DRILL: The session opens with quick brainstorming or topic discussion to prime student writers. Then the teacher sets a timer and tells the students to write for five minutes. The teacher announces when there is one minute remaining in the session and tells students to stop writing when the timer sounds. The following rules are publicly posted and reviewed with students before writing sessions: (1) Write quickly in legible handwriting;(2) Cross out mistakes and continue writing;(3) Write for the full 5 minutes; (4) Refrain from talking or other distracting behavior; and(5) Do not request bathroom or drink breaks during the drill. SCORING: Students count up the number of words written and exchange their writing samples with a neighbor, who re-counts total words written to ensure accuracy. (The teacher resolves any scoring disagreements between students.) GRAPHING AND INCENTIVES: Each student updates a paper or computerized bar graph to include the current day's writing total and cumulative weekly total. Students receive recognition (e.g., praise) for improved daily scores and earn incentives (e.g., 10 minutes free time) for improved weekly scores. The teacher also collects writing scores from all students on a daily basis, with rotating students updating a daily class chart. The teacher acknowledges daily class improvement and provides an incentive for weekly class improvements (e.g., special class game played at the end of the week).	Kasper-Ferguson, S., & Moxley, R. A. (2002). Developing a writing package with student graphing of fluency. Education and Treatment of Children, 25(2), 249-267.

Academic Intervention Strategies	Research Citations
❏ GRAPHOMOTOR: PROVIDE ADDITIONAL PRACTICE ON DIFFICULT LETTERS. Students tend to have the greatest difficulty acquiring these 7 lower-case letters: [q, j, z, u, n, k, and a]. When learning these letters, therefore, a student would benefit from use of models, additional teacher demonstration, supervised practice, and extra opportunities for practice.	Graham, S. (1999). Handwriting and spelling instruction for students with learning disabilities: A review. Learning Disability Quarterly, 22(2), 78-98.
❏ GRAPHOMOTOR: SPACE LETTER-WRITING PRACTICE ACROSS MULTIPLE SESSIONS. When taught to write a new letter, the student should practice it for a short period with teacher supervision and feedback. Before concluding the initial practice session, the student is told to self-evaluate his or her copying efforts by circling the two that are best drawn. The student continues to practice the letter for brief periods daily or several times per week until fluent in writing it. Once sufficient letters have been learned, practice sessions can be made more meaningful by requiring the student first to write all of the letters that he or she knows and then to compose or copy a brief composition (e.g., one to two sentences) to practice letter-writing in context.	Graham, S. (1999). Handwriting and spelling instruction for students with learning disabilities: A review. Learning Disability Quarterly, 22(2), 78-98.
❏ GRAPHOMOTOR: USE COLORED PAPER TO INCREASE WRITING LEGIBILITY. Students with attention or impulsivity issues may improve the legibility of handwriting for spelling and writing tasks through use of colored writing paper. In preparation, the student is offered a range of colored paper choices ranging from pastels to bright, highly saturated (neon) hues. The paper in the color chosen by the student is then prepared by adding ruled lines for writing. Whenever the student has an important writing task in which legibility is important, he or she is encouraged to use writing paper of the preferred color.	Imhof, M. (2004). Effects of color stimulation on handwriting performance of children with ADHD without and with additional learning disabilities. European Child & Adolescent Psychiatry, 13, 191-198.
❏ GRAPHOMOTOR: USE MODELS FOR LETTER FORMATION. To help the student to write letter shapes appropriately, the teacher provides the student with models of each letter with numbered arrows to show the orientation, order, and direction of each stroke that makes up the letter.	Graham, S. (1999). Handwriting and spelling instruction for students with learning disabilities: A review. Learning Disability Quarterly, 22(2), 78-98.

ACADEMIC INTERVENTION SAMPLER: Spelling

Academic Intervention Strategies	Research Citations
❑ SPELLING: ASSESSMENT: EVALUATE STUDENT GROWTH DAILY. Each day, before the student practices spelling words (whether alone, with a peer, or with an adult), the teacher administers a brief spelling pre-test. The daily pre-test contains any spelling words that the student is currently working on or that will be introduced during the day's session.(In addition, the daily pre-test should also contain a sampling of words previously learned as a maintenance check.) At the end of the student's practice period, the same spelling list is readministered to the student--with words presented in a different order-- to formatively track spelling growth. Results are shared with the student.	Graham, S.,& Voth, V. P. (1990). Spelling instruction: Making modifications for students with learning disabilities. Academic Therapy, 25(4), 447-457.
❑ SPELLING: ASSESSMENT: GIVE PRE- AND POST-TESTS. Before assigning a spelling list, the teacher tests students' knowledge of words on the list by giving a non-graded spelling pre-test. Students then study the words they spelled incorrectly--narrowing the number of spelling items to be practiced. At the end of the study period, students are re-tested on the full spelling list and receive a grade.	Graham, S. (1999). Handwriting and spelling instruction for students with learning disabilities: A review. Learning Disability Quarterly, 22(2), 78-98.
❑ SPELLING: MOTIVATE ON-TASK BEHAVIOR THROUGH SELF-MONITORING. During spelling-review sessions, direct the student to keep track of the number of times that he or she practices a particular word (e.g., by putting a series of tally marks next to each word on the spelling list). Self-monitoring can increase the student's rate of on-task behavior and academic engagement.	Graham, S.,& Voth, V. P. (1990). Spelling instruction: Making modifications for students with learning disabilities. Academic Therapy, 25(4), 447-457.
❑ SPELLING: PERSONALIZED DICTIONARY. As a writing aid, help the student to compile her or his own spelling dictionary made up of 'spelling demons' (common words that challenge any speller), as well as other words that the student commonly misspells. When writing and revising a writing assignment, the student consults the dictionary as needed. This dictionary should grow over time as the student encounters more advanced vocabulary and more demanding spelling lists.	Graham, S.,& Voth, V. P. (1990). Spelling instruction: Making modifications for students with learning disabilities. Academic Therapy, 25(4), 447-457.
❑ SPELLING: PRACTICE: ADD-A-WORD. The Add-a-Word program is well-suited for the student who needs a high rate of success and review to maintain spelling motivation. The student is given an initial list of 10 spelling words. For each word, the student applies the Cover-Copy-Compare (CCC) strategy: (1) The student looks the correctly spelled word on the spelling list; (2) The student covers the model word(e.g., with an index card); (3) From memory, the student writes the spelling word; (4) The student uncovers the original model and compares it to the student response; (5) If incorrect, the student repeats the CCC steps with the error word. The student	Schermerhorn, P. K., & McLaughlin, T. F. (1997): Effects of the Add-A-Word spelling program on test accuracy, grades, and retention of spelling words with fifth and sixth

reviews each spelling word on the list using CCC until he or she spells it correctly twice in a row. At the end of the practice session, the student is given an exit spelling test on all 10 words and scores (or has the teacher score) the test. All correct words on the test are added to the student's log of mastered spelling words. Any word spelled correctly on the exit test two days in a row is removed from the current 10-word list, to be replaced by a new word. A week after initial mastery, mastered words are included as review words on the student's daily exit spelling test . If spelled correctly on the one-week checkup, mastered words are placed again as review words on the spelling test one month later. Any mastered word misspelled on either review test goes back onto the student's 10-item current spelling list.	grade regular education students. Child & Family Behavior Therapy, 19(1), 23-35.
❑ SPELLING: PRACTICE: ADOPT A KINESTHETIC APPROACH. The student is trained to practice spelling words using the following sequence: (1) The student says the word aloud; (2) The student writes the word and then says it again; (3) The student checks the word by consulting the spelling list and corrects the word if required; (4) The student traces the letters of the word while saying the word; (5) The student again writes the word from memory, checks the word, and corrects it if required. The student then moves to the next word on the spelling list and repeats the steps above.	Graham, S., & Freeman, S. (1986). Strategy training and teacher vs. student-controlled study conditions: Effects on learning disabled students' spelling performance. Learning Disability Quarterly, 9, 15-22.
❑ SPELLING: PRACTICE: BREAK THE LARGER LIST INTO SMALLER SEGMENTS. Rather than overwhelming the student with a large set of spelling words to be mastered all at once, introduce 3-4 new words per day for the student to practice from the larger list. Once all words from the master list have been introduced, continue to practice until the full list has been mastered.	Graham, S. (1999). Handwriting and spelling instruction for students with learning disabilities: A review. Learning Disability Quarterly, 22(2), 78-98.
❑ SPELLING: PRACTICE: COVER-COPY-COMPARE. The student is trained to practice spelling words using the following sequence: (1) The student looks at a model of the correctly spelled word; (2) The student covers the model word(e.g., with an index card); (3) From memory, the student writes the spelling word; (4) The student uncovers the original model and compares it to the student response; (5) If incorrect, the student repeats steps 1-4 with the error word. If correct, the student goes to the next word on the spelling list and applies steps 1-4.	Skinner, C. H., McLaughlin, T. F., & Logan, P. (1997). Cover, copy, and compare: A self-managed academic intervention effective across skills, students, and settings. Journal of Behavioral Education, 7, 295-306.
❑ SPELLING: PRACTICE: ENGAGE IN A CLASSWIDE GAME. To make the study of spelling words more engaging, the teacher can divide the class at random each week into two teams. Within each team, students are paired off. Each pair meets through the week (e.g., daily) for 10-minute sessions. During the first 5 minutes, one student takes the role of tutor. The tutor reads words from the weekly spelling list aloud to the other student/tutee, who writes the word down and at the same time calls out each letter of the word being written. If the tutee correctly spells the word, he or she is awarded 2 points. If the word is incorrect, the tutor reads the word and spells it correctly aloud; has the tutee successfully write the word three times; and then awards the tutee 1 point. At the end of 5 minutes, the pair reverses the roles of tutor	Graham, S. (1999). Handwriting and spelling instruction for students with learning disabilities: A review. Learning Disability Quarterly, 22(2), 78-98.

and tutee and repeat the process. When finished, the pair reports its cumulative points to the teacher. Team totals are posted each day and added to the weekly team point totals. At the end of the week, students take the final spelling test and receive 3 points for each correct word. These spelling test points are also added to the team totals. At the end of the week, the class team with the most spelling points wins a certificate.	
❏ SPELLING: PRACTICE: HIGHTLIGHT PHONEMIC ELEMENTS. The teach and student practice spelling words using the following sequence: (1) The teacher states the word aloud, then points to each letter and gives its name; (2) The student next states the word aloud, then points to each letter and gives its name; (3) The teacher shows a copy of the word to the student with the onset and rime displayed in different colors; (4) The teacher points first to the onset of the word and pronounces it, then points to the rime and pronounces it; (5) The student then points first to the onset and pronounces it, then points to the rime and pronounces it. NOTE: In a single-syllable word, the onset consists of the consonant(s) appearing at the front of the word, while the rime is the part of the word made up of its vowel and any consonants that follow the vowel. For example, in the word black, the onset is [bl-] and the rime is[–ack].	Berninger, V., Vaughn, K., Abbott, R., Brooks, A., Abbott, S., Rogan, L., Reed, E., & Graham, S. (1998). A multiple connections approach to early intervention for spelling problems: Integrating instructional, learner, and stimulus variables. Journal of Educational Psychology, 90, 587-605.
❏ SPELLING: PRACTICE: OFFER CHOICE OF STRATEGIES. Students can be offered several strategies for effective spelling practice and directed to select one or more to use independently or under teacher supervision. Strategies include (1) pronouncing a word slowly and clearly before writing it; (2) saying the letters aloud while writing them; (3) tracing the word as part of the practice sequence; (4) closing one's eyes and visualizing the letters that make up the word; and (5) circling the problem letters of a word misspelled by the student , studying them, and then studying the correct spelling of that word.	Graham, S. (1999). Handwriting and spelling instruction for students with learning disabilities: A review. Learning Disability Quarterly, 22(2), 78-98.
❏ SPELLING: PRACTICE: REPEATED DRILL WITH SOUNDING OUT. The teach and student practice spelling words using the following sequence: (1) The teacher shows the student a flashcard with the spelling word and reads the word aloud; (2) The student reads the word aloud from the flashcard; (3) The teacher withdraws the flashcard; (4) The student writes the word from memory, saying the name of each letter while writing it; (5) The student reads aloud the word just written; (6) The teacher again shows the correct word model on the flashcard. If the student response is incorrect, the student corrects the spelling using the flashcard model. (7) Teacher and student repeat steps 1-6 twice.	Graham, S. (1999). Handwriting and spelling instruction for students with learning disabilities: A review. Learning Disability Quarterly, 22(2), 78-98. Mann, T. B., Bushell Jr., D., & Morris, E. K. (2010). Use of sounding out to improve spelling in young children. Journal of Applied Behavior Analysis, 43(1), 89-93.
❏ SPELLING: PRACTICE: VISUALIZATION. The student is trained to practice spelling words using the following sequence: (1) The student looks at the target spelling word, reads it aloud, then covers the word (e.g., with an index card); (2) The student closes his or her eyes and pictures the word; (3) Still with eyes closed, the student silently	Berninger, V., Abbott, R., Whitaker, D., Sylvester, L., & Nolan, S. (1995). Integrating

names each letter in the word; (4) The student opens his or her eyes and writes the word; (5) The student uncovers the original model and checks the spelling of the student response. (6) If incorrect, the student repeats steps 1-5 with the current word. If correct, the student advances to the next word to repeat the process.	low- and high-level skills in instructional protocols for writing disabilities. Learning Disability Quarterly, 18, 293-310.
❑ SPELLING: TRAIN SPELLING-WORD PREDICTION SKILLS. When students can accurately assess which words on a spelling list are likely to be the most difficult, they can better and more efficiently allocate study time. Whenever giving the student a spelling list, have the student review the new words and circle those that the student predicts that he or she can spell correctly. In follow-up assessments, compare these initial predictions to actual performance as feedback about how accurately the student can predict success. Over time, the student should become more skilled in judging which spelling words will require the greatest study effort.	Graham, S.,& Voth, V. P. (1990). Spelling instruction: Making modifications for students with learning disabilities. Academic Therapy, 25(4), 447-457.

ACADEMIC INTERVENTION SAMPLER: Math Shortcuts

Academic Intervention Strategies	Research Citations
❏ MATH: SHORTCUTS: ADDITION. Teach the student these shortcuts to help with basic addition: (1) The order of the numbers in an addition problem does not affect the answer. (2) When zero is added to the original number, the answer is the original number. (3) When 1 is added to the original number, the answer is the next larger number.	Miller, S.P., Strawser, S., & Mercer, C.D. (1996). Promoting strategic math performance among students with learning disabilities. LD Forum, 21(2), 34-40.
❏ MATH: SHORTCUTS: SUBTRACTION. Teach the student these shortcuts to help with basic subtraction: (1) When zero is subtracted from the original number, the answer is the original number. (2) When 1 is subtracted from the original number, the answer is the next smaller number. (3) When the original number has the same number subtracted from it, the answer is zero.	4 Miller, S.P., Strawser, S., & Mercer, C.D. (1996). Promoting strategic math performance among students with learning disabilities. LD Forum, 21(2), 34-40.
❏ MATH: SHORTCUTS: MULTIPLICATION. Teach the student these shortcuts to help with basic multiplication: (1) When a number is multiplied by zero, the answer is zero. (2) When a number is multiplied by 1, the answer is the original number. (3) When a number is multiplied by 2, the answer is equal to the number being added to itself. (4) The order of the numbers in a multiplication problem does not affect the answer.	4 Miller, S.P., Strawser, S., & Mercer, C.D. (1996). Promoting strategic math performance among students with learning disabilities. LD Forum, 21(2), 34-40.
❏ MATH: SHORTCUTS: DIVISION. Teach the student these shortcuts to help with basic division: (1) When zero is divided by any number, the answer is zero. (2) When a number is divided by 1, the answer is the original number. (3) When a number is divided by itself, the answer is 1.	Miller, S.P., Strawser, S., & Mercer, C.D. (1996). Promoting strategic math performance among students with learning disabilities. LD Forum, 21(2), 34-40.

ACADEMIC INTERVENTION SAMPLER: Math Facts

Academic Intervention Strategies	Research Citations
❏ MATH: ARITHMETIC FACTS: ACQUISITION: COVER-COPY-COMPARE. To memorize arithmetic facts, the student can be trained to independently use Cover-Copy-Compare: The student is given a worksheet with computation problems and answers appearing on the left side of the sheet, and the right side of the page left	Skinner, C. H., McLaughlin, T. F., & Logan, P. (1997). Cover, copy, and compare: A

blank. The student is also given an index card. For each arithmetic-fact item, the student is directed (1) to study the correct arithmetic problem and answer on the left, (2) to cover the correct model with the index card, (3) from memory, to copy the arithmetic fact and answer onto the work space on the right side of the sheet, and (4) to compare the student version of the arithmetic fact and answer to the original model to ensure that it was copied correctly and completely.	self-managed academic intervention effective across skills, students, and settings. Journal of Behavioral Education, 7, 295-306.
❏ MATH: ARITHMETIC FACTS: ACQUISITION: INCREMENTAL REHEARSAL. Incremental rehearsal is a useful strategy to help the student to acquire arithmetic facts. Sessions last 10-15 minutes. In preparation for this intervention, the teacher prepares a set of arithmetic-fact flashcards displaying equations but no answers. The teacher reviews all of the flashcards with the student. Flashcards that the student correctly answers within 2 seconds are sorted into a 'KNOWN' pile, while flashcards for which the student gives an incorrect answer or hesitates for longer than 2 seconds are sorted into the 'UNKNOWN' pile. During the intervention: (1) the teacher selects a card from the UNKNOWN pile (Card UK1), presents it to the student, reads off the arithmetic problem, and provides the answer (e.g., '4 x 8=32'). The student is then prompted to read the problem and give the correct answer (2) Next, the teacher selects a card from the KNOWN pile (Card K1) and adds it to the previously practiced card (UK1). In succession, the teacher shows the student the unknown (UK1) and the known (K1) card. The student has 2 seconds to provide an answer for each card. Whenever the student responds incorrectly or hesitates for longer than 2 seconds, the teacher corrects student responses as needed and has the student state the correct response. (3) The teacher then selects a second card from the KNOWN pile (card K2) and adds it to the student stack--reviewing cards UK1, K1, and K2. (4) This incremental review process repeats until the student's flashcard stack comprises 10 cards: 1 unknown and 9 known. (5) At this point, the original unknown card (UK1) is now considered to be a 'known' card and is retained in the student's review-card stack. To make room for it, the last known card (K9) is removed, leaving 9 known cards in that student's stack. (6) The teacher then draws a new card from the UNKNOWN pile (card UK2) and repeats the incremental review process described above, each time adding known cards from the 9-card student stack in incremental fashion.	Burns, M. K. (2005). Using incremental rehearsal to increase fluency of single-digit multiplication facts with children identified as learning disabled in mathematics computation. Education and Treatment of Children, 28, 237-249.
❏ MATH COMPUTATION STRATEGY: ACQUISITION: STUDENT HIGHLIGHTING. Students who are inattentive or impulsive can improve their accuracy and fluency on math computation problems through student-performed highlighting. The student is given highlighters of several colors and a math computation sheet. Before completing the worksheet, the student is directed to color-code the problems on the sheet in a manner of his or her choosing (e.g., by level of difficulty, by math operation). The student then completes the highlighted worksheet.	Kercood, S., & Grskovic, J. A. (2009). The effects of highlighting on the math computation performance and off-task behavior of students with attention problems. Education and Treatment of Children, 32, 231-241.
❏ MATH: ARITHMETIC FACTS: FLUENCY: PERFORMANCE FEEDBACK & GOAL-SETTING. The student gets regular feedback about computation fluency and sets performance goals. In preparation for this intervention, the teacher decides on a fixed time limit for worksheet drills (e.g., 5 or 10 minutes) --with an equivalent worksheet to be prepared for each session. In each session, before the student	Codding, R. S., Baglici, S., Gottesman, D., Johnson, M., Kert, A. S., & LeBeouf, P. (2009).Selecting

begins the worksheet, (1) the teacher provides the student with feedback about the number of correct problems and errors on the most recent previous worksheet, and (2) the teacher and student agree on an improvement-goal for the current worksheet (e.g., to increase the number of correct problems by at least 2 and to reduce the errors by at least 1). Student performance on worksheets is charted at each session.	intervention strategies: Using brief experimental analysis for mathematics problems. Journal of Applied School Psychology, 25, 146-168.
❏ MATH: ARITHMETIC FACTS: FLUENCY: PROVIDE INCENTIVES. A student may benefit from incentives to increase fluency with math facts. BRIEF ANALYSIS: The teacher first conducts a brief experimental analysis to determine whether incentives will increase a particular student's performance: (1) The student is given a worksheet with arithmetic facts and allotted two minutes to complete as many items as possible. The student receives a point for each correct digit written on the worksheet. (2) The teacher next prepares an equivalent worksheet with different problems--but composed of the same type and number of problems. (3) Before administering the second worksheet, the teacher presents the student with a 'prize bag' with tangible items (e.g., markers, small toys) and perhaps edible items (e.g., packaged raisins, crackers, etc.). The student is told that if he/she can increase performance on the second worksheet by at least 30%, the student will earn a prize. The student is asked to select a preferred prize from the prize bag. (4) The student is given the second worksheet and works on it for 2 minutes. Again, the worksheet is scored for correct digits. (5) If the student meets the fluency goal, he/she receives the selected prize. If the student fails to meet the goal, he/she is given a sticker as a consolation prize. USE OF INCENTIVES: The teacher uses incentives only if the preceding brief analysis indicates that incentives are an effective motivator. For this intervention, the teacher decides on a fixed time limit for worksheet drills (e.g., 5 or 10 minutes) --with an equivalent worksheet to be prepared for each session. In each session, before the student begins the worksheet, (1) the student is asked to select a potential prize from the prize bag, (2) the student reviews his/her most recent previous worksheet score, and (3) the student and teacher set an improvement goal for the current worksheet (e.g., to exceed the previous score by at least 2 correct digits). If the student meets the goal, he/she is given the prize; if the student falls short, the teacher provides verbal encouragement and perhaps a sticker as a consolation prize. Student performance on worksheets is charted at each session.	Codding, R. S., Baglici, S., Gottesman, D., Johnson, M., Kert, A. S., & LeBeouf, P. (2009).Selecting intervention strategies: Using brief experimental analysis for mathematics problems. Journal of Applied School Psychology, 25, 146-168.
❏ MATH: ARITHMETIC FACTS: FLUENCY: TIME DRILLS. Explicit time-drills are a method to boost students' rate of responding on arithmetic-fact worksheets: (1) The teacher hands out the worksheet. Students are instructed that they will have 3 minutes to work on problems on the sheet. (2) The teacher starts the stop watch and tells the students to start work. (3) At the end of the first minute in the 3-minute span, the teacher 'calls time', stops the stopwatch, and tells the students to underline the last number written and to put their pencils in the air. Then students are told to resume work and the teacher restarts the stopwatch. (4) This process is repeated at the end of minutes 2 and 3. (5) At the conclusion of the 3 minutes, the teacher collects the student worksheets.	Rhymer, K. N., Skinner, C. H., Jackson, S., McNeill, S., Smith, T., & Jackson, B. (2002). The 1-minute explicit timing intervention: The influence of mathematics problem difficulty. Journal of Instructional Psychology, 29(4), 305-311. Skinner, C. H., Pappas,

	D. N., & Davis, K. A. (2005). Enhancing academic engagement: Providing opportunities for responding and influencing students to choose to respond. Psychology in the Schools, 42, 389-403.

ACADEMIC INTERVENTION SAMPLER: Math Computation Strategies

Academic Intervention Strategies	Research Citations
❏ MATH: COMPUTATION STRATEGY: ADDITION: COUNT-UP. Train the student to use this strategy to complete basic addition operations: (1) The student is given a copy of a number-line spanning 0-20. (2) When presented with a two-addend addition problem, the student is taught to start with the larger of the two addends and to 'count up' by the amount of the smaller addend to arrive at the answer to the addition problem.	Fuchs, L. S., Powell, S. R., Seethaler, P. M., Cirino, P. T., Fletcher, J. M., Fuchs, D., & Hamlett, C. L. (2009). The effects of strategic counting instruction, with and without deliberate practice, on number combination skill among students with mathematics difficulties. Learning and Individual Differences 20(2), 89-100.
❏ MATH: COMPUTATION STRATEGY: SUBTRACTION: COUNT-UP. Train the student to use this strategy to complete basic subtraction operations: (1) The student is given a copy of a number-line spanning 0-20. (2) The student is taught to refer to the first number appearing in the subtraction problem (the minuend) as 'the number you start with' and to refer to the number appearing after the minus (subtrahend) as 'the minus number'. (3) The student is directed to start at the minus number on the number-line and --from that start point--to count up to the starting number while keeping a running tally of numbers counted up on his or her fingers. (4) The final tally of digits separating the minus number and starting number is the answer to the subtraction problem.	Fuchs, L. S., Powell, S. R., Seethaler, P. M., Cirino, P. T., Fletcher, J. M., Fuchs, D., & Hamlett, C. L. (2009). The effects of strategic counting instruction, with and without deliberate practice, on number combination skill among students with mathematics difficulties. Learning and Individual Differences 20(2), 89-100.
❏ MATH: COMPUTATION STRATEGY: MULTIPLICATION: COUNT-BY. Train the student to use this strategy to complete basic multiplication operations: (1) The student looks at the two terms of the multiplication problem and chooses one of the terms as a number that he or she can count by (the 'count by' number). (2) The student takes the remaining term from the multiplication problem (the 'count times'	Cullinan, D., Lloyd, J., & Epstein, M.H. (1981). Strategy training: A structured approach to arithmetic instruction.

number) and makes a corresponding number of tally marks to match it. (3) The student starts counting using the 'count by' number. While counting, the student touches each of the tally marks matching the 'count times' number. (4) The student stops counting when he or she has reached the final tally-mark. (5) The student writes down the last number said as the answer to the multiplication problem.	Exceptional Education Quarterly, 2, 41-49.

ACADEMIC INTERVENTION SAMPLER: Word Problems

Academic Intervention Strategies	Research Citations
❏ MATH: WORD PROBLEMS: ACQUISITION: USE WORKED EXAMPLES. Students acquiring math skills in the form of word-problems benefit from being given completed problems ('worked examples') to study. Teachers should observe these recommendations when formatting, teacher, and using worked examples as a student support: (1) FORMAT PROBLEM-SOLVING STEPS: the solution presented in the worked example should be broken down into discrete, labeled sub-steps/sub-goals corresponding to the appropriate process for solving the problem. (2) COMBINE TEXT AND GRAPHICS. If both text and visual elements appear in the worked example, they should be integrated into a single unitary display, if possible, rather than split into separate components--so as not to overwhelm the novice learner. (3) PAIR WORKED WITH UNWORKED EXAMPLES. Whenever the student is given a worked example to study, he or she should then immediately be presented with 1-2 similar examples to solve.	Atkinson, R. K., Derry, S. J., Renkl, A., & Wortham, D. (2000). Learning from examples: Instructional principles from the worked examples research. Review of Educational Research, 70(2), 181-214.
❏ MATH: WORD PROBLEMS: METACOGNITION: PAIRING WORKED EXAMPLES WITH SELF-EXPLANATION. Students who can coach themselves through math problem-solving steps ('self-explanation') demonstrate increased conceptual understanding of the task. The student should be explicitly coached to 'self-explain' each of the steps to be used in solving a particular type of problem--starting with completed problems ('worked examples') before advancing to unworked problems: (1) INTRODUCTION TO SELF-EXPLANATION. The teacher first explains the importance of self-explanation as a student math self-help skill. (2) TEACHER MODELING. Next, the teacher models self-explanation, applying the appropriate problem-solving steps to a worked example. (3) STUDENT MODELING WITH TEACHER FEEDBACK. The teacher then coaches the student's own self-explanation efforts, as the student moves through the steps of a second worked example. (4) INDEPENDENT STUDENT APPLICATION. When the student has successfully mastered the process, he or she is directed to use self-explanation during the problem-solving steps with any unworked problems.	Atkinson, R. K., Derry, S. J., Renkl, A., & Wortham, D. (2000). Learning from examples: Instructional principles from the worked examples research. Review of Educational Research, 70(2), 181-214. Tajika, H., Nakatsu, N., Nozaki, H., Neumann, E., & Maruno, S. (2007). Self-explanation for solving mathematical word problems: Effects of self-explanation as a metacognitive strategy for solving mathematical word problems. Japanese Psychological Research, 49(3), 222-233.

❏ MATH: WORD PROBLEMS: STRATEGY: DRAW THE PROBLEM. The student can clarify understanding of a word problem by making a drawing of it before solving. To teach this strategy: (1) The teacher gives the student a worksheet containing at least six word problems. (2) The teacher explains to the student that making a picture of a word problem can make that problem clearer and easier to solve. (3) The teacher and student independently create drawings of each of the problems on the worksheet. (4) Next, the student shows his or her drawings for each problem while explaining each drawing and how it relates to the word problem. (5) The teacher also participates, explaining his or her drawings to the student. (6) The student is then directed to 'draw the problem' whenever solving challenging word problems.	Van Garderen, D. (2006). Spatial visualization, visual imagery, and mathematical problem solving of students with varying abilities. Journal of Learning Disabilities, 39, 496-506.
❏ MATH: WORD PROBLEMS: STRATEGY: 4-STEP PLANNING PROCESS. The student can consistently perform better on applied math problems when following this efficient 4-step plan: (1) UNDERSTAND THE PROBLEM. To fully grasp the problem, the student may restate the problem in his or her own words, note key information, and identify missing information. (2) DEVISE A PLAN. In mapping out a strategy to solve the problem, the student may make a table, draw a diagram, or translate the verbal problem into an equation. (3) CARRY OUT THE PLAN. The student implements the steps in the plan, showing work and checking work for each step. (4) LOOK BACK. The student checks the results. If the answer is written as an equation, the student puts the results in words and checks whether the answer addresses the question posed in the original word problem.	Pólya, G. (1957). How to solve it (2nd ed.). Princeton University Press: Princeton, N.J. Williams, K. M. (2003). Writing about the problem solving process to improve problem-solving performance. Mathematics Teacher, 96(3), 185-187.
❏ MATH: WORD PROBLEMS: STRATEGY: SELF-CORRECTION CHECKLISTS. The student can improve accuracy on particular types of word and number problems by using an 'individualized self-instruction checklist' to direct attention to his or her unique error patterns: (1) To create such a checklist, the teacher meets with the student. Together they analyze common error patterns that the student tends to commit on a particular problem type (e.g., 'On addition problems that require carrying, I don't always remember to carry the number from the previously added column.'). For each type of error identified, the student and teacher together describe the appropriate step to take to prevent the error from occurring (e.g., 'When adding each column, make sure to carry numbers when needed.'). (2) These self-check items are compiled into a single checklist. (3) The student is encouraged to use the individualized self-instruction checklist when working independently on number or word problems. TIP: As older students become proficient in creating and using these individualized error checklists, they can begin to analyze their own math errors and to make their checklists independently whenever they encounter new problem types.	Uberti, H. Z., Mastropieri, M. A., & Scruggs, T. E. (2004). Check it off: Individualizing a math algorithm for students with disabilities via self-monitoring checklists. Intervention in School and Clinic, 39(5), 269-275.
❏ MATH: WORD PROBLEMS: STRATEGY: 7-STEP PLANNING PROCESS. Students with a consistent strategy to take on math word problems work more efficiently and avoid needless errors. Presented here is an all-purpose 7-step cognitive strategy useful for solving any math word problem: This strategy should be formatted as a checklist for independent student use: (1) READ THE PROBLEM. The student reads the problem carefully, noting and attempting to clear up any areas of uncertainly or	Montague, M. (1992). The effects of cognitive and metacognitive strategy instruction on the mathematical problem solving of

confusion (e.g., unknown vocabulary terms). (2) PARAPHRASE THE PROBLEM. The student restates the problem in his or her own words. (3) DRAW THE PROBLEM. The student creates a drawing of the word problem, converting words to a visual representation of that problem. (4) CREATE A PLAN TO SOLVE. The student decides on the best way to solve the problem and develops a plan to do so. (5) PREDICT/ESTIMATE THE ANSWER. The student estimates or predicts what the answer to the problem will be. The student may compute a quick approximation of the answer, using rounding or other shortcuts. (6) COMPUTE THE ANSWER. The student follows the plan developed previously to solve the problem and arrive at the correct answer. (7) CHECK THE ANSWER. The student methodically checks the calculations for each step of the problem. The student also compares the actual answer to the estimated answer calculated in a previous step to ensure that there is general agreement between the two values.	middle school students with learning disabilities. Journal of Learning Disabilities, 25, 230-248. Montague, M., & Dietz, S. (2009). Evaluating the evidence base for cognitive strategy instruction and mathematical problem solving. Exceptional Children, 75, 285-302.
❑ MATH WORD PROBLEMS: HIGHLIGHT KEY TERMS. Students who have difficulties with inattention or impulsivity can increase rates of on-task behavior and accuracy on math word problems through highlighting of key terms. The teacher prepares the worksheet by using a colored highlighter to highlight a combination of 8-11 key words and numbers for each math word problem. The student then completes the highlighted worksheet.	Kercood, S., Zentall, S. S., Vinh, M., & Tom-Wright, K. (2012). Attentional cuing in math word problems for girls at-risk for ADHD and their peers in general education settings. Contemporary Educational Psychology, 37, 106-112.

How To: Teach Student Writing Skills—
Elements of Effective Writing Instruction

The Common Core State Standards place a heavy emphasis on writing skills. Yet writing instruction in schools often falls short in training students to be accomplished writers (Graham, McKeown, Kiuhare, & Harris, 2012). As a help to teachers, this article identifies nine elements of writing instruction found to be effective in classrooms ranging from later elementary to high school.

Several meta-analyses are the source for these instructional recommendations (Graham, McKeown, Kiuhare, & Harris, 2012; Graham & Herbert, 2010; Graham & Perrin, 2007). Meta-analysis is a statistical procedure that aggregates the findings of various individual studies--all focusing on one writing-instruction component--to calculate for that component a single, global estimate of effectiveness. The results of these meta-analyses are calculated as 'effect sizes'. An effect size is the estimate of the difference between a treatment group (in this case, students receiving a specific writing-instruction treatment) and a control group that does not receive the treatment (Graham & Perrin, 2007). The larger the effect size, the more effective is the treatment. Below is a scale that can be used to evaluate the importance of the effect-sizes that appear with each writing-instruction element (Cohen, 1992; Graham & Herbert, 2010):

- 0.20: Small effect size
- 0.50: Medium effect size
- 0.80: Large effect size

Teachers are encouraged to use this listing of effective writing-instruction practices as a checklist against which to evaluate the quality of their own writing programs. However, the following considerations should be kept in mind:

1. *Recommendations are general--not specific.* Descriptions of these elements of writing instruction are quite general. This lack of specificity is an unavoidable product of the meta-analysis--which isolates from a collection of varied studies the broad, underlying instructional practice common to them all. Nonetheless, teachers can have confidence that, so long as their own classroom practice incorporates these general writing recommendations, they are more likely to deliver high-quality writing instruction.

2. *Ordering and weighting of writing strategies is unknown.* While the instructional strategies presented here have demonstrated their effectiveness in improving student writing, researchers do not yet know the relative importance that each component has in developing student writing skills or in what order the components should appear (Graham & Hebert, 2010). Teacher judgment in the weighting and ordering of each component is required.

3. *Writing components should be explicitly taught.* Struggling writers will need explicit instruction in the various writing components (e.g., in how to work effectively on collaborative writing projects) in order to enjoy the maximum benefit from them (Graham & Hebert, 2010).

Recommended Writing-Instruction Components

Listed in descending order of effectiveness are these components of effective writing instruction:

1	**Students follow a multi-step writing process**. Effect sizes: **1.2** (Graham, McKeown, Kiuhare, & Harris, 2012); **0.82** (Graham & Perrin, 2007).
	Students are trained to use (and can produce evidence of) a multi-step writing process, including the elements of planning, drafting, revision, and editing (e.g., Robinson & Howell, 2008). They make use of this process for all writing assignments.
2	**Students work collaboratively on their writing**. Effect sizes: **0.89** (Graham, McKeown, Kiuhare, & Harris, 2012); **0.75** (Graham & Perrin, 2007).
	Students work on their writing in pairs or groups at various stages of the writing process: planning (pre-writing), drafting, revising, editing.
3	**Students receive timely feedback about the quality of their writing**. Effect sizes: **0.80** for adult feedback, **0.37** for student feedback (Graham, McKeown, Kiuhare, & Harris, 2012).
	Students receive regular performance feedback about the quality of a writing product from adults, peers, or through self-administered ratings (e.g., using rubrics). It should be noted that the impact of timely teacher feedback to young writers is especially large (effect size = 0.80).
4	**Students set writing goals**. Effect sizes: **0.76** (Graham, McKeown, Kiuhare, & Harris, 2012); **0.70** (Graham & Perrin, 2007).
	At various points in the writing process (planning, drafting, writing, revising), students are encouraged to formulate specific goals; they later report out (to the teacher or a peer) whether they have actually accomplished those goals. Examples of goal-setting might include locating at least 3 sources for a research paper, adding 5 supporting details during revision of an argumentative essay, writing the first draft of an introductory paragraph during an in-class writing period, etc.
5	**Students use word processors to write**. Effect sizes: **0.47** (Graham, McKeown, Kiuhare, & Harris, 2012); **0.55** (Graham & Perrin, 2007).
	Students become fluent in keyboarding and have regular access to word-processing devices when writing.
6	**Students write about what they have read**. Effect sizes: **0.40** (Graham & Herbert, 2010); **0.82** (Graham & Perrin, 2007).
	Students are explicitly taught how to summarize and/or reflect in writing on texts that they have recently read. Each of the following writing activities has been found to be effective in promoting writing skills -- as well as improving reading comprehension: • paraphrasing the original text as a condensed student summary • analyzing the text, attempting to interpret the text's meaning, or describing the writer's reaction to it • writing notes (e.g., key words or phrases) that capture the essential text information
7	**Students engage in pre-writing activities**. Effect sizes: **0.54** (Graham, McKeown, Kiuhare, & Harris, 2012); **0.30** (Graham & Perrin, 2007).
	Before beginning a writing assignment, students take part in structured tasks to plan or visualize the topic to be written about. Activities might include having students draw pictures relevant to the topic; write out a writing plan independently or in pairs or groups; read articles linked to the writing topic and discuss them before developing a writing plan, etc.
8	**Students produce more writing**. Effect size: **0.30** (Graham, McKeown, Kiuhare, & Harris, 2012).
	Students have more writing included in their daily instruction (e.g., through daily journaling).
9	**Students study writing models**. Effect size: **0.30** (Graham & Perrin, 2007).
	Students are given models of the kinds of writing that they will be asked to produce: e.g., argumentative or informational essays. Students closely study the structure of these models and attempt to incorporate the important elements of each model into their own writing.

References

Cohen, J. (1992). Statistical power analysis. *Current Directions in Psychological Science, 1*(3), 98-101.

Graham, S., & Hebert, M. (2010). *Writing to Read: Evidence for how writing can improve reading.* Alliance for Excellence in Education. Washington, D.C.

Graham, S., McKeown, D., Kiuhare, S., & Harris, K. R. (2012). A meta-analysis of writing instruction for students in the elementary grades. *Journal of Educational Psychology, 104*(4), 879-896.

Graham, S., & Perrin, D. (2007). *Writing Next: Effective strategies to improve writing of adolescents in middle and high school.* Alliance for Excellence in Education. Washington, D.C.

Robinson, L. K., & Howell, K. W. (2008). Best practices in curriculum-based evaluation and written expression. In A. Thomas & J. Grimes (Eds.), *Best practices in school psychology V* (pp. 439-452). Bethesda, MD: National Association of School Psychologists.

How To: Promote Acquisition of Math Facts or Spelling Words Using Cover-Copy-Compare

DESCRIPTION: In this intervention to promote acquisition of spelling words or math facts, the student is given a sheet with a set of target spelling words or math facts and answers. The student looks at each original spelling word or math-fact (equation and answer), covers the spelling word or math fact briefly and copies the item from memory, then compares the copied spelling word or math fact and answer to the original correct model (Skinner, McLaughlin & Logan, 1997).

GROUP SIZE: Whole class, small group, individual student

TIME: Variable up to 15 minutes per session

MATERIALS:

- *Worksheet: Spelling or Math Cover-Copy-Compare* (attached)

- *Log: Mastered Spelling Words or Math-Facts* (attached)

INTERVENTION STEPS: Here are the steps of Cover-Copy-Compare for spelling words or math facts:

1. *[Teacher] Create a Cover-Copy-Compare Spelling List or Math-Fact Sheet.* The teacher selects up to 10 spelling words/math facts for the student to work on during the session and writes those items as correct models (math facts are copied with both equation and answer) into the left column ('Spelling Words' or 'Math Facts') of the appropriate *Cover-Copy-Compare Worksheet* (attached). The teacher then pre-folds the sheet using as a guide the vertical dashed line ('fold line') bisecting the left side of the student worksheet.

2. *[Student] Use the Cover-Copy-Compare Procedures.* During the Cover-Copy-Compare intervention, the student follows these self-directed steps for each spelling word or math fact:

   - Look at the spelling word or math fact with answer that appears in the left column of the sheet.

   - Fold the left side of the page over at the pre-folded vertical crease to hide the correct model ('Cover').

   - Copy the spelling word or math fact and answer from memory, writing it in the first response blank under the 'Student Response' section of the Cover-Copy-Compare worksheet ('Copy').

   - Uncover the correct model and compare it to the student response ('Compare'). If the student has written the spelling word/math fact and answer CORRECTLY, the student moves to the next item on the list and repeats these procedures. If the student has written the spelling word/math fact and answer INCORRECTLY, the student draws a line through the incorrect response, studies the correct model again, covers the model, copies the model again from memory into the second response blank under the 'Student Response' section of the sheet, and again checks the correctness of the copied item..

   - Continue until all spelling words or math facts on the sheet have been copied and checked against the correct models.

3. *[Teacher] Log: Items Mastered by Student.* The teacher should formulate an objective standard for judging that the student using Cover-Copy-Compare has 'mastered' an individual spelling word or math fact (e.g., when the student is able to copy a spelling word or math fact plus answer from memory without error on three successive occasions). The teacher can then apply this standard for mastery to identify and log items mastered in each session, using the appropriate *Log Sheet* (attached).

References

Skinner, C. H., McLaughlin, T. F., & Logan, P. (1997). Cover, copy, and compare: A self-managed academic intervention effective across skills, students, and settings. *Journal of Behavioral Education, 7*, 295-306.

Worksheet: Cover-Copy-Compare Student: _____ Date: _____

Math Facts		Student Response
1.		1a.
		1b.
2.		2a.
		2b.
3.		3a.
		3b.
4.		4a.
		4b.
5.		5a.
		5b.
6.		6a.
		6b.
7.		7a.
		7b.
8.		8a.
		8b.
9.		9a.
		9b.
10.		10a.
		10b.

Fold Line

Log: Mastered Math Facts

Student: _____ School Yr: _____ Classroom/Course: _____

Math-Facts Cumulative Mastery Log: During the intervention, log each mastered math fact below with date of mastery.

Math Fact: _____ Date: ___/___/___	Math Fact: _____ Date: ___/___/___
Math Fact: _____ Date: ___/___/___	Math Fact: _____ Date: ___/___/___
Math Fact: _____ Date: ___/___/___	Math Fact: _____ Date: ___/___/___
Math Fact: _____ Date: ___/___/___	Math Fact: _____ Date: ___/___/___
Math Fact: _____ Date: ___/___/___	Math Fact: _____ Date: ___/___/___
Math Fact: _____ Date: ___/___/___	Math Fact: _____ Date: ___/___/___
Math Fact: _____ Date: ___/___/___	Math Fact: _____ Date: ___/___/___
Math Fact: _____ Date: ___/___/___	Math Fact: _____ Date: ___/___/___
Math Fact: _____ Date: ___/___/___	Math Fact: _____ Date: ___/___/___
Math Fact: _____ Date: ___/___/___	Math Fact: _____ Date: ___/___/___
Math Fact: _____ Date: ___/___/___	Math Fact: _____ Date: ___/___/___
Math Fact: _____ Date: ___/___/___	Math Fact: _____ Date: ___/___/___
Math Fact: _____ Date: ___/___/___	Math Fact: _____ Date: ___/___/___
Math Fact: _____ Date: ___/___/___	Math Fact: _____ Date: ___/___/___
Math Fact: _____ Date: ___/___/___	Math Fact: _____ Date: ___/___/___
Math Fact: _____ Date: ___/___/___	Math Fact: _____ Date: ___/___/___
Math Fact: _____ Date: ___/___/___	Math Fact: _____ Date: ___/___/___
Math Fact: _____ Date: ___/___/___	Math Fact: _____ Date: ___/___/___
Math Fact: _____ Date: ___/___/___	Math Fact: _____ Date: ___/___/___
Math Fact: _____ Date: ___/___/___	Math Fact: _____ Date: ___/___/___
Math Fact: _____ Date: ___/___/___	Math Fact: _____ Date: ___/___/___
Math Fact: _____ Date: ___/___/___	Math Fact: _____ Date: ___/___/___

Worksheet: Cover-Copy-Compare   Student: _____   Date: _____

Spelling Words	Student Response
1.	1a.
	1b.
2.	2a.
	2b.
3.	3a.
	3b.
4.	4a.
	4b.
5.	5a.
	5b.
6.	6a.
	6b.
7.	7a.
	7b.
8.	8a.
	8b.
9.	9a.
	9b.
10.	10a.
	10b.

Fold Line

Log: Mastered Spelling Words

Student: _____ School Yr: _____ Classroom/Course: _____

Spelling Cumulative Mastery Log: During the spelling intervention, log each mastered word below with date of mastery.

Word 1: _____ Date: ___/___/___   Word 21: _____ Date: ___/___/___

Word 2: _____ Date: ___/___/___   Word 22: _____ Date: ___/___/___

Word 3: _____ Date: ___/___/___   Word 23: _____ Date: ___/___/___

Word 4: _____ Date: ___/___/___   Word 24: _____ Date: ___/___/___

Word 5: _____ Date: ___/___/___   Word 25: _____ Date: ___/___/___

Word 6: _____ Date: ___/___/___   Word 26: _____ Date: ___/___/___

Word 7: _____ Date: ___/___/___   Word 27: _____ Date: ___/___/___

Word 8: _____ Date: ___/___/___   Word 28: _____ Date: ___/___/___

Word 9: _____ Date: ___/___/___   Word 29: _____ Date: ___/___/___

Word 10: _____ Date: ___/___/___   Word 30: _____ Date: ___/___/___

Word 11: _____ Date: ___/___/___   Word 31: _____ Date: ___/___/___

Word 12: _____ Date: ___/___/___   Word 32: _____ Date: ___/___/___

Word 13: _____ Date: ___/___/___   Word 33: _____ Date: ___/___/___

Word 14: _____ Date: ___/___/___   Word 34: _____ Date: ___/___/___

Word 15: _____ Date: ___/___/___   Word 35: _____ Date: ___/___/___

Word 16: _____ Date: ___/___/___   Word 36: _____ Date: ___/___/___

Word 17: _____ Date: ___/___/___   Word 37: _____ Date: ___/___/___

Word 18: _____ Date: ___/___/___   Word 38: _____ Date: ___/___/___

Word 19: _____ Date: ___/___/___   Word 39: _____ Date: ___/___/___

Word 20: _____ Date: ___/___/___   Word 40: _____ Date: ___/___/___

How To: Use Peers as Tutors—Math Computation with Constant Time Delay

DESCRIPTION: This intervention employs students as reciprocal peer tutors to target acquisition of basic math facts (math computation) using constant time delay (Menesses & Gresham, 2009; Telecsan, Slaton, & Stevens, 1999). Each tutoring 'session' is brief and includes its own progress-monitoring component--making this a convenient and time-efficient math intervention for busy classrooms.

MATERIALS:

Student Packet: A work folder is created for each tutor pair. The folder contains:

❑ 10 math fact cards with equations written on the front and correct answer appearing on the back. NOTE: The set of cards is replenished and updated regularly as tutoring pairs master their math facts.

❑ Progress-monitoring form for each student.

❑ Pencils.

PREPARATION: To prepare for the tutoring program, the teacher selects students to participate and trains them to serve as tutors.

Select Student Participants. Students being considered for the reciprocal peer tutor program should at minimum meet these criteria (Telecsan, Slaton, & Stevens, 1999, Menesses & Gresham, 2009):

❑ Is able and willing to follow directions;

❑ Shows generally appropriate classroom behavior;

❑ Can attend to a lesson or learning activity for at least 20 minutes.

❑ Is able to name all numbers from 0 to 18 (if tutoring in addition or subtraction math facts) and name all numbers from 0 to 81 (if tutoring in multiplication or division math facts).

❑ Can correctly read aloud a sampling of 10 math-facts (equation plus answer) that will be used in the tutoring sessions. (NOTE: The student does not need to have memorized or otherwise mastered these math facts to participate—just be able to read them aloud from cards without errors).

❑ [To document a deficit in math computation] When given a two-minute math computation probe to complete independently, computes **fewer** than 20 correct digits (Grades 1-3) or **fewer** than 40 correct digits (Grades 4 and up) (Deno & Mirkin, 1977).

NOTE: Teachers may want to use the attached *Reciprocal Peer Tutoring in Math Computation: Teacher Nomination Form* to compile a list of students who would be suitable for the tutoring program.

Train the Student Tutors. Student tutors are trained through explicit instruction (Menesses & Gresham, 2009) with the teacher clearly explaining the tutoring steps, demonstrating them, and then having the students practice the steps with performance feedback and encouragement from the teacher. The teacher also explains, demonstrates, and observes students practice the progress-monitoring component of the program. (NOTE: Teachers can find a handy listing of all the tutoring steps in which students are to be trained on the attached form *Peer Tutoring in Math*

Computation with Constant Time Delay: Integrity Checklist. This checklist can also be used to evaluate the performance of students to determine their mastery of the tutoring steps during practice sessions with the teacher.)

When students have completed their training, the teacher has each student role-play the tutor with the teacher assuming the role of tutee. The tutor-in-training works through the 3-minute tutoring segment and completes the follow-up progress-monitoring activity. The teacher then provides performance feedback. The student is considered to be ready to tutor when he or she successfully implements all steps of the intervention (100% accuracy) on three successive training trials (Menesses & Gresham, 2009).

INTERVENTION STEPS: Students participating in the tutoring program meet in a setting in which their tutoring activities will not distract other students. The setting is supervised by an adult who monitors the students and times the tutoring activities. These are the steps of the tutoring intervention:

1. **Complete the Tutoring Activity.** In each tutoring pair, one of the students assumes the role of tutor. The supervising adult starts the timer and says 'Begin'; after 3 minutes, the adult stops the timer and says 'Stop'.

   While the timer is running, the tutor follows this sequence:

   a. *Presents Cards.* The tutor presents each card to the tutee for 3 seconds.
   b. *Provides Tutor Feedback.* [When the tutee responds correctly] The tutor acknowledges the correct answer and presents the next card.

      [When the tutee does not respond within 3 seconds or responds incorrectly] The tutor states the correct answer and has the tutee repeat the correct answer. The tutor then presents the next card.
   c. *Provides Praise.* The tutor praises the tutee immediately following correct answers.
   d. *Shuffles Cards.* When the tutor and tutee have reviewed all of the math-fact carts, the tutor shuffles them before again presenting cards.
   e. *Continues to the Timer.* The tutor continues to presents math-fact cards for tutee response until the timer rings.

2. **Assess the Progress of the Tutee.** The tutor concludes each 3-minute tutoring session by assessing the number of math facts mastered by the tutee. The tutor follows this sequence:

   a. *Presents Cards.* The tutor presents each card to the tutee for 3 seconds.
   b. *Remains Silent.* The tutor does not provide performance feedback or praise to the tutee, or otherwise talk during the assessment phase.
   c. *Sorts Cards.* Based on the tutee's responses, the tutor sorts the math-fact cards into 'correct' and 'incorrect' piles.
   d. *Counts Cards and Records Totals.* The tutor counts the number of cards in the 'correct' and 'incorrect' piles and records the totals on the tutee's progress-monitoring chart.

3. **Switch Roles.** After the tutor has completed the 3-minute tutoring activity and assessed the tutee's progress on math facts, the two students reverse roles. The new tutor then implements steps 2 and 3 described above with the new tutee.

4. **Conduct Tutoring Integrity Checks and Monitor Student Performance.** As the student pairs complete the tutoring activities, the supervising adult monitors the integrity with which the intervention is carried out. At the conclusion of the tutoring session, the adult gives feedback to the student pairs, praising successful implementation and providing corrective feedback to students as needed. NOTE: Teachers can use the attached form *Peer Tutoring in Math Computation with Constant Time Delay: Integrity Checklist* to conduct integrity checks of the intervention and student progress-monitoring components of the math peer tutoring.

    The adult supervisor also monitors student progress. After each student pair has completed one tutoring cycle and assessed and recorded their progress, the supervisor reviews the score sheets. If a student has successfully answered all 10 math fact cards three times in succession, the supervisor provides that student's tutor with a new set of math flashcards.

References

Deno, S. L., & Mirkin, P. K. (1977). Data-based program modification: A manual. Reston, VA: Council for Exceptional Children.

Menesses, K. F., & Gresham, F. M. (2009). Relative efficacy of reciprocal and nonreciprocal peer tutoring for students at-risk for academic failure. *School Psychology Quarterly, 24,* 266–275.

Telecsan, B. L., Slaton, D. B., & Stevens, K. B. (1999). Peer tutoring: Teaching students with learning disabilities to deliver time delay instruction. *Journal of Behavioral Education, 9,* 133-154.

Reciprocal Peer Tutoring in Math Computation: Teacher Nomination Form

Teacher: _____ **Classroom:** _____ **Date:** _____

Directions: Select students in your class that you believe would benefit from participation in a peer tutoring program to boost math computation skills. Write the names of your student nominees in the space provided below. Remember, students who are considered for the peer tutoring program should—*at minimum*—meet these criteria:

- Show generally appropriate classroom behaviors and follow directions.

- Can pay attention to a lesson or learning activity for at least 20 minutes.

- Are able to wait appropriately to hear the correct answer from the tutor if the student does not know the answer.

- When given a two-minute math computation probe to complete independently, computes **fewer** than 20 correct digits (Grades 1-3) or **fewer** than 40 correct digits (Grades 4 and up) (Deno & Mirkin, 1977).

- Can name all numbers from 0 to 18 (if tutoring in addition or subtraction math facts) and name all numbers from 0 to 81 (if tutoring in multiplication or division math facts).

- Can correctly read aloud a sampling of 10 math-facts (equation plus answer) that will be used in the tutoring sessions. (NOTE: The student does not need to have memorized or otherwise mastered these math facts to participate—just be able to read them aloud from cards without errors).

Number	Student Name	NOTES
1.		
2.		
3.		
4.		
5.		
6.		
7.		
8.		

Peer Tutoring in Math Computation with Constant Time Delay: Integrity Checklist

Tutoring Session: Intervention Phase

Directions: Observe the tutor and tutee for a full intervention session. Use this checklist to record whether each of the key steps of the intervention were correctly followed.

Correctly Carried Out?	Step	Tutor Action	NOTES
__ Y __ N	1.	**Promptly Initiates Session.** At the start of the timer, the tutor immediately presents the first math-fact card.	
__ Y __ N	2.	**Presents Cards.** The tutor presents each card to the tutee for 3 seconds.	
__ Y __ N	3.	**Provides Tutor Feedback.** [When the tutee responds correctly] The tutor acknowledges the correct answer and presents the next card. [When the tutee does not respond within 3 seconds or responds incorrectly] The tutor states the correct answer and has the tutee repeat the correct answer. The tutor then presents the next card.	
__ Y __ N	4.	**Provides Praise.** The tutor praises the tutee immediately following correct answers.	
__ Y __ N	5.	**Shuffles Cards.** When the tutor and tutee have reviewed all of the math-fact carts, the tutor shuffles them before again presenting cards.	
__ Y __ N	6.	**Continues to the Timer.** The tutor continues to presents math-fact cards for tutee response until the timer rings.	

		Tutoring Session: Assessment Phase	

Directions: Observe the tutor and tutee during the progress-monitoring phase of the session. Use this checklist to record whether each of the key steps of the assessment were correctly followed.

Correctly Carried Out?	Step	Tutor Action	NOTES
__ Y __ N	1.	**Presents Cards.** The tutor presents each card to the tutee for 3 seconds.	
__ Y __ N	2.	**Remains Silent.** The tutor does not provide performance feedback or praise to the tutee, or otherwise talk during the assessment phase.	
__ Y __ N	3.	**Sorts Cards.** The tutor sorts cards into 'correct' and 'incorrect' piles based on the tutee's responses.	
__ Y __ N	4.	**Counts Cards and Records Totals.** The tutor counts the number of cards in the 'correct' and 'incorrect' piles and records the totals on the tutee's progress-monitoring chart.	

Math Tutoring: Score Sheet

Tutor 'Coach': _____ Tutee 'Player': _____

Directions to the Tutor: Write down the number of math-fact cards that your partner answered *correctly* and the number answered *incorrectly*.		
Date:	Cards Correct:	Cards Incorrect:
Date:	Cards Correct:	Cards Incorrect:
Date:	Cards Correct:	Cards Incorrect:
Date:	Cards Correct:	Cards Incorrect:
Date:	Cards Correct:	Cards Incorrect:
Date:	Cards Correct:	Cards Incorrect:
Date:	Cards Correct:	Cards Incorrect:
Date:	Cards Correct:	Cards Incorrect:

Chapter 4

Managing Behaviors to Promote Student Learning

The focus of the Common Core State ELA and Math Standards is academic, but woven throughout those standards are also very high expectations for student behavior. To cite one example, the initial Grade 6 ELA Standard for Comprehension & Collaboration (ELA.SL.6.1.a-b) sets as a goal that students "will engage effectively in a range of collaborative discussions...", "come to discussions prepared...", and "follow rules for collegial discussions...". If we analyze the behavioral requirements for success in just this single standard, it is plain that students must have the skill-set and willingness to focus on and take part in group discussion, engage in turn-taking, politely acknowledge and respond to views other than their own and be motivated to review in advance the academic material to be discussed.

Yet many students either lack the appropriate behaviors necessary for success on the standards or are inconsistent in displaying those positive behaviors at the 'point of performance' when they are most needed. In their role as behavior managers, then, teachers must establish, teach, and reinforce classwide behavioral expectations needed by all students to take part in productive academic work. Additionally, however, teachers must be ready to respond appropriately to just about any behavior that a particular student might bring through the classroom door. While having a toolkit of specific behavioral strategies is important, one secret of educators who maintain smoothly running classrooms with minimal behavioral disruptions is that they are able to view problem student behaviors through the lens of these 7 'big ideas' in behavior management:

1. *Manage behaviors through strong instruction.* A powerful method to prevent misbehavior is to keep students actively engaged in academic responding (Lewis, Hudson, Richter, & Johnson, 2004). A teacher is most likely to 'capture' a student's behavior for academic purposes when that teacher ensures that the student has the necessary academic skills to do the assigned classwork, is given explicit instruction to master difficult material, and receives timely feedback about his or her academic performance (Burns, VanDerHeyden, & Boice, 2008).

2. *Check for academic problems.* The correlation between classroom misbehavior and deficient academic skills is high (Witt, Daly, & Noell, 2000). Teachers should, therefore, routinely assess a student's academic skills as a first step when attempting to explain why a particular behavior is occurring. And it logically follows that, when poor academics appear to drive problem behaviors, at least some of the interventions that the teacher selects should address the student's academic deficit.

3. *Identify the underlying function of the behavior.* Problem behaviors occur for a reason. Such behaviors serve a function for the student (Witt, Daly, & Noell, 2000). The most commonly observed behavioral functions in classrooms are escape/avoidance and peer or adult attention (Packenham, Shute, & Reid, 2004). When the probable function sustaining a particular set of behaviors can be identified, the teacher has confidence that interventions selected to match the function will be correctly targeted and therefore are likely to be effective. For example, if a teacher decides that a student's call-outs in class are sustained by the function of adult attention, that teacher may respond by shifting the flow of that attention. For example, the teacher may interact minimally with the student during call-outs but boost attention during times when the student shows appropriate behavior.

4. *Eliminate behavioral triggers.* Problem behaviors are often set off by events or conditions within the instructional setting (Kern, Choutka, & Sokol, 2002). Sitting next to a distracting classmate or being handed an academic task that is too difficult to complete are two examples of events that might trigger student misbehavior. When the teacher is able to identify and eliminate triggers of negative conduct, such actions tend to work quickly and, by preventing class disruptions, result in more time available for instruction (Kern & Clemens, 2007).

5. *Redefine the behavioral goal as a replacement behavior.* When a student displays challenging behaviors, it can be easy to fall into the trap of simply wishing that those misbehaviors would go away. The point of a behavioral intervention, however, is to expand the student's repertoire of pro-social, pro-academic behaviors, rather than just extinguish aberrant behaviors. By selecting a positive behavioral goal that is an appropriate replacement for the student's original problem behavior, the teacher reframes the student concern in a manner that allows for more effective intervention planning (Batsche, Castillo, Dixon, & Forde, 2008). For example, a teacher who is concerned that a student is talking with peers about non-instructional topics during independent seatwork might select as a replacement behavior that the student will engage in "active, accurate academic responding."

6. *Rule out the most likely causes for misbehavior first.* Teachers can access a wealth of information sources when attempting to identify the cause of misbehavior. These can include student work products, direct observation, interviews with the student, other teachers, parents, etc. However, when trying to understand misbehavior, educators may be too quick to choose global explanations that fit preconceptions of the student that are not supported by the data. For example, a teacher may describe a student who is non-compliant and fails to complete classwork as 'apathetic', 'unmotivated', or 'lazy'. However, students are rarely so sealed off from the world that their behavioral problems are

determined solely by their own attitudes or work ethic. It is far more likely that a student displays challenging behavior because of significant interactions with elements of his or her environment, such as attempting to escape work that is too difficult or seeking the attention of peers in the classroom. Teachers should first collect and analyze information on the student from several sources and rule out the most common ('low-inference') explanations for misbehavior (Christ, 2008) before considering whether that student's internal levels of motivation could be the primary cause of the problem behavior.

7. *Be flexible in responding to misbehavior.* Teachers have greater success in managing the full spectrum of student misbehaviors when they respond flexibly by evaluating each individual case and applying strategies that logically address the likely cause(s) of that student's problem conduct (Marzano, Marzano, & Pickering, 2003). A teacher may choose to respond to a non-compliant student with a warning and additional disciplinary consequences, for example, if evidence suggests that the misbehavior stems from his seeking peer attention and approval. However, that same teacher may respond to non-compliance with a behavioral conference and use of defusing strategies if the misbehavior appears to have been triggered by a negative peer comment.

Roadmap to This Chapter

This chapter includes several resources to assist teachers in managing the behaviors of all students in the class, address the problem behaviors of individual students, and build student motivation. These resources include:

• *How To: Write Behavior Statements to Identify Cause/s of Student Misbehavior.* When the teacher has a clear understanding of the student problem behavior and its probable cause(s), that teacher is then able to select intervention ideas that are likely to fix the problem. This resource walks the teacher through the process of writing a behavior statement and then using that statement to link the student's behavior to its underlying behavior function.

- *How To: Motivate Students Through Teacher Praise.* This resource provides teachers with advice on how to increase motivation in the classroom with well-structured praise statements, as well as recommendations for adjusting praise to match a student's stage of learning.

- *How To: Handle Common Classroom Problem Behaviors Using a Behavior Management Menu.* Teachers who can manage low-level student misbehaviors in the classroom rather than referring those students to the office with a disciplinary referral have fewer disruptions to instruction and are able to enhance their own authority with their students. This resource provides teachers with 8 categories of classroom 'disciplinary' response and provides examples. A teacher can use this to assemble a classroom Behavior Management Menu to prompt more consistent, flexible, and positive responses when student misbehavior occurs.

- *How To: Calm the Agitated Student: Tools for Effective Behavior Management.* Students who are highly agitated need to be calm before a teacher can help them to decide on the steps necessary to resolve whatever problem triggered that emotional upset. This resource provides teachers with common-sense recommendations for structuring interactions with agitated students to help to de-escalate these high-stress situations.

- *How To: Improve Classroom Management Through Flexible Rules: The Color Wheel.* This resource is a classwide behavior management system that enforces uniform group expectations for conduct while also responding flexibly to the differing behavioral demands of diverse learning activities. It presents full instructions for implementing this group intervention.

- *How To: Use the Power of Personal Connection to Motivate Students.* When students feel that they have a significant, positive relationship with the teacher, they are more likely to internalize and follow that teacher's behavioral expectations. This resource presents 4 simple strategies to promote student-teacher relationships.

- *How to: Focus Students With ADHD Through Antecedent Teaching Strategies: Cuing.* The inattentive student may benefit from easy-to-implement cuing strategies that can increase academic engagement while reducing problem behaviors. This resource provides several classroom-friendly ideas for cuing the student.

- *How To: Build a Student Motivation Trap to Increase Academic Engagement.* When instruction and learning tasks are built around a student's high-interest topics, that student is likely to become motivated to participate. This resource walks the teacher through a 6-step process for building a positive 'motivation trap' that infuses instruction with topics that engage the student.

- *How To: Increase Motivation in Students: High-Probability Requests.* Teacher use of high-probability requests is a classroom technique that can be effective in motivating reluctant students to engage in assigned classwork. This resource provides teachers with instructions on how to use this approach to build student success and momentum to complete assignments.

References

Batsche, G. M., Castillo, J. M., Dixon, D. N., & Forde, S. (2008). Best practices in designing, implementing, and evaluating quality interventions. In A. Thomas & J. Grimes (Eds.), *Best practices in school psychology V* (pp. 177-193). Bethesda, MD: National Association of School Psychologists.

Burns, M. K., VanDerHeyden, A. M., & Boice, C. H. (2008). Best practices in intensive academic interventions. In A. Thomas & J. Grimes (Eds.), *Best practices in school psychology V* (pp.1151-1162). Bethesda, MD: National Association of School Psychologists.

Christ, T. (2008). Best practices in problem analysis. In A. Thomas & J. Grimes (Eds.), *Best practices in school psychology V* (pp. 159-176). Bethesda, MD: National Association of School Psychologists.

Kern, L., Choutka, C. M., & Sokol, N. G. (2002). Assessment-based antecedent interventions used in natural settings to reduce challenging behaviors: An analysis of the literature. *Education & Treatment of Children,* 25, 113-130.

Kern, L. & Clemens, N. H. (2007). Antecedent strategies to promote appropriate classroom behavior. *Psychology in the Schools,* 44, 65-75.

Lewis, T. J., Hudson, S., Richter, M., & Johnson, N. (2004). Scientifically supported practices in emotional and behavioral disorders: A proposed approach and brief review of current practices. *Behavioral Disorders,* 29, 247-259.

Marzano, R. J., Marzano, J. S., & Pickering, D. J. (2003). *Classroom management that works: Research-based strategies for every teacher.* Alexandria, VA: Association for Supervision and Curriculum Development.

Packenham, M., Shute, R., & Reid, R. (2004). A truncated functional behavioral assessment procedure for children with disruptive classroom behaviors. *Education and Treatment of Children,* 27(1), 9-25.

Witt, J. C., Daly, E. M., & Noell, G. (2000). *Functional assessments: A step-by-step guide to solving academic and behavior problems.* Longmont, CO: Sopris West.

How To: Write Behavior Statements to Identify Causes of Student Misbehavior

When a teacher is confronted with a misbehaving or non-compliant student, the challenging behavior presents a puzzle to be solved. Instructors skilled in resolving behavior problems know that effective behavior management is built upon 3 assumptions (Packenham, Shute, & Reid, 2004). First, students engage in specific behaviors for a purpose (e.g., to seek peer attention; to avoid academic work). Second, events in the school environment play a central role in shaping student conduct, whether as behavioral triggers or reinforcers. Third, the teacher who can accurately identify both the purpose (function) of a student's problem behavior and events in the environment that sustain that behavior will be able to select appropriate intervention strategies to replace or eliminate it.

A classroom teacher has access to a great deal of information that could potentially be helpful in analyzing a student's behavior: direct observation, interviews with the student, interviews with past teachers and parents; work products, school records, and more. In fact, as Hosp (2008) notes, a problem that teachers frequently face is not that they lack sufficient data to understand a student, but rather that they are saturated with too much global information to easily analyze.

Behavioral statement: Template for analysis. What is needed is a simple template that helps teachers to narrow their problem-solving focus, productively tap into their reservoir of knowledge about a student, and—hopefully—solve the behavioral puzzle. Such a template exists in the form of the 'behavioral statement' (Moreno & Bullock, 2011). The behavioral statement—also known as the 'ABC' (Antecedent-Behavior-Consequence) statement—describes (a) *antecedents:* events that precede and trigger the problem behavior; (b) *behavior:* the problem behavior itself; and (c) *consequences:* events occurring as a result of the behavior that reinforce it in the future.

Sample Behavioral (ABC) Statements		
Antecedent	**Behavior**	**Consequence**
During large-group lectures in social studies	Brian talks with peers about non-instructional topics	and receives positive peer attention.
During independent seatwork assignments involving writing tasks	Angela verbally refuses to comply with teacher requests to start work	and is sent to the office with a disciplinary referral.

The behavioral statement neatly encapsulates the behavior and its context and places the student's behavior on a timeline (trigger, behavior, outcome). The statement's format allows the teacher to examine what antecedent events or conditions may precipitate a problem behavior and think about how to reengineer aspects of the learning activity to prevent the problem behavior. In the same manner, the statement prompts the instructor to look at the current consequences that accompany the problem behavior, consider whether they are actually supporting misbehavior, and perhaps seek to replace them with alternative consequences to extinguish undesired behaviors.

Classroom Behavioral Statement Organizer. While teachers can certainly draw upon their knowledge of students to write their own behavior statements, the process does require time and reflection. Yet time is a scarce commodity in busy classrooms. Teachers need access to streamlined tools to speed their understanding of mild problem behaviors and make behavior analysis feasible in general-education classrooms (Packenham, Shute, & Reid, 2004).

The *Classroom Behavioral Statement Organizer,* which appears later in this document, is just such a tool, created to help instructors in a classroom setting to quickly draft behavior statements in ABC format and use those statements to link student behaviors to their underlying purpose or function. The chart is a table divided into four columns: (1) *Antecedent/Activity;* (2) *Student Behavior;* (3) *Consequence/ Outcome;* and (4) *Behavior Function.* The teacher browses the elements in the first 3 columns to assemble a behavior/ABC statement that describes a student's problem behavior and its context. Based on this statement and the teacher's comprehensive knowledge of the student, the instructor then selects the underlying behavioral 'function' or purpose, a hypothesis that best explains why the problem behavioral is occurring.

A brief explanation of the sections of the *Classroom Behavioral Statement Organizer* follows:

• *Antecedent/Activity.* The chart lists a range of classroom activities (e.g., student work-pairs; reading activities; independent seat work) typically taking place when the student problem behavior occurs. If a teacher finds that a student behavior is displayed across *multiple* classroom settings/activities, it is recommended that the instructor make the analysis more manageable by choosing only the one or two most important settings/activities where the student's behavior is most problematic. Also, while this antecedent/activity list covers the majority of common classroom activities, the teacher is encouraged to write out his or her own description of any antecedents or activities not listed here.

• *Student Behavior.* A listing of the more common types of student misbehavior (e.g., talks to other students about non-instructional topics; fails to comply with routine teacher requests) appear in this section of the chart. The instructor identifies those problem behaviors that the student most often displays during the 'antecedent/activity' previously selected. It is recommended that teachers select no more than 2-3 behaviors to keep the behavior statement (and classroom intervention) manageable. If the teacher does not see a particular behavior listed, the instructor can use the examples from the chart as models to craft his or her own behavior definition.

• *Consequence/Outcome.* The teacher chooses outcomes/consequences that typically follow the problem behavior (e.g., student fails to complete work; student is sent from the classroom to the office or to in-school suspension). The instructor should try to limit the number of consequences/ outcomes selected to 3. If, in the teacher's opinion, several consequences (e.g., positive peer attention; student fails to finish work) occur with the same frequency, each selected consequence can simply be indicated with a check mark. However, if several consequences are linked to the behavior but one consequence (e.g., student fails to complete work) clearly occurs more often than another (e.g., student is sent to the office with a disciplinary referral), the teacher should number the relevant consequences in descending (i.e., 1, 2, 3) order of frequency. The value of rank-ordering when consequences happen with differing frequencies is that such ranking can provide insight into what 'pay-off' is actually sustaining the problem student behavior. For example, the instructor may note that the number-one consequence for a misbehaving student is that she reliably gets positive attention from her classmates but that a more sporadic disciplinary consequence such as teacher reprimand or office referral ranks a distant third. From this differential rate of consequences, the teacher may conclude that the more frequent peer attention is driving the behavior and that the sparser disciplinary consequence is not sufficient to change that pattern.

• *Behavior Function.* Having reviewed the behavior statement, the teacher chooses a behavior function that appears to be the most likely driver or cause of the student problem behavior(s). Seven possible functions are listed in this column. The most commonly observed behavioral functions in classrooms are escape/avoidance and peer or adult attention (Packenham, Shute, & Reid, 2004), but other functions can appear as well. If the teacher is unsure of the function sustaining the behavior but has 2-3 candidates (e.g., peer attention; escape or avoidance of a situation or activity), that instructor should continue to observe the target student's behaviors and note accompanying antecedents and consequences in an effort to rule out all but one of the competing hypotheses.

References

Hosp, J. L. (2008). Best practices in aligning academic assessment with instruction. In A. Thomas & J. Grimes (Eds.), *Best practices in school psychology V* (pp.363-376). Bethesda, MD: National Association of School Psychologists.

Moreno, G., & Bullock, L. M. (2011). Principles of positive behaviour supports: Using the FBA as a problem-solving approach to address challenging behaviours beyond special populations. *Emotional and Behavioural Difficulties,* 16(2), 117-127.

Packenham, M., Shute, R., & Reid, R. (2004). A truncated functional behavioral assessment procedure for children with disruptive classroom behaviors. *Education and Treatment of Children,* 27(1), 9-25.

Classroom Behavioral Statement Organizer

Antecedent/Activity

- ☐ Start of class/bell-ringer activities
- ☐ Large-group lecture
- ☐ Large group teacher-led discussion
- ☐ Large-group: when called on by the teacher
- ☐ Student work-pairs
- ☐ Student groups: cooperative learning
- ☐ Reading activities
- ☐ Writing activities
- ☐ Math activities
- ☐ Independent seat work
- ☐ Independent computer work
- ☐ Transitions between academic activities
- ☐ Homework collection
- ☐ In-class homework review
- ☐ Tests and/or quizzes
- ☐ Class dismissal
- ☐ Other: _____

Student Behavior

- ☐ Sits inactive
- ☐ Puts head on desk
- ☐ Is inattentive (e.g., staring into space, looking out the window)
- ☐ Leaves seat without permission
- ☐ Requests bathroom or water breaks
- ☐ Uses cell phone, music player, or other digital device against class rules
- ☐ Whispers/talks/mutters to self
- ☐ Makes loud or distracting noises
- ☐ Calls out with non-instructional comments
- ☐ Calls out with instructionally relevant comments
- ☐ Plays with/taps objects
- ☐ Throws objects
- ☐ Destroys work materials/instructional materials (e.g., ripping up a worksheet, breaking a pencil)
- ☐ Whispers/talks to other students about non-instructional topics
- ☐ Whispers/talks to other students about instructional/academic topics: e.g., seeking answers or help with directions
- ☐ Makes verbal threats toward peers
- ☐ Uses inappropriate language (e.g., obscenities) with peers
- ☐ Taunts/teases/makes fun of peers
- ☐ Makes comments to encourage or 'egg on' other students to misbehave
- ☐ Fails to begin in-class assignments (verbal refusal)
- ☐ Fails to begin in-class assignments (silent refusal)
- ☐ Fails to comply with routine teacher requests (verbal refusal)
- ☐ Fails to comply with routine teacher requests (silent refusal)
- ☐ Makes verbal threats toward adult
- ☐ Uses inappropriate language (e.g., obscenities) with adult
- ☐ Taunts/teases/makes fun of adult
- ☐ Seeks academic help from adult when not needed
- ☐ Perseverates with previous academic activity after the class/group has transitioned to a new activity
- ☐ Other: _____

Consequence/Outcome

- - Student fails to complete work.
- - Teacher ignores the behavior ('planned ignoring').
- - Teacher redirects the student.
- - Teacher reprimands the student.
- - Teacher conferences w/ the student.
- - Student receives positive peer attention
- - Student receives negative peer attention.
- - Student is briefly timed-out within the classroom.
- - Student is briefly timed-out outside of the classroom.
- - Student is sent from the classroom to the office or to in-school suspension (disciplinary referral).
- - Student receives a disciplinary consequence outside of class time (e.g., afterschool detention).
- - Student receives a 'respite' break away from peers to calm down before rejoining class.
- - Student is sent from the classroom to talk with a counselor/psychologist/social worker.
- - Student receives a snack, nap, or other support.
- - Other: _____

Behavior Function

- ☐ Peer attention
- ☐ Acceptance/affiliation with individuals or peer group(s)
- ☐ Power/control in interactions with peer(s)
- ☐ Adult attention
- ☐ Power/control in interactions with adult(s)
- ☐ Escape or avoidance of a situation or activity (e.g., because the student lacks the skills to do the academic work)
- ☐ Fulfillment of physical needs: e.g., sleep
- ☐ Other: _____

Behavioral (ABC) Statement: Use the organizer below to write a behavioral statement, based on your selections from the Classroom Behavior Chart.		
Antecedent	**Behavior**	**Consequence**

How To: Motivate Students Through Teacher Praise

As the majority of states across America adopt the Common Core Standards for reading and mathematics, teachers at all grade levels are eager to find tools that will encourage students to work harder to reach those ambitious outcome goals. Additionally, schools adopting Response to Intervention are seeking evidence-based strategies to motivate struggling students that can also be easily delivered in general-education classrooms.

Teacher praise is one tool that can be a powerful motivator for students. Surprisingly, research suggests that praise is underused in both general- and special-education classrooms (Brophy, 1981; Hawkins & Heflin, 2011; Kern, 2007).

Praise: What the Research Says

Effective teacher praise consists of two elements: (1) a description of noteworthy student academic performance or general behavior, and (2) a signal of teacher approval (Brophy, 1981; Burnett, 2001). The power of praise in changing student behavior is that it both indicates teacher approval and informs the student about how the praised academic performance or behavior conforms to teacher expectations (Burnett, 2001). As with any potential classroom reinforcer, praise has the ability to improve student academic or behavioral performance—but only if the *student* finds it reinforcing (Akin-Little et al., 2004). Here are several suggestions for shaping praise to increase its effectiveness:

• **Describe Noteworthy Student Behavior.** Praise statements that lack a specific account of student behavior in observable terms are compromised—as they fail to give students performance feedback to guide their learning. For example, a praise statement such as *'Good job!'* is inadequate because it lacks a behavioral description (Hawkins & Heflin, 2011). However, such a statement becomes acceptable when expanded to include a behavioral element: *"You located eight strong source documents for your essay. Good job!"*

• **Praise Effort and Accomplishment, Not Ability.** There is some evidence that praise statements about general ability can actually reduce student appetite for risk-taking (Burnett, 2001). Therefore, teachers should generally steer clear of praise that includes assumptions about global student ability (e.g., *"You are a really good math student!"*; *"I can tell from this essay that writing is no problem for you."*). Praise should instead focus on specific examples of student effort or accomplishment (e.g., *"It's obvious from your grade that you worked hard to prepare for this quiz. Great work!"*). When praise singles out exertion and work-products, it can help students to see a direct link between the effort that they invest in a task and improved academic or behavioral performance.

• **Match the Method of Praise Delivery to Student Preferences.** Teachers can deliver praise in a variety of ways and contexts. For example, an instructor may choose to praise a student in front of a class or work group or may instead deliver that praise in a private conversation or as written feedback on the student's assignment. When possible, the teacher should determine and abide by a student's preferences for receiving individual praise. It is worth noting that, while most students in elementary grades may easily accept public praise, evidence suggests that middle and high-school students actually prefer private praise (Burnett, 2001). So, when in doubt with older students, deliver praise in private rather than in public.

Praise: Use in the Classroom

Praise is a powerful motivating tool because it allows the teacher to selectively encourage different aspects of student production or output. For example, the teacher may use praise to boost the student's performance, praising effort, accuracy, or speed on an assignment. Or the teacher may instead single out the student's work product and use praise to underscore how closely the actual product matches an external standard or goal set by the student. The table below presents descriptions of several types of praise-statements tied to various student goals:

Praise: Goal	Example
Student Performance: Effort. Learning a new skill requires that the student work hard and put forth considerable effort--while often not seeing immediate improvement. For beginning learners, teacher praise can motivate and offer encouragement by focusing on effort ('seat-time') rather than on product (Daly et al., 2007).	*"Today in class, you wrote non-stop through the entire writing period. I appreciate your hard work."*
Student Performance: Accuracy. When learning new academic material or behaviors, students move through distinct stages (Haring et al., 1978). Of these stages, the first and most challenging for struggling learners is acquisition. In the acquisition stage, the student is learning the rudiments of the skill and strives to respond correctly. The teacher can provide encouragement to students in this first stage of learning by praising student growth in accuracy of responding.	*"This week you were able to correctly define 15 of 20 biology terms. That is up from 8 last week. Terrific progress!"*
Student Performance: Fluency. When the student has progressed beyond the acquisition stage, the new goal may be to promote fluency (Haring et al., 1978). Teacher praise can motivate the student to become more efficient on the academic task by emphasizing that learner's gains in fluency (a combination of accuracy and speed of responding).	*"You were able to compute 36 correct digits in two minutes on today's math time drill worksheet. That's 4 digits more than earlier this week--impressive!"*
Work Product: Student Goal-Setting. A motivating strategy for a reluctant learner is to have him or her set a goal before undertaking an academic task and then to report out at the conclusion of the task about whether the goal was reached. The teacher can then increase the motivating power of student goal-setting by offering praise when the student successfully sets and attains an ambitious goal. The praise statement states the original student goal and describes how the product has met the goal.	*"At the start of class, you set the goal of completing an outline for your paper. And I can see that the outline that you produced today looks great—it is well-structured and organized."*
Work Product: Using External Standard. Teacher praise often evaluates the student work product against some external standard. Praise tied to an external standard reminds the student that objective expectations exist for academic or behavioral performance (e.g., Common Core State Standards in reading and mathematics) and provides information about how closely the student's current performance conforms to those expectations. When comparing student work to an external standard, the teacher praise-statement identifies the external standard and describes how closely the student's work has come to meeting the standard.	*"On this assignment, I can see that you successfully converted the original fractions to equivalent fractions before you subtracted. Congratulations—you just showed mastery of one of our state Grade 5 math standards!"*

Praise: Troubleshooting

One reason that praise is often underused in middle and high school classrooms may be that teachers find it very difficult both to deliver effective group instruction and to provide (and keep track of) praise to individual students. Here are several informal self-monitoring ideas to help teachers to use praise with greater frequency and consistency:

• **Keep Daily Score.** The teacher sets a goal of the number of praise-statements that he or she would like to deliver during a class period. During class, the teacher keeps a tally of praise statements delivered and compares that total to the goal.

• **Select Students for Praise: Goal-Setting and Checkup.** Before each class, the teacher jots down the names of 4-5 students to single out for praise. (This activity can be done routinely as an extension of lesson-planning.) After the class, the teacher engages in self-monitoring by returning to this list and placing a checkmark next to the names of those students whom he or she actually praised at least once during the class period.

• **Make It Habit-Forming: Tie Praise to Classroom Routines.** Like any other behavior, praise can be delivered more consistently when it becomes a habit. Here is an idea that takes advantage of the power of habit-formation by weaving praise into classroom routine: (1) The teacher first defines various typical classroom activities during which praise is to be delivered (e.g., large-group instruction; student cooperative-learning activities; independent seatwork, etc.). (2) For each type of activity, the teacher decides on a minimum number of group and/or individual praise statements that the instructor would like to deliver each day or class period as a part of the instructional routine (e.g., 'Large-group instruction: 5 praise-statements or more to the class or individual students', 'Independent seatwork: 4 praise-statements or more to individual students'). (3) The teacher initially monitors the number of praise-statements actually delivered during each activity and strives to bring those totals into alignment with the minimum levels previously established as goals. (4) As delivery of praise becomes associated with specific activities, the onset of a particular class activity such as large-group instruction serves as a reminder (trigger or stimulus) to deliver praise. In effect, praise becomes a habit embedded in classroom routine.

References

Akin-Little, K. A., Eckert, T. L., Lovett, B. J., & Little, S. G. (2004). Extrinsic reinforcement in the classroom: Bribery or best practice. *School Psychology Review,* 33, 344-362.

Brophy, J. (1981). Teacher praise: A functional analysis. *Review of Educational Research,* 51, 5-32.

Burnett, P. C. (2001). Elementary students' preferences for teacher praise. Journal of Classroom Interaction, 36(1), 16-23.

Daly, E. J., Martens, B. K., Barnett, D., Witt, J. C., & Olson, S. C. (2007). Varying intervention delivery in response to intervention: Confronting and resolving challenges with measurement, instruction, and intensity. *School Psychology Review,* 36, 562-581.

Haring, N.G., Lovitt, T.C., Eaton, M.D., & Hansen, C.L. (1978). *The fourth R: Research in the classroom.* Columbus, OH: Charles E. Merrill Publishing Co.

Hawkins, S. M., & Heflin, L. J. (2011). Increasing secondary teachers' behavior-specific praise using a video self-modeling and visual performance feedback intervention. *Journal of Positive Behavior Interventions,* 13(2) 97–108.

Kern, L. & Clemens, N. H. (2007). Antecedent strategies to promote appropriate classroom behavior. *Psychology in the Schools,* 44, 65-75.

How To: Handle Common Classroom Problem Behaviors Using a Behavior Management Menu

Teachers who can draw on a range of responses when dealing with common classroom misbehaviors are more likely to keep those students in the classroom, resulting in fewer disruptions to instruction, enhanced teacher authority, and better learning outcomes for struggling students (Sprick, Borgmeier, & Nolet, 2002). A good organizing tool for teachers is to create a classroom menu that outlines a range of response options for behavior management and discipline. Teachers are able to assert positive classroom control when they apply such a behavior management menu consistently and flexibly—choosing disciplinary responses that match each student's presenting concerns (Marzano, Marzano, & Pickering, 2003).

This document groups potential teacher responses to classroom behavior incidents into 8 'menu' categories: (1) Behavior reminder, (2) academic adjustment, (3) environmental adjustment, (4) warning, (5) time-out, (6) response cost, (7) behavior conference, and (8) defusing strategies. Teachers can use these categories as a framework for organizing their own effective strategies for managing student problem behaviors.

1. Behavioral Reminder

Description: A behavioral reminder is a brief, neutral prompt to help the student to remember and follow classroom behavioral expectations (Simonsen, Fairbanks, Briesch, Myers, & Sugai, 2008).

When to Use: This strategy is used when the student appears to be distracted or otherwise requires a simple reminder of expected behaviors.

Examples: Here are examples of behavioral reminders:
- ☐ The teacher makes eye contact with the student who is misbehaving and points to a classroom rules chart.
- ☐ The teacher approaches the off-task student to remind him/her of the specific academic task the student should be doing.
- ☐ The teacher proactively provides behavioral reminders just when the student needs to use them.

2. Academic Adjustment

Description: An academic adjustment is a change made to the student's academic task(s) to improve behaviors. Such changes could include the amount of work assigned, provision of support to the student during the work, giving additional time to complete the work, etc. (Kern, Bambara & Fogt, 2002).

When to Use: Academic adjustments can be useful when the teacher judges that the student's problem behaviors are triggered or exacerbated by the required academic task(s).

Examples: Here are examples of academic adjustments:
- ☐ The teacher pre-teaches challenging vocabulary to the student prior to a large-group discussion.
- ☐ The teacher adjusts the difficulty of the assigned academic work to match the student's abilities ('instructional match').
- ☐ The teacher allows the student additional time to complete an academic task.

3. Environmental Adjustment

Description: An environmental adjustment is a change made to some aspect of the student's environment to improve behaviors (Kern & Clemens, 2007).

When to Use: This strategy is used when the teacher judges that an environmental element (e.g., distracting activities, proximity of another student) is contributing to the student's problem behavior.

Examples: Here are examples of environmental adjustments:
- ☐ The teacher moves the student's seat away from distracting peers.
- ☐ The teacher collects distracting objects from a student (e.g., small toys, paperclips) during a work session.
- ☐ The student is given a schedule of the day to prepare her for upcoming academic activities.

4. Warning

Description: A warning is a teacher statement informing the student that continued misbehavior will be followed by a specific disciplinary consequence (Simonsen, Fairbanks, Briesch, Myers, & Sugai, 2008).

When to Use: A warning is appropriate when the teacher judges (a) that the student has control over his or her behavior and (b) that a pointed reminder of impending behavioral consequences may improve the student's behavior. Whenever possible, it is recommended that proactive strategies such as providing behavioral reminders or eliminating environmental/academic triggers be tried before using warnings.

Examples: Here are examples of warnings:
- ☐ The teacher tells the student that if the problem behavior continues, the student will lose the opportunity for free time later that day.
- ☐ The student is warned that continued misbehavior will result in the teacher's calling the parent.

5. Time-Out

Description: Time-out (from reinforcement) is a brief removal of the student from the setting due to problem behaviors (Yell, 1994).

When to Use: Time-out from reinforcement can be effective in situations when the student would prefer to be in the classroom setting rather than in the time-out setting. Time-out sessions should typically be brief (e.g., 3-10 minutes). Because time-out is a punishment procedure, the teacher should first ensure that appropriate, less intrusive efforts to improve student behavior (e.g., behavior reminders, warnings, elimination of behavioral triggers) have been attempted before using it. If a teacher finds that a student does not improve behaviors despite several repetitions of time-out, other behavior management strategies should be tried instead.

Preparation: If time-out is to occur within the classroom, the teacher should identify the time-out location in advance and ensure that students placed there can be easily observed but are sufficiently removed from the current classroom activity. If the time-out location is out of the classroom, the teacher should arrange with other adults in advance (e.g., participating teachers whose classrooms may be time-out locations) to work out details for students to enter and exit time-out and for supervising students during time-out.

Examples: Here are examples of time-out from reinforcement:

☐ The teacher sends a student to a study carrel in the corner of the classroom for 5 minutes for misbehavior.

☐ The teacher sends a misbehaving student to a neighboring classroom for 10 minutes, where the student is to sit alone and complete classwork.

6. Response Cost

Description: Response cost is the taking away of privileges or other valued elements ('cost') in response to student misbehavior (DuPaul & Stoner, 2002).

When to Use: Response cost can be an effective response to misbehavior, provided that the student actually values the privilege or element being taken away. Because response cost is a punishment procedure, the teacher should first ensure that appropriate, less intrusive efforts to improve student behavior (e.g., behavior reminders, warnings, elimination of behavioral triggers) have been attempted before using it.

Examples: Here are examples of response-cost:

☐ Because of misbehavior, a student loses access to classroom free time at the end of the day.

☐ A student is given 5 good-behavior points at the start of class--and then has one deducted for each incident of misbehavior.

7. Behavior Conference

Description: A behavior conference is a brief meeting between teacher and student to discuss the student's problem behavior(s) (Fields, 2004). While the structure and content of a behavior conference will vary based on circumstances, it will typically include some or all of the following elements:

1. *Description of the problem behavior.* The teacher describes the student's behavior and explains why it is presenting a problem in the classroom.
2. *Open-ended questions and student input.* The teacher asks open-ended questions to fully understand what factors are contributing to the problem behavior.
3. *Problem-solving.* Teacher and student discuss solutions to the problem behavior and agree to a plan.
4. *Disciplinary reminder.* If appropriate, the teacher concludes the conference by informing the student of the disciplinary consequence that will occur if the problem behavior continues.

When to Use: The behavior conference is a useful tool for the teacher who:

• wishes to better understand reasons of the student problem behavior before acting.

• wants to model that it is better for the student to communicate his or her needs to the teacher through discussion than by engaging in acting-out behaviors.

Examples: Here are examples of a behavior conference:

☐ A teacher approaches the desk of a student who appears upset to explore what triggered that student's current emotional distress and to figure out how best to respond to the situation.

☐ A non-compliant student is taken aside by the teacher for a brief in-class conference, in which the teacher establishes that the student is in control of her behavior, states the behavioral expectations for the classroom, and informs the student that she will be given a disciplinary referral if her behaviors do not improve immediately.

8. Defusing Techniques

Description: Defusing techniques are any teacher actions taken to calm a student or otherwise defuse a situation with the potential for confrontation or emotional escalation (Daly & Sterba, 2011).

When to Use: When the teacher judges that the student's negative emotions are a significant contributor to the problem behaviors, defusing techniques are appropriate to stabilize the situation.

Examples: Here are examples of defusing techniques:
- ☐ The teacher temporarily removes academic work from a student who is reacting negatively to the assignment.
- ☐ The teacher encourages a student to sit in a quiet corner of the room for a few minutes to collect herself before conferencing with the teacher.
- ☐ The teacher sends a student to the guidance counselor to discuss the issue(s) causing him anger.

Behavior Management Menu: Example

A teacher, Mrs. Stevenson, decides to develop a behavior management menu to help her to respond more flexibly and effectively to common student misbehaviors in her classroom. Once that menu is in place, Mrs. Stevenson is able to manage two different student situations with success:

Episode 1: Francine. A student, Francine is whispering to two of her friends sitting nearby. Mrs. Stevenson can see that the whispering is beginning to distract students in proximity to Francine.
- *Behavioral Reminder.* The teacher makes eye contact with Francine while teaching and puts a finger to her lips to signal that the student should stop talking and attend to instruction.
- *Environmental Adjustment.* When Francine continues to talk to peers, the teacher moves her to a seat near the front of the room, away from her friends and close to the teacher.
- *Warning.* Francine continues to clown at her desk, making faces and whispering comments to no one in particular. The teacher approaches her desk and tells Francine quietly that if she continues to talk and distract other students, she will need to stay after class for a teacher conference, which will probably make her late for lunch. Francine's behaviors improve immediately.

Episode 2: Jay. A student, Jay, walks into class after lunch one day appearing visibly upset. When Mrs. Stevenson directs the class to pull out a homework assignment for review, Jay sits in his seat looking flushed and angry. He does not take out his work.
- *Behavioral Reminder.* The teacher approaches Jay and quietly asks that he pull out his homework. She then returns to the front of the room.
- *Behavior Conference.* The teacher sees that Jay is still not getting out his homework. She gives the class a 5-minute assignment to review their homework before submitting and uses that time to meet briefly with Jay in the hallway. She asks open-ended questions and discovers that Jay is angry about an incident that occurred at lunch.
- *Defusing Techniques.* Based on information gathered during the behavior conference, the teacher decides that Jay needs to meet with a mental health staff member to talk through and resolve his issue from lunch. She issues Jay a pass. Ultimately, he meets for 20 minutes with the school psychologist, calms down, and is able to return to class.

References

Daly, D. L., & Sterba, M. N. (2011). *Working with aggressive youth: Positive strategies to teach self-control and prevent violence.* Boys Town, NE: Boys Town Press.

DuPaul & Stoner, 2002 DuPaul, G.J., & Stoner, G. (2002). Interventions for attention problems. In M. Shinn, H.M. Walker, & G. Stoner (Eds.) *Interventions for academic and behavioral problems II: Preventive and remedial approaches* (pp. 913-938). Bethesda, MD: National Association of School Psychologists.

Fields, B. (2004). Breaking the cycle of office referrals and suspensions: Defensive management. *Educational Psychology in Practice, 20,* 103-115.

Kern, L., Bambara, L., & Fogt, J. (2002). Class-wide curricular modification to improve the behavior of students with emotional or behavioral disorders. *Behavioral Disorders, 27,*317-326.

Kern, L, & Clemens, N.(2007). Antecedent strategies to promote appropriate classroom behavior. *Psychology in theSchools, 44*(1), 65-75.

Marzano, R. J., Marzano, J. S., & Pickering, D. J. (2003). *Classroom management that works: Research-based strategies for every teacher.* Alexandria, VA: Association for Supervision and Curriculum Development.

Simonsen, B., Fairbanks, S., Briesch, A., Myers, D., & Sugai, G. (2008). Evidence-based practices in classroom management: Considerations for research to practice. *Evaluation and Treatment of Children, 31*(3), 351-380.

Sprick, R. S., Borgmeier, C., & Nolet, V. (2002). Prevention and management of behavior problems in secondary schools. In M. A. Shinn, H. M. Walker & G. Stoner (Eds.), *Interventions for academic and behavior problems II: Preventive and remedial approaches* (pp.373-401). Bethesda, MD: National Association of School Psychologists.

Yell, M.L. (1994). Timeout and students with behavior disorders: A legal analysis. *Education and Treatment of Children*, 17, 293-301.

Classroom Behavior Incident: Teacher Response Plan

Directions: Complete this form to document strategies used to manage individual students' problem classroom behaviors.

Student Name: _____ Date: _____

Person Completing Form: _____ Classroom: _____

	Behavior Management Strategy	Details. Include a description of each strategy used.
1	Behavioral Reminder	
2	Academic Adjustment	
3	Environmental Adjustment	
4	Warning	
5	Time-Out	
6	Response Cost	
7	Behavioral Conference	
8	Defusing Techniques	

Narrative of Incident [Optional]: _____

_____

How To: Calm the Agitated Student—
Tools for Effective Behavior Management

Students can sometimes have emotional outbursts in school settings. This fact will not surprise many teachers, who have had repeated experience in responding to serious classroom episodes of student agitation. Such outbursts can be attributed in part to the relatively high incidence of mental health issues among children and youth. It is estimated, for example, that at least one in five students in American schools will experience a mental health disorder by adolescence (U.S. Department of Health and Human Services, 1999). But even students not identified as having behavioral or emotional disorders may occasionally have episodes of agitation triggered by situational factors such as peer bullying, frustration over poor academic performance, stressful family relationships, or perceived mistreatment by educators.

Since virtually any professional working in schools might at some point find him/herself needing to 'talk down' a student who presents as emotionally upset, all educators should know the basics of how to de-escalate the agitated student. The advice offered in this checklist is adapted for use by schools from research on best practices in calming individuals in medical or psychiatric settings (Cowin et al., 2003; Fishkind, 2002; Richmond et al., 2012). These strategies are intended to be used in a flexible manner to increase the odds that an educator can respond efficiently and effectively to students who present with a wide range of emotional issues.

> **CAUTION**: The guidelines presented below are intended for use with a student whose agitated behavior is largely verbal, shows no signs of escalating beyond that point, and does not present as potentially physically aggressive or violent. Educators who suspect that a student may present a safety risk to self or others should immediately seek additional assistance. Schools should also conduct Functional Behavioral Assessments (FBAs), assemble appropriate Behavior Intervention Plans (BIPs) and—if needed— create Crisis Response Plans to manage the behaviors of students who show patterns of escalating, potentially violent behaviors.

☐ *Create a 'safe' setting.* An educator attempting to calm an agitated student cannot always select the setting in which that interaction plays out. When a student outburst occurs in the classroom, however, the educator should attempt to engage the student in a semi-private conversation (e.g., off to the side of the room) rather than having an exchange in front of classmates. As part of the protocol for conducting a de-escalation conference, adults should also ensure that they are never left alone with agitated students.

☐ *Limit the number of adults involved.* Having too many educators (e.g., teacher and a teaching assistant) participating in a de-escalation conference can be counter-productive because of possible confusion and communication of mixed messages to the agitated student. If more than one adult is available in the instructional setting, select the one with the most experience with de-escalation techniques to engage the student one-to-one, while the additional educator(s) continue to support the instruction or behavior management of other students.

☐ *Provide adequate personal space.* Stand at least 2 arm's length of distance away from the agitated student. If the student tells you to 'back off' or 'get away', provide the student with additional space.

☐ *Do not block escape routes.* When individuals are agitated, they are more likely to experience a 'fight-or-flight' response that can express itself in the need to have escape routes available. When engaging a student in a de-escalation conference, do not position yourself between the student and the door. If the student says, "Get out of my way", step back to give that student additional personal space and reposition yourself out of his or her potential escape path.

☐ *Show open, accepting body language.* Convey through stance and body language that you are calm and accepting of the student—and will treat that student respectfully and maintain his or her safety. Stand at an angle rather than facing the student directly in a 'confrontational' pose. Keep hands open and visible to the student. Stand comfortably, with knees slightly bent. Avoid 'clenched' body language such as crossing arms or balling hands into fists.

☐ *Keep verbal interactions respectful.* It is natural for educators to experience feelings of defensiveness, embarrassment, anxiety, or irritation when attempting to talk down a student from an emotional outburst. However, you should strive to appear calm and to treat the student respectfully at all times. Avoid use of teasing, reprimands, or other negative comments and abstain as well from sarcasm or an angry tone of voice.

☐ *Communicate using simple, direct language.* When people are emotionally upset, they may not process language quickly or with complete accuracy. In talking with the student, keep your vocabulary simple and your sentences brief. Be sure to allow sufficient time for the student to think about and respond to each statement before continuing. In particular, if the student does not respond to a statement, avoid falling into the trap of assuming too quickly that the student is simply 'ignoring you'. Instead, calmly repeat yourself--several times if necessary. So long as the student's behavior is not escalating, give him or her the benefit of the doubt and use gentle repetition to help the student to focus on and respond to you.

☐ *Coach the student to take responsibility for moderating behavior.* At the point in an encounter with an agitated student when you feel that you have established rapport, you can use a positive, assertive tone to prompt the student to take responsibility for controlling his or her own behavior (e.g., "John, it is hard for me to follow what you are saying when you raise your voice and pace around the room. If you sit down and calmly explain what the problem is, I think that I can help.").

☐ *Reassure the student and frame an outcome goal.* You can often help to defuse the student's agitation by reassuring the student (e.g., "You're not in trouble. This is your chance to give me your side of the story") and stating an outcome goal ("Let's figure out how to take care of this situation in a positive way" ; "I want to understand why you are upset so that I can know how to respond"). Also, if you do not know the agitated student whom you are approaching, introduce yourself and state both your name and position.

☐ *Identify the student's wants and feelings.* Use communication tools such as active listening (e.g., "Let me repeat back to you what I thought I heard you say ...."), open-ended questions (e.g., "What do you need right now to be able to calm yourself?"), and labeling of emotions ("Rick, you look angry. Tell me what is bothering you") to better understand how the student feels and what may be driving the current emotional outburst.

☐ *Identify points of agreement.* A powerful strategy to build rapport with an agitated student is to find points on which you can agree. At the same time, of course, you must preserve your professional integrity as an educator and therefore cannot falsely express agreement on issues that you in fact disagree with. Here are suggestions for finding authentic common ground with the student in response to different situations. (1) Agreement with student's account: If you essentially agree with the student's account of (and/or emotional reaction to) the situation, you can say so (e.g., "I can understand why you were upset when you lost your book on the field trip. I would be upset too."); (2) Agreement with a principle expressed or implied by the student: If you are unsure of the objectivity of the student's account, you might still discern within it a principle that you can support (e.g., If the student claims to have been disrespected by a hall monitor, you can say, "I think everybody has the right to feel respected."); (3) Agreement with the typicality of the student response: If you decide that the student's emotional response would likely be shared by a substantial number of peers, you can state that observation (e.g., "So I gather that you were pretty frustrated when you learned that you are no longer sports-eligible because of your report card grades. I am sure that there are other students here who feel the same way.";(4) Agreement to disagree: If you cannot find a point on which you can agree with the student or validate an aspect of his or her viewpoint, you should simply state that you and the student agree to disagree.

References

Cowin, L, Davies, R., Estall, G., Berlin, T., Fitzgerald, M., & Hoot, S. (2003). De-escalating aggression and violence in the mental health setting. *International Journal of Mental Health Nursing,* 12, 64-73.

Fishkind, A. (2002). Calming agitation with words, not drugs: 10 commandments for safety. *Current Psychiatry,* 1(4), 32-39.Available at: http://www.currentpsychiatry.com/pdf/0104/0104_Fishkind.pdf

Richmond, J. S., Berlin, J. S., Fishkind, A. B., Holloman, G. H., Zeller, S. L., Wilson, M. P., Rifai, M. A., & Ng, A. T. (2012). Verbal de-escalation of the agitated patient: Consensus statement of the American Association for Emergency Psychiatry Project BETA de-escalation work-group. *Western Journal of Emergency Medicine,* 13(1), 17-25.

U.S. Department of Health and Human Services. (1999). *Mental health: A report of the Surgeon General.* Rockville, MD: Author.

How To: Improve Classroom Management Through Flexible Rules— The Color Wheel

The posting of classwide rules can help teachers to teach behavioral expectations and prevent problem behaviors (Simonsen et al., 2008). However, a single set of rules lacks flexibility. As students move from large group instruction to cooperative learning groups to less-structured free time (often during the same day and in the same classroom), behavioral expectations shift as well. The teacher who attempts to apply an unchanging set of behavioral rules across so varied a range of activities will be forced to suspend, amend, or ignore certain rules at certain times, creating potential uncertainty and confusion among students (Kirk et al., 2010). For example, the simple rule "To speak, raise hand for teacher permission" is useful in large-group instruction but does not transfer well to discussions in student-led groups.

The Color Wheel is one solution that enforces uniform group expectations for conduct while also responding flexibly to the differing behavioral demands of diverse learning activities. This classwide intervention divides all activities into 3 categories and links each category to a color: green for free time/ low-structure activities; yellow for large- or small-group instruction/independent work; and red for brief transitions between activities. The student learns a short list of behavioral rules for each category and, when given a color cue, can switch quickly from one set of rules to another.

Color Wheel: Steps. Here are the 5 steps to implementing the Color Wheel in the classroom (Fudge et al., 2008; Kirk et al., 2010):

1. *Define behavioral expectations for each color.* The teacher develops a short list of rules summarizing the behavioral expectations for each of the color levels in the Color Wheel: green (free time/ low-structure activities); yellow (large- or small-group instruction/independent work); and red (transitioning between activities). The table on the right provides a starter-set of appropriate behaviors by color condition that the teacher can edit to match the developmental level of a particular classroom.

2. *Create Color rules posters.* The teacher next creates posters to be publicly posted for this intervention. The instructor copies the rules for each color level in large, legible script onto posterboard of a matching color (e.g., green color level rules are copied onto green posterboard, etc.). (See Figure 1 below for an example of Color Wheel posters.)

3. *Create the Color Wheel.* The teacher assembles the Color Wheel, a simple device for alerting students to the current color condition in effect in the classroom. The simplest way to create a Color Wheel is to cut a large disk (12 inches or greater) from white posterboard. The disk is partitioned into thirds with heavy black lines--like a pie divided into 3 large slices. Each of the 3 pie-slices is then colored in with one of the green/yellow/red colors. The teacher then affixes a large posterboard arrow in the center of the circle -- using a brad (paper fastener) to allow the arrow to rotate. (See Figure 1 below for an example of a Color Wheel.)

4. *Train students in the Color Wheel procedures.* The teacher posts the Color Wheel and colored behavior posters in a location visible to all students. The instructor explains the color levels and describes the activities associated with each. Next, the teacher uses the colored posters to review the behavioral expectations associated with each color level. The teacher gives specific descriptions of acceptable behaviors and their boundaries (e.g., "At the

Color Wheel Behaviors: Sample List
Green Condition: Free Time/Low-Structure Activities
• Talk in a quiet voice
• Keep hands and feet to self
• Comply with directions
Yellow Condition: Large- or Small-Group Instruction/Independent Work
• To speak, raise hand for teacher permission
• To leave seat, raise hand for teacher permission
• Look at the speaker or your work
• Comply with directions
Red Condition: Transitions Between Activities
• Return to your seat
• Clear your desk
• Look at the teacher
• Do not talk

red level, when you clear your desks, your materials go into desks, backpacks, and cubbies--you should not stack any materials on the floor."). The teacher next demonstrates the Color Wheel, showing how the arrow indicator will always point to the color condition currently in effect as a guide to which colored rules poster the students will follow.

5. *Begin the Color Wheel intervention.* The teacher then starts the Color Wheel intervention. To prepare students to adjust quickly to new color conditions, the instructor always gives a 30-second warning when the Color Wheel is about the change. (If students have difficulty with this single reminder, the instructor may want to give both a 2-minute and 30-second warning.) The teacher also regularly praises students for following posted behaviors. For maximum effectiveness, classwide praise should be intermixed with praise to small groups and individuals. Praise should also be 'labeled', clearly describing the behaviors that are praise-worthy (e.g., "This reading group transitioned quickly and quietly to the math lesson. Nice work!").

Figure 1: Sample Posters and Color Wheel

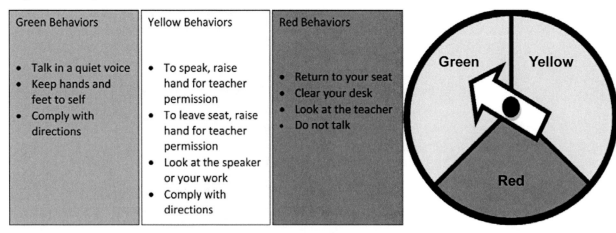

Green Behaviors	Yellow Behaviors	Red Behaviors
• Talk in a quiet voice • Keep hands and feet to self • Comply with directions	• To speak, raise hand for teacher permission • To leave seat, raise hand for teacher permission • Look at the speaker or your work • Comply with directions	• Return to your seat • Clear your desk • Look at the teacher • Do not talk

Color Wheel: Additional Considerations. Although the Color Wheel system is fairly easy to implement, teachers should be mindful of these recommendations (Fudge, et al., 2008)

1. *Keep the Color Wheel 'red' periods short.* The red condition of the Color Wheel covers transitions between activities--which should always be brief in duration. Teachers should therefore keep students on the red phase only long enough complete the transition to a new green or yellow activity. Once students are trained to make efficient transitions, 3-5 minutes should be sufficient to move into and out of a red phase.

2. *Do not use the 'red' Color Wheel setting as punishment.* The behavioral expectations for the red (transitions) Color Wheel condition are the most restrictive, as students need to be seated, quiet, and focused on the teacher to learn the details of the upcoming activity. However, teachers should never set the classroom color condition to red simply to punish students for misbehavior. Linking the red condition with punishment raises the possibility that students will fail to comply with the red behavioral rules because they are seen as punitive rather than necessary to support an effective learning environment.

References

Fudge, D. L., Skinner, C. H., Williams, J. L., Cowden, D., Clark, J., & Bliss, S. L. (2008). Increasing on-task behavior in every student in a second-grade classroom during transitions: Validating the color wheel system. *Journal of School Psychology, 46*, 575-592.

Kirk, E. R., Becker, J. A., Skinner, C. H., Fearrington, J. Y., McCane-Bowling, S. J., Amburn, C., Luna, E., & Greear, C. (2010). Decreasing inappropriate vocalizations using classwide group contingencies and color wheel procedures: A component analysis. *Psychology in the Schools, 47*, 931-943.

Simonsen, B., Fairbanks, S., Briesch, A., Myers, D., & Sugai, G. (2008). Evidence-based practices in classroom management: Considerations for research to practice. *Evaluation and Treatment of Children, 31*(3), 351-380.

How To: Use the Power of Personal Connection to Motivate Students— 4 Strategies

A positive relationship with the teacher is often a crucial factor in motivating a struggling student. The power of positive teacher-student interactions is illustrated in one recent study, which found that—when instructors took just a few seconds to greet inattentive students by name at the start of class—the percentage of time those students spent academically engaged during the first 10 minutes of instruction soared from 45% to 72% (Allday & Pakurar, 2007).

Teachers who are 'proactively positive' in their classroom interactions can foster strong student connections with a minimum of effort. However, in the push to increase the academic rigor of classrooms to implement the Common Core State Standards, teachers can sometimes forget to use simple but effective tools such as praise (Kern & Clemens, 2007) that motivate students even as they strengthen teacher-student relationships. In this discussion, we review efficient strategies to use in connecting with students, along with pointers for integrating those practices into teachers' instructional routines.

Connecting With Students: 4 Strategies. Here are four recommendations for building student relationships that work--but do not require a great deal of time or effort--with fuller explanations of each strategy appearing in the table at the end of this document:

1. *Greet students at the start of class.* As students arrive at the start of class, the teacher stands at the door and briefly greets each student by name (Allday & Pakurar, 2007). This modest effort has been shown to substantially increase student attention and focus. Teachers who commit to using student greetings rearrange their start-of-class routine to allow them consistently to be standing just outside or inside the classroom door as the students arrive.

2. *Promote positive interactions via the 3-positives:1-negative ratio.* To keep relationships on a positive footing throughout the classroom, the teacher self-monitors encounters with particular students and sets the goal of having at least 3 positive interactions for each disciplinary interaction (Sprick, Borgmeier & Nolet, 2002). Positive teacher-student interactions can vary in format: for example, greeting, praise, conversation, smile, thumbs-up sign. By maintaining at least a 3:1 ratio between relationship-enhancing vs. disciplinary interactions, the teacher bends the odds in his or her favor that every student in the class will view the instructor as fair and caring.

3. *Use targeted praise.* Teachers can enhance the positive climate of the classroom, motivate learners, and shape student performance in the desired direction by using frequent praise-statements (Kern & Clemens, 2007). To maximize its impact, praise should describe in specific terms the behavior that is praise-worthy and be delivered as soon as possible after the observed student behavior.

   A significant challenge for any instructor who wishes to increase use of praise statements is to employ them with consistency. After all, it is easy for teachers to forget to praise when faced with competing instructional demands. One idea to improve delivery is for the teacher to select as a goal a minimum number of praise statements to be given in a class period (e.g., 10). The teacher then keeps a running count of praise statements as they are delivered throughout the period to verify that the daily goal is reached. A second idea to self-monitor frequency of praise statements is for the teacher to decide on a minimum time-interval for delivering those statements to students —for example, every 3 minutes. The instructor can then use an audio tape with tones at 3-minute intervals to signal when praise should be given. NOTE: Free self-monitoring audio tapes in MP3 format with a range of fixed intervals playable on smart phones or other devices are available at: http://www.interventioncentral.org/free-audio-monitoring-tapes

4. *Provide teacher attention for positive behavior: The 'two-by-ten' intervention.* If a teacher has a strained (or non-existent) relationship with a particular student, that teacher may want to jump-start a more positive pattern of interaction using the 'two-by-ten' intervention (Mendler, 2000). With this time-efficient strategy, the teacher commits to having a positive 2-minute conversation with the student at least once per day across 10 consecutive school days. The active ingredient in the intervention is regular and positive teacher attention delivered at times when the student is not misbehaving. After the 10-day intervention, teachers often find that their relationships with formerly problematic students have improved markedly.

Teachers know that building relationships with students is not a process that occurs by magic—but instead requires thoughtful planning and effort. However, the four ideas presented here are a good starting point for instructors who seek efficient ways to promote interpersonal connections that motivate and inspire students.

References

Allday, R. A., & Pakurar, K. (2007). Effects of teacher greetings on student on-task behavior. *Journal of Applied Behavior Analysis,* 40, 317-320.

Kern, L. & Clemens, N. H. (2007). Antecedent strategies to promote appropriate classroom behavior. *Psychology in the Schools*, 44, 65-75.

Mendler, A. N. (2000). *Motivating students who don't care.* Bloomington, IN: National Educational Service.

Sprick, R. S., Borgmeier, C., & Nolet, V. (2002). Prevention and management of behavior problems in secondary schools. In M. A. Shinn, H. M. Walker & G. Stoner (Eds.), *Interventions for academic and behavior problems II: Preventive and remedial approaches* (pp.373-401). Bethesda, MD: National Association of School Psychologists.

How To: Focus Students With ADHD Through Antecedent Teaching Strategies—Cuing

Because of inattention, students with Attention-Deficit Hyperactivity Disorder (ADHD) often perform below their level of ability on academic tasks such as math computation, word problems, or reading comprehension. However, teachers can often use simple verbal or visual cuing techniques to substantially improve these students' academic performance. Cuing techniques are considered to be positive antecedents that set the student up for greater success (Kern, Choutka, & Sokol, 2002). Such techniques are time-efficient, quick-acting, and non-intrusive.

Here is a sampling of ideas for cuing student attention to improve academic performance:

Academic Strategy Examples: Visual & Verbal Attentional Cuing	
VISUAL CUING: MATH COMPUTATION: STUDENT HIGHLIGHTING. Students who are inattentive or impulsive can improve their accuracy and fluency on math computation problems through student-performed highlighting. The student is given highlighters of several colors and a math computation sheet. Before completing the worksheet, the student is directed to color-code the problems on the sheet in a manner of his or her choosing (e.g., by level of difficulty, by math operation). The student then completes the highlighted worksheet.	Kercood, S., & Grskovic, J. A. (2009). The effects of highlighting on the math computation performance and off-task behavior of students with attention problems. Education and Treatment of Children, 32, 231-241.
VISUAL CUING: MATH WORD PROBLEMS: HIGHLIGHT KEY TERMS. Students who have difficulties with inattention or impulsivity can increase rates of on-task behavior and accuracy on math word problems through highlighting of key terms. The teacher prepares the worksheet by using a colored highlighter to highlight a combination of 8-11 key words and numbers for each math word problem. The student then completes the highlighted worksheet.	Kercood, S., Zentall, S. S., Vinh, M., & Tom-Wright, K. (2012). Attentional cuing in math word problems for girls at-risk for ADHD and their peers in general education settings. Contemporary Educational Psychology, 37, 106-112.
VISUAL CUING: WRITING: USE COLORED PAPER TO INCREASE WRITING LEGIBILITY. Students with attention or impulsivity issues may improve the legibility of handwriting for spelling and writing tasks through use of colored writing paper. In preparation, the student is offered a range of colored paper choices ranging from pastels to bright, highly saturated (neon) hues. The paper in the color chosen by the student is then prepared by adding ruled lines for writing. Whenever the student has an important writing task in which legibility is important, he or she is encouraged to use writing paper of the preferred color.	Imhof, M. (2004). Effects of color stimulation on handwriting performance of children with ADHD without and with additional learning disabilities. European Child & Adolescent Psychiatry, 13, 191-198.
VERBAL CUING: READING COMPREHENSION: PROMPT WITH INCENTIVE. To boost student comprehension of a passage, use a verbal prompt before the reading paired with an incentive. Before the student begins reading a story or informational-text passage, the teacher says: "Read this story/passage out loud. Try to remember as much as you can about the story/passage. Then I will have you retell the main points of the story/passage. If you remember enough of the reading, you will get a sticker [or other prize or incentive]." If the student needs a reminder during the reading, the teacher says: "Work on remembering as much of the reading as you can." At the end of the reading, the student is told to recount the main points of the passage and is awarded the promised incentive at the discretion of the teacher.	O'Shea, L. J., Sindelar, P. T., & O'Shea, D. J. (1985). The effects of repeated reading and attentional cues on reading fluency and comprehension. Journal of Literacy Research, 17(2), 129-142.

Some of the strategies presented here can also be adapted for use with groups. For example, students could pair off to discuss and highlight math computation worksheets. Or the teacher could use an overhead projector to highlight key terms in assigned math word problems, while the students highlight the same terms on their own worksheets.

Reference

Kern, L., Choutka, C. M., & Sokol, N. G. (2002). Assessment-based antecedent interventions used in natural settings to reduce challenging behavior: An analysis of the literature. *Education and Treatment of Children, 25*(1), 113-130.

How To: Build a Student Motivation Trap to Increase Academic Engagement

Motivating a reluctant student to complete schoolwork is not easy. In a typical classroom, students can choose from a number of sources of potential reinforcement (Billington & DiTommaso, 2003)--and academic tasks often take a back seat to competing behaviors such as talking with peers. One way that teachers can increase the attractiveness of schoolwork is by structuring lessons or assignments around topics or activities of high interest to the student (Miller et al., 2003).In fact, with planning, the teacher can set up a 'trap' that uses motivating elements to capture a student's attention to complete academic tasks (Alber & Heward, 1996). Here is a 6-step blue-print for building an academic 'motivation trap' (adapted from Alber & Heward, 1996):

How to Set a 'Positive Motivation Trap': 6 Steps	
1	*Choose an Academic Skill-Area.* The teacher selects a significant academic-skill area in which the student is deficient--and this becomes the focus for the motivation trap. Examples include spelling, math computation, vocabulary development, reading comprehension, letter identification, writing/text production, and independent reading. The key question to be answered in this step is: *"What academic area presents the greatest hurdle to this student's success and requires his/her motivation and engagement?"*
2	*Identify a Target Behavior.* Within the more general area of academic skill, the teacher identifies specific student academic behaviors that the instructor would like to increase via the motivation trap. Examples include working to acquire basic-multiplication math facts (academic skill: math computation), reading assigned articles without adult prompting (academic skill: independent reading), and writing in-class compositions of appropriate length (academic skill: writing/text production). When selecting specific target behaviors to increase, the teacher should consider starting small: that is, selecting modest academic behaviors that are easy to perform and of short duration. As the motivation trap takes effect and the student shows increased investment in the academic activity, the teacher can always lengthen student sessions or even revise the target behavior to be more ambitious. For example, an instructor might set as an initial behavior goal for math-computation that the student will respond to math-fact flashcards in 5-minute tutoring sessions. Later, as the motivation trap takes effect and the student shows increased energy and engagement, the teacher may lengthen the tutoring sessions to 10 minutes or alter the behavior target to have the student take responsibility for reviewing flashcards independently. When possible, it is also a good idea to select as targets those academic behaviors that can be practiced frequently and have the potential to give the student sustainable, real-world pay-offs (e.g., teacher praise, improved grades, positive peer interactions, etc.). The key question to be answered in this step is: *"What specific academic behaviors are feasible, important targets for the student to increase?"*
3	*Identify the Motivator: High-Interest Activities or Topics.* The driving force behind the motivation trap is an activity or topic that is of high interest to the student, such as a sports team, fashion, music, a career interest. The teacher who is uncertain what motivates a particular student can pick up clues by talking with or observing the student (e.g., noting recurring topics he/she brings up, book or article themes that he/she is drawn to, preferred websites) or by talking with adults with a deeper knowledge

	of the student (e.g., last year's teacher, parent). The key question to be answered in this step is: *"What activity or topic is highly motivating for this student?"*
4	*Link the Motivator and the Target Academic Behavior.* The teacher 'sets the motivational trap' by connecting the motivator (activity or topic of high interest to the student) with the targeted academic behavior (Alber & Heward,1996). The ways that an instructor might weave together student motivator and target behavior are limited only by the teacher's creativity. For example, the student who avidly follows a baseball team and is working on multiplication facts might be allowed to review a favorite baseball card after every ten correct responses to flashcards. On another day, the same student might draw a 2-column table in her notebook with the names of her favorite team and their fiercest rival at the top of the respective columns. As the student solves math-facts, she records the answers in the table--alternating between home team and rival--and at the end of the tutoring session adds up the 'score' to determine the winning team. The key question to be answered in this step is: *"In what ways can the motivator (high-interest activity or topic) be linked to the academic activity to engage the student?"*
5	*Assess Improvement in Student Engagement and on the Target Academic Behavior.* Before a judgment can be made about whether the motivation trap is effective, the teacher must collect data on the academic skill and student interest-level . While the teacher has wide latitude in determining what kind of data will be collected, that instructor will probably want to know two important outcomes: (1) Has the student's rate of academic engagement increased? (measure of motivation), and (2) are the student's target academic skills improving? (measure of academic mastery). For example, a tutor using math flashcards with a student may rate the student's daily level of participation (measure of motivation) and also keep a cumulative record of mastered facts by day (measure of academic mastery). The key question to be answered in this step is: *"Does the data show that the motivation trap is improving student engagement and academic skills?"*
6	*Revise and Troubleshoot the Intervention.* A positive motivation trap is always dynamic, because conditions are always changing. So the teacher monitors the effectiveness of the trap and is ready to make revisions and corrections as needed. For example, as a student masters a target skill, the teacher will want to replace it with a more ambitious academic behavior goal. Or as a student is able to tolerate 5-minute tutoring sessions, those sessions may be extended to 10 minutes. Or, at different times of the year, a teacher may update the professional leagues used to motivate a sports-focused student to match real-world sports schedules. The key question to be answered in this step is: *"What revisions or corrections might be needed to maintain or strengthen the motivation trap?"*

References

Alber, S. R., & Heward, W. L. (1996). "GOTCHA!" Twenty-five behavior traps guaranteed to extend your students' academic and social skills. *Intervention in School and Clinic, 31,* 285-289.

Billington, E., & DiTommaso, N. M. (2003). Demonstrations and applications of the matching law in education. *Journal of Behavioral Education, 12*(2), 91-104.

Miller, K.A., Gunter, P.L., Venn, M.J., Hummel, J., & Wiley, L.P. (2003). Effects of curricular and materials modifications on academic performance and task engagement of three students with emotional or behavioral disorders. *Behavioral Disorders, 28,* 130-149.

How To: Increase Motivation in Students—High-Probability Requests

Non-compliance is a frequent source of problem classroom behavior--driven by student attempts to escape or avoid challenging academic tasks (Packenham, Shute & Reid, 2004). For instance, when transitioning between educational activities a work-avoidant student may stall in beginning the next assignment. Or, during independent assignments, that same student may run out the clock by dawdling between work items. To increase compliance and work completion, teachers should identify strategies that prevent off-task behaviors but must also continue to hold students accountable for attaining rigorous academic standards.

High-probability requests are one feasible classroom technique that can be effective in motivating students to engage in assigned classwork (Lee, 2006). The teacher first identifies an academic activity in which the student historically shows a low probability of completing because of non-compliance. The teacher then embeds within that low-probability activity an introductory series of simple, brief 'high-probability' requests or tasks that this same student has an established track record of completing (Belfiore, Basile, & Lee, 2008).

As the student completes several embedded high-probability tasks in succession, he or she builds 'behavioral momentum' in responding that increases the likelihood that the student will apply full effort when encountering the 'main event'--the more challenging, low-probability activity. (See the table *Use of High-Probability Requests to Increase Student Compliance: Examples from Research Studies* for descriptions of how high-probability requests have been used successfully in school settings.)

Use of high-probability requests offers the twin advantages of motivating students while encouraging high academic standards. Students can find the experience of completing simple, high-probability tasks to be intrinsically reinforcing--which fuels the behavioral momentum that gives this strategy its power (Lee et al., 2004). At the same time, this approach offers teachers a means of holding non-compliant students to the same high academic expectations as their more cooperative classmates (Belfiore et al., 2008).

A potential instructional advantage of the high-probability request strategy should also be noted. Research suggests that student retention of learned material is heightened if that material is reviewed at intervals of several months or more from the initial learning (Pashler et al., 2007). If teachers are able to fold previously learned academic material (e.g., math

Use of High-Probability Requests to Increase Student Compliance: Examples from Research Studies

Transitioning within academic tasks: Letter/word copying (Lee et al., 2004). During independent work, two 2nd-grade students were directed to copy a letter several times from a model (a preferred, high-probability task) before being asked to copy a whole word from a model (less-preferred, low-probability task).

Transitioning within academic tasks: Math computation (Lee et al., 2004). Three students with IEPs from intermediate grades were presented with flashcards containing math computation problems. The students were to read off and solve each problem, flip the card over to check the actual answer against their solution, and then advance to the next card. For the activity, the teacher first created a series of cards containing low-probability computation problems that were less-preferred because of their difficulty. Then, before each low-probability problem, the teacher inserted flashcards with three easy (more-preferred, high-probability) computation problems.

Transitioning between academic tasks: Independent math assignment (Wehby & Hollahan, 2000). This study focused on a middle-school student who often would not initiate independent math assignments. The teacher compiled a list of high-probability requests related to the independent math assignment that the student would typically respond to--e.g., 'write your name on the worksheet", "pick up your pencil", "take out a sheet of paper for the assignment", "look over the first problem". At the start of the independent seatwork activity, the teacher approached the student and randomly selected and delivered 3 requests from the high-probability list. If the student ignored a request, the teacher would simply deliver another from the list until the student had successfully complied with 3 high-probability requests. Then the teacher delivered the less-preferred, low-probability request: "Begin your independent assignment."

computation facts; course vocabulary items) into high-probability requests, they can both boost student work compliance and promote retention of essential skills or knowledge.

Here are more detailed teacher guidelines from Lee (2006) for embedding high-probability requests to build behavioral momentum sufficient to motivate students to tackle less-preferred, low-probability academic activities:

1. *Identify incidents of non-compliant behavior.* The teacher notes academic work-situations that initially have a low probability for completion because of student non-compliance (e.g., writing a journal entry; completing a worksheet with reflective questions tied to a reading assignment). The teacher also determines whether non-compliance in each situation occurs within that task or in transitioning to that task.

2. *List high-probability tasks.* Next, the teacher generates a list of high-probability tasks that the student is likely to comply with. These tasks should be brief (i.e., take 5 seconds or fewer to complete) and should logically link to the low-probability activity. For example, if the low-probability event is getting the student to start the writing of a journal entry (transitioning between academic activities), easy, high-probability tasks associated with beginning the writing task might include 'organize your writing materials', 'write a title', and 'list 3 ideas for the journal entry'. If the low-probability event is having the student complete a worksheet with reflective questions tied to an assigned reading (within-task), sample high-probability tasks associated with the worksheet could include questions asking the student to 'copy the title of this reading', or 'write down one interesting vocabulary term from the first paragraph'.

3. *Create activities with embedded high-probability tasks.* The teacher then reworks the low-probability work-situation to embed within it a series of high-probability tasks. If the target is to get the student to transition efficiently from one activity to another, the teacher inserts 3 high-probability requests at the start of the activity to create behavioral momentum. If the goal is to prod the student to efficiently complete an independent assignment without hesitating between items, the teacher inserts 3 high-probability requests before each challenging item on the assignment.

4. *Introduce the activities.* The teacher rolls out the activities, now retooled to include embedded high-probability tasks or requests. The teacher is careful, when presenting directives aloud to the student, to pace those directives briskly: letting no more than 10 seconds elapse between student completion of one request and teacher delivery of the next request. The teacher should also monitor the student's performance. If the student does not comply quickly with selected high-probability requests, the teacher should replace those requests on future assignments with others that elicit prompt compliance.

The guidelines offered here demonstrate how strategic use of high-probability requests can generate behavioral momentum and prevent compliance problems with individual students. However, teachers may also be able to creatively use high-probability sequences to motivate whole groups or even an entire class. For example, an instructor might decide to intersperse 3 'easy' (high-probability) items between each 'challenge' item on a math computation worksheet to be assigned to all students for independent seatwork. Or a teacher may routinely introduce in-class writing assignments by first verbally directing students to 'take out paper and pen', 'write your name on the paper', and 'copy this journal topic onto your paper'. The crucial factor in group use of high-probability sequences is that the teacher accurately identify what tasks are indeed motivating and likely to build behavioral momentum among the majority of students.

References

Belfiore, P. J., Basile, S. P., & Lee, D. L. (2008). Using a high probability command sequence to increase classroom compliance: The role of behavioral momentum. *Journal of Behavioral Education, 17,* 160-171.

Lee, D. L. (2006). Facilitating transitions between and within academic tasks: An application of behavioral momentum. *Remedial and Special Education, 27,* 312-317.

Lee, D. L., Belfiore, P. J., Scheeler, M. C., Hua, Y., & Smith, R. (2004). Behavioral momentum in academics: Using embedded high-p sequences to increase academic productivity. *Psychology in the Schools, 41,* 789-801.

Packenham, M., Shute, R., & Reid, R. (2004). A truncated functional behavioral assessment procedure for children with disruptive classroom behaviors. Education *and Treatment of Children, 27*(1), 9-25.

Pashler, H., Bain, P., Bottge, B., Graesser, A., Koedinger, K., McDaniel, M., and Metcalfe, J. (2007) *Organizing instruction and study to improve student learning.* Washington, DC: National Center for Education Research, Institute of Education Sciences, U.S. Department of Education. Retrieved from http://ncer.ed.gov.

Wehby, J. H., & Hollahan, M. S. (2000). Effects of high-probability requests on the latency to initiate academic tasks. *Journal of Applied Behavior Analysis, 33,* 259–262.

Chapter 5

Collecting Data to Track Interventions: General Classroom Measures

When teachers create individualized classroom academic or behavioral intervention plans, they should also routinely collect data to judge whether the intervention is actually working to fix the student problem(s). There are several reasons that data collection is an integral part of all individual student intervention plans. To begin with, teachers cannot know beforehand that a particular intervention strategy is certain to be effective for a given student. Also, teachers have only limited time and other resources to provide intervention support, and so cannot afford to waste those resources on strategies that are not working. By collecting data during the intervention, therefore, they can be reassured that their efforts are paying off and, if needed, quickly discontinue practices that are ineffective and try other strategies instead.

An additional reason that teachers will want to collect data on intervention impact is that they can use that information to communicate with important stakeholders (e.g., the student, parents, fellow teachers, administrators) about the intervention and its effectiveness. Furthermore, data collected during an intervention can sometimes demonstrate whether a student has attained a particular Common Core State Standard. And finally, records of an intervention plan and related progress-monitoring data have the potential of being archived and made available to future teachers to inform them of previous strategies that were (or were not) found to be effective for a particular student.

However, if teachers are expected to collect classroom data to monitor interventions, such data collection must be feasible to carry out in classrooms of 20-30 students. To define 'feasibility', then, it is necessary at the start to determine what specifically are the essential quality indicators that must always be a part of data collection. These are just four: problem definition, baseline, goal-setting, and a progress-monitoring plan; if even one of these data-related elements is missing, however, the student intervention that they connect to will have "fatal flaws" (Witt, VanDerHeyden, & Gilbertson, 2004; p. 366) and success of the intervention will be unlikely. Brief descriptions of the 4 components of intervention data collection follow:

1. *Problem identification.* A concise, specific definition of the academic or behavioral problem is necessary before data can be collected. The guiding motto for this step is: "If you can't name the problem, you can't measure it."

2. *Baseline.* Prior to putting an intervention into place, the teacher collects initial (baseline) data to verify the nature and extent of the student's academic or behavioral problem. Baseline data serves as a pre-intervention snap-shot or point of comparison. When the intervention is over, the teacher compares the intervention outcome data to baseline to judge the overall magnitude of student progress. The saying that highlights the importance of baseline data is: "If you don't know the student's pre-intervention starting point, you cannot know if that student has made progress during the intervention."

3. *Goal-setting.* Before starting the intervention, the teacher selects an outcome goal. If this outcome goal is reached by the end of the intervention period, of course, that intervention is judged to be a success. The power of an outcome goal is that it makes any judgment of intervention effectiveness clear-cut and objective: either the student reaches the goal or does not. The motto for goal-setting is: "If you have no outcome goal, you cannot judge if the intervention is successful—no matter how much data you collect."

4. *Progress-monitoring plan.* While the intervention plan is in place and being delivered, the teacher periodically collects data to judge in real time whether the student is showing adequate growth toward the outcome goal. While the frequency of classroom data collection will depend in part on the type of measure used, a good rule of thumb is to monitor student progress at least once per instructional week. The saying that sums up the importance of a progress-monitoring plan is: "If you don't actually collect the data, you are blind about the intervention outcome."

The essential elements of data collection will remain unchanged across different types of intervention. However, teachers who intervene early gain considerable freedom in what data-collection methods they can select to use with particular students. As Hosp (2008) points out, the freedom of an educator to choose monitoring measures is tied directly to "the costs of being wrong" (p. 365). For high-stakes cases with severe academic or behavioral problems, drawing the wrong conclusion from progress-monitoring data could cost the student a great deal, e.g., course failure, special education referral, school suspension or expulsion. In such high-stakes cases, then, the teacher is restricted to using only high-quality data that may be more time-consuming to collect and interpret. However, when the teacher is proactive and intervenes at the first sign of student academic or behavioral trouble, the stakes of the case are lower because the student problem has not yet escalated and the teacher can therefore make use of a range of classroom-friendly measures for data collection that may be less rigorous but are easier to collect (Hosp, 2008).

Roadmap to This Chapter

The remainder of this chapter provides resources to help teachers collect classroom data to monitor student academic and behavioral interventions. While the chapter presents an array of monitoring tools (e.g., rubrics, behavior report cards, academic survival skills checklists) that teachers can use even in busy classrooms, it also offers guidance on how to bring rigor to any type of data collection by ensuring that such progress-monitoring information is placed within a meaningful 'data context' that includes components such as baseline, setting of an outcome goal, and so on. Additional resources are also included in this chapter to address specialized data-collection scenarios. Included are:

- *How To: Match a Progress-Monitoring Tool to Every Classroom Problem.* This resource lists 6 common types of student problems (e.g., acquisition of basic academic skills, behavior, homework issues) and makes recommendations for what data sources teachers can use to track each problem type.

- *How To: Structure Classroom Data Collection for Individual Students.* Teachers can use this convenient resource to structure data collection for any academic or behavioral intervention. It moves through the process of describing the student problem, collecting and interpreting baseline data, setting an intervention outcome goal, creating a plan to monitor student progress, and judging whether the intervention goal is met.

- *How To: Organize Data to Answer Questions About Student Academic Performance and Behavior: The RIOT/ICEL Matrix.* When teachers need to sample information from a broad range of sources to zero in on the cause/s of a student's academic or behavioral problems, they can use the RIOT/ICEL matrix. This matrix helps identify what relevant information to collect on student academic performance and behavior—and also how to organize that information to identify probable reasons why the student is not experiencing academic or behavioral success.

- *How To: Set Academic Goals for the Acquisition Stage of Learning.* When the focus of classroom interventions is to help students acquire a fixed set of academic-skill items (e.g., naming numbers 1-10 or calculating a basic math-fact), teachers can use this 8-step guide to set up a progress-monitoring plan.

- *How To: Use Rubrics in Student Assessment.* This resource provides an introduction to designing rubrics. Rubrics are a type of classroom assessment that teachers can use to evaluate multi-dimensional assignments; they often incorporate a sliding scale to rate the quality of student work.

- *How To: Use Checklists to Measure Academic Survival Skills.* Students must cultivate a set of general academic survival skills that they can apply to any coursework. But measuring these global skills can be difficult. The trick is to convert global skills into a checklist. This section describes how teachers can create observational checklists to measure academic survival skills and offers 5 sample checklists that instructors can use immediately.

- *How To: Use the Cumulative Mastery Log to Record Progress in the Acquisition Stage of Learning.* During academic interventions in which the student is newly learning a fixed set of academic items (e.g., math facts, spelling words, sight words, vocabulary terms), the teacher can conveniently track the impact of the intervention by recording and dating mastered items in a cumulative log. This resource provides a description of how to set up and use such a log.

- *How To: Enlist Students to Monitor Their Own Academic Goals.* Research suggests that, if possible, the teacher should routinely include students in academic intervention plans by having them select and self-monitor academic performance goals. This resource explains how to enlist the student to carry out academic self-monitoring.

References

Hosp, J. L. (2008). Best practices in aligning academic assessment with instruction. In A. Thomas & J. Grimes (Eds.), *Best practices in school psychology V* (pp.363-376). Bethesda, MD: National Association of School Psychologists.

Witt, J. C., VanDerHeyden, A. M., & Gilbertson, D. (2004). Troubleshooting behavioral interventions. A systematic process for finding and eliminating problems. *School Psychology Review,* 33, 363-383.

How To: Match a Progress-Monitoring Tool to Every Classroom Problem

Whenever teachers put an academic or behavioral intervention in place for a student, they will also want to collect classroom progress-monitoring data to judge whether that intervention is effective (Witt, VanDerHeyden, & Gilbertson, 2004). For teachers, the six most frequent intervention targets are the following:

1. Academics: Acquisition of basic skills
2. Academics: Fluency in basic skills
3. Academics: Complex skills
4. Academics: Survival skills
5. Behaviors
6. Homework

The table below is designed as a' look-up' resource to help instructors quickly to select appropriate monitoring tools to track the success of academic and behavioral interventions. Under each intervention target are listed one or more data sources that can measure the target--along with information about how to make or find examples of recommended measurement tools.

1. Academics: Acquisition of Basic Skills

What to assess: Basic academic skills are those 'building-block' skills that are the foundation for more advanced learning. When students are just acquiring basic skills, they often are expected to learn a finite set of items--such as letter sounds, multiplication math-facts 0-9, Dolch pre-primer sight word list, or 50 vocabulary terms necessary for success in a biology course. At this acquisition stage of learning, the teacher's measurement objective is to monitor which items the student has mastered from the larger set.

How to assess and where to find materials:
Cumulative mastery log. The simplest way for the teacher to track which items the student has learned from a larger pool is to maintain a cumulative mastery log. First, the teacher develops objective guidelines for judging that a student has mastered an item: e.g., "to know a math-fact, the student must answer the fact correctly from a flash-card within 3 seconds and repeat the feat twice in a row during a session". Then the teacher conducts a baseline assessment. That is, the instructor (1) reviews with the student all items in the larger pool (e.g., letters; multiplication math-facts 0-9, etc.) Using the previously developed guidelines for judging mastery, the teacher (2) identifies and (3) records those items that the student already knows at baseline. Then during the intervention, whenever the student masters an additional item, the teacher logs the item and date acquired. Over time, this log becomes a cumulative, date-stamped record of items acquired by the student.

A tutorial on setting up and using a cumulative mastery log is presented elsewhere in this assessment chapter (chapter 5), along with a sample form.

2. Academics: Fluency in Basic Skills

What to assess: When a student has acquired basic academic skills, the next goal is often to build fluency in those skills. Examples of fluency goals are increasing a student's oral reading speed and working toward automatic recall of math-facts. In this fluency stage of learning, the instructor's measurement objective is to continue to monitor accuracy while also tracking increasing speed of performance.

How to assess and where to find materials:
Curriculum-based measurement. A very useful way to assess a student's growing fluency (as well as accuracy) in foundation academic skills is via curriculum-based measurement (CBM)—a family of quick assessments of basic academic skills. While CBM covers a wide range of different assessments, all are brief; timed; use standard procedures to prepare materials, administer, and score; and include decision rules to help educators to make appropriate instructional decisions (Hosp, Hosp & Howell, 2007). Examples of CBM include oral reading fluency (1-minute passages that the student reads aloud) and math computation (2-minute math-fact worksheets with the student receiving credit for number of digits computed correctly).

In chapter 6, teachers can find a series of CBM resources covering letter knowledge, oral reading, reading comprehension, number sense, math computation, and writing mechanics.

3. Academics: Complex Skills

What to assess: Teachers often find that they must evaluate a student on higher-level academic skills that are multi-dimensional and complex (Moskal, 2000). For example, the Common Core ELA Standard for grade 5-speaking and listening (CCSSELA.5.SL.1) sets the expectation that, in collaborative discussions, the student will come prepared, participate, engage in appropriate turn-taking and follow other discussion rules, etc. Similarly, a standard for grade 4 writing (CCSSELA.4.W.1) presents as a goal that the student will write an opinion essay supporting a specific point of view that includes specific elements such as introductory and concluding statements and supporting details. In both examples, a student may show evidence of at least partial fulfillment of some elements within the standard. So teachers need a flexible evaluation format for rating complex academic skills, one that can handle several dimensions simultaneously, while defining for each dimension a sliding-scale, or continuum, for rating success.

How to assess and where to find materials:
Rubrics. Rubrics are well-suited for measuring a student on complex tasks. In a rubric, the teacher defines the categories that make up the important dimensions of a task, develops exemplars representing mastery for each dimension, and creates a rating scale to be used in evaluating a particular student's work for each dimension (Schafer, Swanson, Bene', & Newberry, 2001).

A detailed description of how to create rubrics for classroom use can be found elsewhere in this chapter (chapter 5) on student assessment.

4. Academics: Survival Skills

What to assess: Academic survival skills are those global 'academic enablers'--such as time management, study skills, homework completion, note-taking--required to support a strong academic performance (DiPerna, 2006).

How to assess and where to find materials:
Academic survival skills checklists. A global academic survival skill (e.g., study skills) can be made measureable by dividing that overarching category into specific, observable component sub-skills (e.g., maintains clear work space for study; creates a study schedule; allocates adequate time each day for study) to create a checklist. Each element of that checklist can then be verified through direct observation, student interview, and/or examination of student work products.

A series of academic survival skills checklists appears elsewhere in this chapter (chapter 5) on student assessment. Teachers can also create their own customized checklists using a free online application, the Academic Survival Skills Checklist Maker:
www.interventioncentral.org/teacher-resources/student-academic-success-strategies-checklist-maker

5. Behaviors

What to assess: Classroom behaviors are specific, observable behaviors that relate to such categories as general conduct (e.g., remaining in seat, calling out), compliance (e.g., following teacher directives); and academic readiness and engagement (e.g., paying attention to the teacher during a lesson, completing independent seatwork, bringing work materials to class).

How to assess and where to find materials:
Behavior report card. A behavior report card is a type of rating scale that the teacher fills out on a regular basis—e.g., daily—to rate targeted student behaviors (Riley-Tillman, Chafouleas, & Briesch, 2007). Behavior report cards have several advantages: They are quick to complete, can be customized by the teacher to measure any observable behavior, and are an excellent vehicle for communicating classroom behavioral expectations to students and parents.

Teachers can create their own behavior report cards using the Behavior Report Card Maker, a free online application: *www.interventioncentral.org/teacher-resources/behavior-rating-scales-report-card-maker*

Frequency count. In a frequency count, the teacher keeps count of the number of times that the student engages in a target behavior (e.g., number of call-outs; episodes of non-compliance with teacher requests) during an observation period. If frequency-count data are collected across multiple observation periods of the same duration, the teacher can directly compare the data across those observations to look for trends of improvement.

In chapter 7, the handout on student self-monitoring contains an observation sheet for collecting frequent-count data.

6. Homework

What to assess: Homework can be evaluated in a number of ways. Depending on the nature of the student's presenting problem(s), the teacher may use one or more of the data sources below to track homework timeliness, completion, accuracy, and/or quality.

How to assess and where to find materials:
Existing data. If the teacher's focus is on getting homework turned in reliably and on time, that instructor can use existing data, such as gradebook information about homework submission, to monitor this intervention goal.

Quality: Percentage of work attempted/grade. If the teacher is monitoring the quality of the submitted homework, two simple but useful metrics are (1) an estimate of the amount of work attempted (presented as a percentage of the entire assignment) and (2) homework grades.

Quality: Rubric. Because some homework assignments (e.g., term paper; PowerPoint presentation) are complex and must be rated across several dimensions, the teacher may choose the rubric as an evaluation tool.

A detailed description of how to create rubrics for classroom use can be found elsewhere in this chapter (chapter 5) on student assessment.

References

DiPerna, J. C. (2006). Academic enablers and student achievement: Implications for assessment and intervention services in the schools. *Psychology in the Schools,* 43, 7-17.

Hosp, M.K., Hosp, J. L., & Howell, K. W. (2007). *The ABCs of CBM.* New York: Guilford.

Moskal, Barbara M. (2000). Scoring rubrics: what, when and how? *Practical Assessment, Research & Evaluation,* 7(3). Retrieved June 3, 2013 from http://PAREonline.net/getvn.asp?v=7&n=3

Riley-Tillman, T. C., Chafouleas, S. M., & Briesch, A. M. (2007). A school practitioner's guide to using daily behavior report cards to monitor student behavior. *Psychology in the Schools,* 44(1), 77-89.

Schafer, W. D., Swanson, G., Bene', N., & Newberry, G. (2001). Effects of teacher knowledge of rubrics on student achievement in four content areas. *Applied Measurement in Education,* 12(2), 151-170.

Witt, J. C., VanDerHeyden, A. M., & Gilbertson, D. (2004). Troubleshooting behavioral interventions. A systematic process for finding and eliminating problems. *School Psychology Review,* 33, 363-383.

How To: Structure Classroom Data Collection for Individual Students

When a student is struggling in the classroom, the teacher will often implement an intervention matched to the student's deficient academic skills. However, classroom interventions are incomplete if the teacher is not also collecting data to document whether those interventions are actually benefiting students. Indeed, an intervention can be viewed as 'fatally flawed' (Witt, VanDerHeyden & Gilbertson, 2004) if it lacks any one of these 4 data elements:

- *Problem definition.* The teacher clearly and specifically defines the presenting student problem(s) needing intervention. If the student problem is not clearly defined, the teacher cannot accurately measure or fix it.

- *Baseline performance.* The teacher assesses the student's current skill or performance level (baseline performance) in the identified area(s) of concern. If the teacher lacks baseline information, he or she cannot judge at the end of the intervention how much progress was actually made.

- *Intervention goal.* Before starting the intervention, the teacher sets a specific outcome goal for student improvement. Without a goal in place before the start of the intervention, the teacher cannot judge at the end of the intervention whether it has in fact been a success.

- *Ongoing progress-monitoring.* The teacher selects a method to monitor the student's progress formatively during the intervention. Without ongoing monitoring of progress, the teacher is 'flying blind', unable to judge to judge whether the intervention is effective in helping the student to attain the outcome goal..

Bringing Structure to Classroom Data-Collection. The *Student Intervention: Monitoring Worksheet.* As teachers take on the role of 'first responder' interventionist, they are likely to need guidance – at least initially—in the multi-step process of setting up and implementing classroom data collection, as well as interpreting the resulting data.

A form designed to walk teachers through the data-collection process-- The *Student Intervention: Progress-Monitoring Worksheet*—appears at the end of this document, along with a completed example. The *Worksheet* is a 7-step 'wizard' form to show teachers how to structure their progress-monitoring to ensure that their data collection is adequate to the task of measuring the impact of their classroom interventions:

A. *Identify the student problem.* The teacher defines the student problem in clear, specific terms that allow the instructor to select an appropriate source of classroom assessment to measure and monitor the problem.

B. *Decide on a data collection method.* The teacher chooses a method for collecting data that can be managed in the classroom setting and that will provide useful information about the student problem. Examples of data collection methods are curriculum-based measurement (e.g., oral reading fluency; correct writing sequences), behavior-frequency counts, and daily behavior report cards. When selecting a data collection method, the teacher also decides how frequently that data will be collected during intervention progress-monitoring. In some cases, the method of data collection being used will dictate monitoring frequency. For example, if homework completion and accuracy is being tracked, the frequency of data collection will be equal to the frequency of homework assignments. In other cases, the level of severity of the student problem will dictate monitoring frequency. In schools implementing Response to Intervention (RTI), students on Tier 2 (standard-protocol) interventions should be monitored 1-2 times per month, for example, while students on Tier 3 (intensive problem-solving protocol) interventions should be monitored at least weekly (Burns & Gibbons, 2008).

C. *Collect data to calculate baseline.* The teacher should collect 3-5 data-points prior to starting the intervention to calculate the student's baseline, or starting point, in the skill or behavior that is being targeted for intervention. The student's baseline performance serves as an initial marker against which to compare his or her outcome performance at the end of the intervention. (Also,--because baseline data points are collected prior to the start of the intervention-- they collectively can serve as an prediction of the trend, or rate of improvement, if the student's current academic program were to remain unchanged with no additional interventions attempted.). In calculating baseline, the teacher has the option of selecting the median, or middle, data-point, or calculating the mean baseline performance.

D. *Determine the timespan of the intervention.* The length of time reserved for the intervention should be sufficient to allow enough data to be collected to clearly demonstrate whether that intervention was successful. For example, it is recommended that a high-stakes intervention last at least 8 instructional weeks (e.g., Burns & Gibbons, 2008).

E. *Set an intervention goal.* The teacher calculates a goal for the student that, if attained by the end of the intervention period, will indicate that the intervention was successful.

F. *Decide how student progress is to be summarized.* A decision that the teacher must make prior to the end of the intervention period is how he or she will summarize the actual progress-monitoring data. Because of the variability present in most data, the instructor will probably not elect simply to use the single, final data point as the best estimate of student progress. Better choices are to select several (e.g. 3) of the final data points and either select the median value or calculate a mean value. For charted data with trendline, the teacher may calculate the student's final performance level as the value of the trendline at the point at which it intercepts the intervention end-date.

G. *Evaluate the intervention outcome.* At the conclusion of the intervention, the teacher directly compares the actual student progress (summarized in the previous step) with the goal originally set. If actual student progress meets or exceeds the goal, the intervention is judged to be successful.

References

Burns, M. K., & Gibbons, K. A. (2008). Implementing *response-to-intervention in elementary and secondary schools.* Routledge: New York.

Witt, J. C., VanDerHeyden, A. M., & Gilbertson, D. (2004). Troubleshooting behavioral interventions. A systematic process for finding and eliminating problems. *School Psychology Review, 33,* 363-383.

Student Intervention: Progress-Monitoring Worksheet

Student: ___Brian Jones___ Teacher: _____Mrs. Braniff_____ Classroom or Course: _Gr 3_____

SET-UP

A. Identify the Student Problem: Describe in clear, specific terms the student academic or behavioral problem:
   _Need to Become Fluent in Multiplication Facts: 0 to 9_____

B. Select a Data Collection Method: Choose a method of data collection to measure whether the classroom intervention actually improves the identified student problem (e.g., curriculum-based measurement, etc.).
   _Curriculum-Based Measurement: 2-Minute Timed Math Computation Probes_____

   How frequently will this data be collected?: _1_ times per _Week_

BASELINE

C. Collect Data to Calculate Baseline: What method from the choices below will be used to estimate the student's baseline (starting) performance? (NOTE: Generally, at least 3-5 baseline data points are recommended.)

   ☑ From a total of _3_ observations, select the **median** value.   ❑ Other: _____

   ❑ From a total of _____ observations, calculate the **mean** value.   _____

Baseline	3. Date: _11_/_21_/2011 Obsv: _34___
1. Date: _11_/_14_/2011 Obsv: _31___	4. Date: ___/___/____ Obsv: _____
2. Date: _11_/_17_/2011 Obsv: _28___	5. Date: ___/___/____ Obsv: _____

   Baseline Performance: Based on the method selected above, it is calculated that the student's baseline performance is:
   _____31 Correct Digits in 2 minutes_____

PROGRESS-MONITORING

D. Determine Intervention Timespan: The intervention will last _6_ instructional weeks and end on _1_/_13_/2012

E. Set a Performance Goal: What goal is the student expected to achieve if the intervention is successful?
   At the end of the intervention, it is predicted that the student will reach this performance goal:
   _____40 Correct Digits in 2 minutes_____

F. Decide How Student Progress is to Be Summarized: Select a method for summarizing student progress ('outcome') attained when the intervention ends. *Student progress at the end of the intervention is to be summarized by:*

   ❑ Selecting the **median** value from the final ____ data-points (e.g.,3).

   ☑ Computing the **mean** value from the final _2_ data-points (e.g.,3).

   ❑ [For time-series graphs]: Calculating the **value on the graph trend line** at the point that it intercepts the intervention end date.

G. Evaluate the Intervention Outcome:
   At the end of the intervention, compare student progress to goal. If **actual progress** meets or exceeds **goal,** the intervention is judged successful.

The student's ACTUAL Progress (Step F) is:	▶	42
The PERFORMANCE GOAL for improvement (Step E) is:	▶	40

Progress-Monitoring	5. Date: _01_/_06_/2012 Obsv: _41___
1. Date: _12_/_02_/2011 Obsv: _29___	6. Date: _01_/_13_/2012 Obsv: _43___
2. Date: _12_/_09_/2011 Obsv: _34___	7. Date: ___/___/____ Obsv: _____
3. Date: _12_/_16_/2011 Obsv: _35___	8. Date: ___/___/____ Obsv: _____
4. Date: _12_/_22_/2011 Obsv: _39___	9. Date: ___/___/____ Obsv: _____

Student Intervention: Progress-Monitoring Worksheet

Student: _____ Teacher: _____ Classroom or Course: _____

A. Identify the Student Problem: Describe in clear, specific terms the student academic or behavioral problem:

_____

B. Select a Data Collection Method: Choose a method of data collection to measure whether the classroom intervention actually improves the identified student problem (e.g., curriculum-based measurement, etc.).

_____

How frequently will this data be collected?: _____ times per _____

C. Collect Data to Calculate Baseline: What method from the choices below will be used to estimate the student's baseline (starting) performance? (NOTE: Generally, at least 3-5 baseline data points are recommended.)

❏ From a total of _____ observations, select the **median** value.   ❏ Other: _____

❏ From a total of _____ observations, calculate the **mean** value.   _____

Baseline	3. Date: ___/___/___ Obsv: _____
1. Date: ___/___/___ Obsv: _____	4. Date: ___/___/___ Obsv: _____
2. Date: ___/___/___ Obsv: _____	5. Date: ___/___/___ Obsv: _____

Baseline Performance: Based on the method selected above, it is calculated that the student's baseline performance is:

_____

D. Determine Intervention Timespan: The intervention will last _____ instructional weeks and end on ___/___/___.

E. Set a Performance Goal: What goal is the student expected to achieve if the intervention is successful?
At the end of the intervention, it is predicted that the student will reach this performance goal:

_____

F. Decide How Student Progress is to Be Summarized: Select a method for summarizing student progress ('outcome') attained when the intervention ends. *Student progress at the end of the intervention is to be summarized by:*

❏ Selecting the **median** value from the final ____ data-points (e.g.,3).

❏ Computing the **mean** value from the final ____ data-points (e.g.,3).

❏ [For time-series graphs]: Calculating the **value on the graph trend line** at the point that it intercepts the intervention end date.

G. Evaluate the Intervention Outcome:
At the end of the intervention, compare student progress to goal. If **actual progress** meets or exceeds **goal,** the intervention is judged successful.

The student's ACTUAL Progress (Step F) is:	▶
The PERFORMANCE GOAL for improvement (Step E) is:	▶

Progress-Monitoring	5. Date: ___/___/___ Obsv: _____
1. Date: ___/___/___ Obsv: _____	6. Date: ___/___/___ Obsv: _____
2. Date: ___/___/___ Obsv: _____	7. Date: ___/___/___ Obsv: _____
3. Date: ___/___/___ Obsv: _____	8. Date: ___/___/___ Obsv: _____
4. Date: ___/___/___ Obsv: _____	9. Date: ___/___/___ Obsv: _____

Student: _____ Grade: _____

Teacher: _____ School Year: _____

Progress-Monitoring (Cont.)	Progress-Monitoring (Cont.)
10. Date: ___/___/___ Obsv: _____	30. Date: ___/___/___ Obsv: _____
11. Date: ___/___/___ Obsv: _____	31. Date: ___/___/___ Obsv: _____
12. Date: ___/___/___ Obsv: _____	32. Date: ___/___/___ Obsv: _____
13. Date: ___/___/___ Obsv: _____	33. Date: ___/___/___ Obsv: _____
14. Date: ___/___/___ Obsv: _____	34. Date: ___/___/___ Obsv: _____
15. Date: ___/___/___ Obsv: _____	35. Date: ___/___/___ Obsv: _____
16. Date: ___/___/___ Obsv: _____	36. Date: ___/___/___ Obsv: _____
17. Date: ___/___/___ Obsv: _____	37. Date: ___/___/___ Obsv: _____
18. Date: ___/___/___ Obsv: _____	38. Date: ___/___/___ Obsv: _____
19. Date: ___/___/___ Obsv: _____	39. Date: ___/___/___ Obsv: _____
20. Date: ___/___/___ Obsv: _____	40. Date: ___/___/___ Obsv: _____
21. Date: ___/___/___ Obsv: _____	41. Date: ___/___/___ Obsv: _____
22. Date: ___/___/___ Obsv: _____	42. Date: ___/___/___ Obsv: _____
23. Date: ___/___/___ Obsv: _____	43. Date: ___/___/___ Obsv: _____
24. Date: ___/___/___ Obsv: _____	44. Date: ___/___/___ Obsv: _____
25. Date: ___/___/___ Obsv: _____	45. Date: ___/___/___ Obsv: _____
26. Date: ___/___/___ Obsv: _____	46. Date: ___/___/___ Obsv: _____
27. Date: ___/___/___ Obsv: _____	47. Date: ___/___/___ Obsv: _____
28. Date: ___/___/___ Obsv: _____	48. Date: ___/___/___ Obsv: _____
29. Date: ___/___/___ Obsv: _____	49. Date: ___/___/___ Obsv: _____

How To: Organize Data to Answer Questions About Student Academic Performance and Behavior—The RIOT/ICEL Matrix

When a student displays serious academic or behavioral deficits, the Response to Intervention model adopts an inductive approach that begins with educators collecting a range of information to better analyze and understand the student's intervention needs (Fuchs, Fuchs & Compton, 2010).

However, this investigative RTI problem-solving approach can be compromised at the outset in several ways (Hosp, 2008). For example, educators may draw from too few sources when pulling together information about the presenting problem(s)—e.g., relying primarily on interviews with one classroom teacher—which can bias the findings. Also, educators may not consider the full range of possible explanations for the student's academic or behavioral problems—such as instructional factors or skill-deficits—and thus fail to collect information that would confirm or rule out those competing hypotheses. And finally, educators may simply not realize when they have reached the 'saturation point' in data collection (Hosp, 2008) when stockpiling still more data will not significantly improve the understanding of the student problem.

One tool that can assist schools in their quest to sample information from a broad range of sources and to investigate all likely explanations for student academic or behavioral problems is the RIOT/ICEL matrix. This matrix helps schools to work efficiently and quickly to decide what relevant information to collect on student academic performance and behavior—and also how to organize that information to identify probable reasons why the student is not experiencing academic or behavioral success.

The RIOT/ICEL Matrix, Form 1, is not itself a data collection instrument. Instead, it is an organizing framework, or heuristic, that increases schools' confidence both in the quality of the data that they collect and the findings that emerge from the data (Hosp, 2006, May). The top horizontal row of the RIOT/ICEL table includes four potential sources of student information: **R**eview, **I**nterview, **O**bservation, and **T**est (RIOT). Schools should attempt to collect information from a range of sources to control for potential bias from any one source.

The leftmost vertical column of the RIOT/ICEL table includes four key domains of learning to be assessed: **I**nstruction, **C**urriculum, **E**nvironment, and **L**earner (ICEL). A common mistake that schools often make is to assume that student learning problems exist primarily in the learner and to underestimate the degree to which teacher instructional strategies, curriculum demands, and environmental influences impact the learner's academic performance. The ICEL elements ensure that a full range of relevant explanations for student problems are examined.

Select Multiple Sources of Information: RIOT. The elements that make up the top horizontal row of the RIOT/ICEL table (**R**eview, **I**nterview, **O**bservation, and **T**est) are defined as follows:
• **Review.** This category consists of past or present records collected on the student. Obvious examples include report cards, office disciplinary referral data, state test results, and attendance records. Less obvious examples include student work samples, physical products of teacher interventions (e.g., a sticker chart used to reward positive student behaviors), and emails sent by a teacher to a parent detailing concerns about a student's study and organizational skills.

• **Interview.** Interviews can be conducted face-to-face, via telephone, or even through email correspondence. Interviews can also be structured (that is, using a pre-determined series of questions) or follow an open-ended format, with questions guided by information supplied by the respondent. Interview targets can include those teachers, paraprofessionals, administrators, and support staff in the school setting who have worked with or had interactions with the student in the present or past. Prospective interview candidates can also consist of parents and other relatives of the student as well as the student himself or herself.

- **Observation.** Direct observation of the student's academic skills, study and organizational strategies, degree of attentional focus, and general conduct can be a useful channel of information. Observations can be more structured (e.g., tallying the frequency of call-outs or calculating the percentage of on-task intervals during a class period) or less structured (e.g., observing a student and writing a running narrative of the observed events). Obvious examples of observation include a teacher keeping a frequency count of the times that she redirects an inattentive student to task during a class period and a school psychologist observing the number of times that a student talks with peers during independent seatwork Less obvious examples of observation include having a student periodically rate her own academic engagement on a 3-point scale (self-evaluation) and encouraging a parent to send to school narrative observations of her son's typical routine for completing homework.

- **Test.** Testing can be thought of as a structured and standardized observation of the student that is intended to test certain hypotheses about why the student might be struggling and what school supports would logically benefit the student (Christ, 2008). Obvious examples of testing include a curriculum-based measurement Oral Reading Fluency probe administered to determine a student's accuracy and fluency when reading grade-level texts and a state English Language Arts test that evaluates students' mastery of state literacy standards. A less obvious example of testing might be a teacher who teases out information about the student's skills and motivation on an academic task by having that student complete two equivalent timed worksheets under identical conditions—except that the student is offered an incentive for improved performance on the second worksheet but not on the first ('Can't Do/Won't Do Assessment'). Another less obvious example of testing might be a student who has developed the capacity to take chapter pre-tests in her math book, to self-grade the test, and to write down questions and areas of confusion revealed by that test for later review with the math instructor.

Investigate Multiple Factors Affecting Student Learning: ICEL. The elements that compose the leftmost vertical column of the RIO/ICEL table (Instruction, Curriculum, Environment, and Learner) are described below:

- **Instruction.** The purpose of investigating the 'instruction' domain is to uncover any instructional practices that either help the student to learn more effectively or interfere with that student's learning. More obvious instructional questions to investigate would be whether specific teaching strategies for activating prior knowledge better prepare the student to master new information or whether a student benefits optimally from the large-group lecture format that is often used in a classroom. A less obvious example of an instructional question would be whether a particular student learns better through teacher-delivered or self-directed, computer-administered instruction.

- **Curriculum.** 'Curriculum' represents the full set of academic skills that a student is expected to have mastered in a specific academic area at a given point in time. To adequately evaluate a student's acquisition of academic skills, of course, the educator must: (1) know the school's curriculum (and related state academic performance standards); (2) be able to inventory the specific academic skills that the student currently possesses; and then (3) identify gaps between curriculum expectations and actual student skills. (This process of uncovering student academic skill gaps is sometimes referred to as 'instructional' or 'analytic' assessment.) More obvious examples of curriculum questions include checking whether a student knows how to compute a multiplication problem with double-digit terms and regrouping or whether that student knows key facts about the Civil War. A less obvious curriculum-related question might be whether a student possesses the full range of essential academic vocabulary (e.g., terms such as 'hypothesis') required for success in the grade 10 curriculum.

- **Environment.** The 'environment' includes any factors in students' school, community, or home surroundings that can directly enable their academic success or hinder that success. Obvious questions about environmental factors that impact learning include whether a student's educational performance is better or worse in the presence of certain peers and whether having additional adult supervision during a study hall results in higher student work productivity. Less obvious questions about the learning environment include whether a student has a setting at home that is conducive to completing homework or whether chaotic hallway conditions are delaying that student's transitioning between classes and therefore reducing available learning time.

- **Learner.** While the student is at the center of any questions of instruction, curriculum, and [learning] environment, the 'learner' domain includes those qualities of the student that represent their unique capacities and traits. More obvious examples of questions that relate to the learner include investigating whether a student has stable and high rates of inattention across different classrooms or evaluating the efficiency of a student's study habits and test-taking skills. A less obvious example of a question that relates to the learner is whether a student harbors a low sense of self-efficacy in mathematics that is interfering with that learner's willingness to put appropriate effort into math courses.

Integrating the RIOT/ICEL Matrix into a Building's Problem-Solving. The power of the RIOT/ICEL matrix lies in its use as a cognitive strategy, one that helps educators to verify that they have asked the right questions and sampled from a sufficiently broad range of data sources to increase the probability that they will correctly understand the student's presenting concern(s). Viewed in this way, the matrix is not a rigid approach but rather serves as a flexible heuristic for exploratory problem-solving.

At the very least, RTI consultants should find that the RIOT/ICEL matrix serves as a helpful mental framework to guide their problem-solving efforts. And as teachers over time become more familiar with the RTI model, they also might be trained to use the RIOT/ICEL framework as they analyze student problems in their classrooms and prepare Tier 1 interventions. Form 2 provides space for using this model.

References

Christ, T. (2008). Best practices in problem analysis. In A. Thomas & J. Grimes (Eds.), *Best practices in school psychology V* (pp. 159-176). Bethesda, MD: National Association of School Psychologists.

Fuchs L. S., Fuchs, D., and Compton, D. L. (2010). Rethinking response to intervention at middle and high school. *School Psychology Review, 39*, 22-28.

Hosp, J. L. (2006, May) *Implementing RTI: Assessment practices and response to intervention.* NASP Communiqué, 34(7). Retrieved September 8, 2010, from: http://www.nasponline.org/publications/cq/cq347rti.aspx

Hosp, J. L. (2008). Best practices in aligning academic assessment with instruction. In A. Thomas & J. Grimes (Eds.), *Best practices in school psychology V* (pp.363-376). Bethesda, MD: National Association of School Psychologists.

RIOT/ICEL Matrix Example: The matrix below is filled out with some possible sources of information on a student, Rick, whose mathematics teacher is concerned at his apparent *lack of academic engagement in large-group settings*. NOTE: The examples in the matrix are for purposes of illustration only. It is probably somewhat unlikely that all of these sources of information would be collected for a single student, unless his or her needs were intensive.

	Review	Interview	Observe	Test
Instruction	• [Review-Instruction] **Review of past report cards:** The teacher searches for comments from former instructors about instructional techniques to which Rick did or did not respond.	• [Interview-Instruction] **Teacher interview:** The instructor is asked by the guidance counselor which instructional elements help Rick to attend in large-group instruction and which are less effective.	• [Observe-Instruction] **Classroom observation:** During large-group instruction, an observer calculates Rick's rate of on-task behavior (e.g., through momentary time-sampling).	• [Test-Instruction] **Note-taking conditions:** The teacher structures two large-group instruction conditions—regular note-taking and guided note —and observes whether Rick's level of academic engagement improves with guided notes.
Curriculum	• [Review-Curriculum] **Work products:** The teacher collects the student's math homework and examines it for evidence about whether Rick is able correctly to use the algorithms taught in class.	• [Interview-Curriculum] **Student interview:** The guidance counselor meets with Rick to ask him a series of questions about his math skills.	• [Observe-Curriculum] **Classroom observation:** The teacher pairs students, directs each to describe to the other his/her reasoning for solving a multi-step word problem with math graphic. Rick is observed during this exercise.	• [Test-Curriculum] **Diagnostic test:** The teacher prepares and administers to the class a diagnostic test with problems that test essential foundation math knowledge required for success in the course. Rick's test results are carefully reviewed.
Environment	• [Review-Environment] **Folder review:** Rick's cumulative folder is reviewed for past instructor comments about aspects of the instructional environment (e.g., presence or absence of peers, teacher proximity) that helped or hindered academic performance.	• [Interview-Environment] **Parent interview:** At a parent conference, the teacher asks Rick's father to describe the student's nightly homework routine, as well as those factors in the homework setting that appear to help or hinder Rick's homework completion.	• [Observe-Environment] **Classroom observation:** During observations of Rick in a large-group math setting, the observer looks for environmental factors—e.g., presence or absence of peers, teacher proximity) that help or hinder academic performance.	• [Test-Environment] **Peer seating conditions:** On different occasions, the instructor (a) allows Rick to choose his own seat-mates and (b) seats Rick next to positive peer role models. The instructor observes whether Rick's level of academic engagement improves in the peer role-model condition.
Learner	• [Review-Learner] **Math journal:** The math teacher collects Rick's math journal and reviews the entries for hints about the student's attitude and level of self-confidence toward mathematics [Learner characteristic: math self-efficacy].	• [Interview-Learner] **Parent interview:** In an email exchange with the student's mother, the teacher asks her to describe her son's study habits [Learner characteristic: study & organizational skills]	• [Observe-Learner] **Behavior rating based on observation:** For one week, the math teacher rates the student daily on a behavior report card. One of the several rating items is the student's 'time on task' [Learner characteristic: attentional focus].	• [Test-Learner] **Reward conditions:** On different occasions, the teacher (a) has Rick participate in large-group instruction with no reward and (b) offers Rick an incentive (reward) if he requires no more than 1 teacher prompt per session to direct him back to task. The instructor observes whether Rick's engagement increases in the reward condition [Learner characteristic: attentional focus].

RIOT/ICEL Assessment Worksheet

Student: _____

Person Completing Worksheet: _____

Date: _____ Statement of Student Problem: _____

Directions: Fill out the grid below to develop an assessment plan for the targeted student.

	Review	Interview	Observe	Test
Instruction				
Curriculum				
Environment				
Learner				

How To: Set Academic Goals for the Acquisition Stage of Learning

The focus of classroom interventions is often to help students to acquire a fixed set of academic-skill items (e.g., naming numbers 1-10). During the acquisition stage of learning, the primary goal is to have the student identify the item (e.g., read a sight-word) or perform a skill (e.g., calculate a basic math-fact) with accuracy (Haring et al., 1978; Martens & Witt, 2004).

When an intervention targets the acquisition of a finite set of items, timelines tend to be short (e.g., 1-8 weeks) and the goal is typically mastery of all items in the academic-item set. Here are the 8 steps that teachers can follow in defining and monitoring a student goal to acquire a limited set of academic items:

1. **Select a Set of Academic Items as the Intervention Target.** The teacher decides on a finite set, or 'pool', of academic items to be targeted in the intervention. Examples of possible academic-item sets suitable for intervention are naming of all mixed-case letters; answering 2-term multiplication math facts 0-12; and giving definitions for 20 key biology terms.

2. **Establish Criteria for Item Mastery.** The teacher next defines the criteria that allow him or her to judge when the student has mastered any particular item from the academic-item pool. Creating criteria for determining item mastery is useful because these criteria allow the teacher both to be more consistent and to have greater confidence in judging whether the student has mastered a particular item.

   Along with the expectation of a correct response, mastery criteria usually include expectations for speed of responding. TIP: If a student tends to have a high degree of variability in responding—e.g., on one day responding correctly to an item but on the next day responding incorrectly to the same item--the teacher may want to set as a condition of mastery that the student respond successfully to an item across 2 or more sessions.

   As an example of criteria for item mastery, a first-grade teacher decides that mastery on a mixed-case letter-naming intervention should be defined as:
   "When shown a flash-card with an upper- or lower-case letter, the student will correctly name the letter within 3 seconds and repeat this performance twice in a row during the session."

   To cite a second example, a middle-school science teacher whose intervention is intended to promote definitions of 20 key biology terms defines mastery as follows:
   "When shown a biology term, the student will correctly state the definition orally within 10 seconds. The student will repeat this performance across at least two sessions."

3. **Collect Baseline Data.** Before beginning the intervention, the teacher determines the student's baseline level of performance. The easiest way to collect baseline data is to present each of the items from the item-pool to the student in random order, have the student respond, apply the mastery criteria (developed in the previous step) to determine whether each item is correct or incorrect, and record the student's responses.

   For example, a first-grade teacher collects baseline data by showing her student flash-cards with all 52 mixed-case letters while applying her mastery criteria: The teacher sorts each card whose letter the student can correctly name within 3 seconds into a 'known' pile and sorts into an 'unknown' pile those flash-cards that the student identifies incorrectly or hesitates in responding beyond 3 seconds. At the end of the session, the teacher tallies the student's responses and discovers that at baseline he can correctly identify 38 of a possible 52 mixed-case letters.

4. **Set an Intervention Exit Goal.** The teacher next sets a student exit goal that defines a successful intervention. In most cases, the teacher will probably decide that the intervention is to be judged a success when the student has met the standard for mastery on all items in the academic-item pool. For example, a high school science teacher may set, as an intervention exit goal, that a student will be able to correctly define all of the items from a list of 20 key biology terms.

5. **Decide on the Frequency and Session Length of the Intervention.** The teacher decides how long each intervention session is to last and how many intervention sessions the student will receive per week. For students with mild academic deficits, intervention sessions can be as short as 20 minutes per day, 3 days per week. For students with greater deficits, intervention sessions may last 30-45 minutes per session and occur as often as 4-5 days per week.

6. **Set a Timespan for the Intervention.** The teacher estimates the number of instructional weeks the intervention should be attempted and sets an end-date by which the student is predicted to attain success. An intervention that targets the student's acquisition of a specific set of academic items is typically of short duration: between 1 and 8 instructional weeks.

   However, predicting how long an acquisition intervention should last is more of an art than a science. The teacher must exercise professional judgment, selecting a timespan that is both ambitious and realistic. Also, the frequency and session length of a particular intervention will affect the timespan. For example, a student whose intervention is scheduled at a higher 'dosage' (e.g., daily for 40-minute sessions) can be expected to reach the exit goal faster than a similar student whose intervention is scheduled at a lower 'dosage' (e.g., 3 times per week for 20-minute sessions).

7. **Calculate Expected Weekly Progress.** Once the teacher has determined the number of weeks that the intervention will last, the instructor can calculate expected weekly progress by dividing the number of items in the pool that the student has not yet mastered by the number of weeks set aside for intervention.

   For example, a student is found to know 17 of 41 sight words from a first-grade word list at baseline-leaving 24 words still to be mastered. The teacher designs a sight-word intervention to last 4 instructional weeks. Dividing the 24 unknown words by 4 intervention weeks, the teacher calculates that the student must learn at least 6 additional sight words per week to meet the goal of 100% mastery by the end of the intervention.

8. **Monitor the Student's Progress.** Throughout the intervention, the teacher can monitor the student's progress periodically (e.g., weekly or even more frequently) by having the student attempt all of the items in the item-pool and recording the results.

   For example, the first-grade teacher whose intervention targets a student's letter-naming skills for mixed-case letters measures her student's progress by reviewing all 52 letter flash-cards once per week and, each time, tracking the number of letters that the student is able to name correctly within 3 seconds of being shown the flash-card.

   As a second example, the high school science teacher working with a student on acquiring 20 key biology terms and their definitions ends each intervention session by having the student attempt to define all terms, with each vocabulary word counted as correct if the student defines it correctly within 10 seconds.

References

Haring, N.G., Lovitt, T.C., Eaton, M.D., & Hansen, C.L. (1978). *The fourth R: Research in the classroom.* Columbus, OH: Merrill.

Martens, B. K., & Witt, J. C. (2004). Competence, persistence, and success: The positive psychology of behavioral skill instruction. *Psychology in the Schools,* 41(1), 19-30.

How To: Set Off-Level Academic Goals for Reading Fluency

Students with *significant* deficits in reading fluency can present particular challenges as teachers attempt to match them to appropriate academic interventions. Often, these more intensive interventions are 'off-level'; that is, they target academic skills that are well below the student's grade placement.

If that student has significant academic delays , it might be a mistake, however, to measure the student using only assessments from the student's grade of record. The problem with monitoring the progress of an off-level student using only assessments from the current grade level is that these assessments could prove so difficult that they fail to show the true gains that the student is making on the off-level intervention. For students with significant academic delays, then, the school must follow sensible and consistent guidelines for matching those students to appropriate supplemental off-level interventions, for setting performance goals, and for measuring their academic progress that will both benefit the student and accurately reflect actual student growth.

The remainder of this article describes how the formulation of academic goals in reading fluency for students who receive 'off-level' supplemental interventions will always contain the four universal goal-setting elements described above—but includes special instructions for estimating typical peer performance and expected weekly progress for this group.

Below is a 6-step process adapted from Shapiro (2008) for finding the optimal 'off-level' grade for monitoring a student with substantial reading fluency delays, for setting progress-monitoring goals for that student, and for adjusting periodically the student's intervention and monitoring to reflect growth in student skills:

1. **Obtain Research-Derived Academic Screening Norms With Percentile Cut-Points.** The process of finding a student's appropriate off-level placement in academic intervention begins with the school selecting a set of research-derived academic screening norms. These norms should include values for fall, winter, and spring of each grade and should be broken down into percentile cut-offs (e.g., norms at the 10th percentile, 25th percentile, 50th percentile, etc.). Commercially available screening packages such as AIMSweb (http://www.aimsweb.com) provide such norms. Or schools can go to other sources to obtain research norms with percentile cut-points for reading fluency (e.g., Tindal & Hasbrouck, 2005; EasyCBM, 2010) and additional academic areas (e.g., EasyCBM, 2010).

   Case Example: Mrs. Chandler is a 4th-grade teacher in a school whose district has adopted AIMSweb literacy screening tools. The district selected AIMSweb in part because the product includes national norms spanning elementary and middle-school grades that are divided into percentile cut-offs at each grade level.

2. **Determine Cut-Points on Research Norms That Indicate Optimal Instructional Placement.** Research norms with percentile cut-offs are essential for deciding a student's appropriate instructional match for supplemental intervention. When reviewing its research-derived screening norms, the school sets percentile cut-offs that designate appropriate instructional placement and mastery at each grade level. Shapiro (2008) recommends that, when consulting research norms at any grade level:

   • the 25th percentile serve as the cut-point for determining that a student has the *minimum* academic skills needed to experience success in that material. (Please note, though, that norms from other popular academic screening tools –e.g., easyCBM.com—set the 20th percentile as the minimum-skills cut-point.)

• the 50th percentile should serve as the cut-point for defining that the student has attained 'mastery' on the grade-level academic skill.

Case Example: Using the AIMSweb norms, Mrs. Chandler's school decides that when assessed on literacy screening tools at any grade level, a student will be considered as falling within the instructional range if he or she performs within the 25th to 49th percentile and as having achieved mastery if he or she performs at or above the 50th percentile.

3. **Find the Target Student's Optimal 'Off-Level' Instructional Match Through a 'Survey-Level' Assessment.** The school must next find the struggling student's appropriate 'instructional match'—the level of task difficulty that will allow the student to experience sufficient success on off-level interventions while also ensuring a monitoring plan that can accurately track the student's true growth on that intervention. The process used to find the student's instructional match is called a 'survey-level' assessment.

The school administers to the target student a series of standardized curriculum-based measures (CBMs) in the area of academic concern. These CBMs start at the level of the student's **current** grade placement and work downward, testing the student at successively earlier grade levels.

For each grade-level CBM administered, the teacher scores that 'off-level' CBM and compares the student results to research norms.

• If the student performs *at or above* the 25th percentile with materials drawn from a particular 'off-level' grade, the teacher judges that the student is likely to experience a good match using intervention and assessment materials at this grade level—and the Survey Level Assessment ends here.

• However, if the student performs *below* the 25th percentile, it is judged that material at that lower, 'off-level' grade is too challenging for use in monitoring the student's progress on intervention. The teacher instead continues to administer CBMs from successively earlier grade levels, stopping only at the grade-level at which the student performs at or above the 25th percentile according to the research norms.

Case Example: In January, Mrs. Chandler reviews her classwide reading fluency screening results. She notes that a student who has recently transferred to her classroom, Randy, performed at 35 Words Read Correct (WRC) on the 1-minute AIMSweb Grade 4 fluency probes.

Mrs. Chandler consults AIMSweb reading-fluency research norms and finds that a reasonable minimum reading rate for students by winter of grade 4 (25th percentile) is 89 WRC. Because Randy's reading fluency rate is so far below the grade-level norms (a gap of 54 WRC), his teacher decides to conduct a Survey Level Assessment to find the student's optimal grade level placement for supplemental reading instruction.

• *On Grade 3-level probes, Randy attains a median score of 48 WRC. The AIMSweb winter norm (25th percentile) for a 3rd grade student is 69 WRC. The student is still in the 'frustration' range and the Survey Level Assessment continues.*

• *On Grade 2-level probes, Randy attains a median score of 64 WRC. The AIMSweb winter norm (25th percentile) for a 2nd grade student is 53 WRC. Because Randy's Grade 2 WRC score exceeds the 25th percentile cut-point, the student is now in the 'instructional' range and the Survey Level Assessment ends.*

4. **Determine an 'Off-Level' Progress-Monitoring Goal Based on Norms.** To set an intervention progress-monitoring goal, the teacher looks up and uses the academic performance norm for the 50th percentile at the student's off-level 'instructional' grade level previously determined through the Survey Level Assessment.

   Case Example: To find the progress-monitoring goal for Randy, his teacher Mrs. Chandler looks up the benchmark Words Read Correct (WRC) for the 50th percentile on the winter screening norms at Grade 2 (Randy's off-level 'instructional' grade level)—which is 79 WRC. This becomes the progress-monitoring goal for the student.

5. **Translate the Student's Long-Term Progress-Monitoring Goal into Weekly Increments.** The teacher's final task before beginning to monitor the student's progress on intervention is to translate the student's ultimate intervention goal into 'ambitious but realistic' weekly increments. A useful method (Shapiro, 2008) for determining weekly growth rates is to start with research-derived growth norms and to then use a 'multiplier' to make the expected rate of weekly growth more ambitious.

   The teacher first looks up the average rate of weekly student growth supplied in the research norms.

   • If available, a good rule of thumb is to use the growth norms for the 50th percentile at the 'off-level' grade at which the student is receiving intervention and being monitored.

   • If a screening tool's academic-performance norms do not also include growth norms, schools can compute the 'typical' rate of weekly progress for any grade-level by (1) subtracting the fall screening results (50th percentile) for the off-level grade from the spring screening results (50th percentile) and (2) dividing the difference by 32--representing the typical 32 weeks that separate fall and spring screenings in most schools. The resulting quotient represents 'average' expected rate of student progress per instructional week on that academic screening measure at that grade level.

   The teacher then multiplies this grade norm for weekly growth by a multiplier whose value falls between 1.5 and 2.0 (Shapiro, 2008). Because the original weekly growth rate represents only a typical rate of academic improvement, this multiplier is used to boost the target student's weekly growth estimate to a point at which learning is accelerated and the gap separating that student from peers will likely close if the intervention is successful.

   Case Example: Randy, the 4th-grade student, is to be monitored on intervention at grade 2. Mrs. Chandler finds—using AIMSweb norms—that a typical student in Grade 2 (at the 50th percentile) has a rate of improvement of 1.1 Words Read Correct (WRC) per week. Based on her own judgment, Mrs. Chandler selects 1.8 as her multiplier—although any figure between 1.5 and 2.0 would be acceptable. She multiplies the 1.1 WRC figure by 1.8 to obtain an ambitious weekly growth goal for Randy of about 2.0 additional WRCs.

   Randy's ultimate 'graduation goal' that would allow him to advance beyond grade 2 as his supplemental intervention level is 79 WRC (the 50th percentile norm for grade 2). During the Survey Level Assessment, Randy was found to read 64 WRC at the 2nd grade level. There is a 15-WRC gap to be closed to get Randy to his goal. At a growth rate of 2 additional WRC per week during the intervention, Randy should close the gap within about 8 instructional weeks.

6. **Advance the Student to Higher Grade Levels for Intervention & Progress-Monitoring.** The teacher monitors the student's growth in the target academic skill at least once per week (twice per week is ideal). When, according to the research norms for his or her off-level grade, the student's performance exceeds the 50th percentile, this triggers a teacher reassessment of the student's academic skills at the next higher grade, again using the research-based norms. If the student performs at or above the 25th percentile on probes from that next grade level, the teacher can move the student up with confidence and begin to monitor at the higher grade level. The process repeats until the student eventually closes the gap with peers and is being monitored at grade of placement.

Case Example: His teacher, Ms. Chandler, notes that after 7 weeks of intervention, Randy is now reading 82 Words Read Correct (WRC)—exceeding the 79 WRC for the 50th percentile of students in Grade 2 (winter norms). So Mrs. Chandler assesses Randy on AIMSweb reading fluency probes for Grade 3 and finds that he reads on average 72 WRC—exceeding the 3rd grade 25th percentile cut-off of 69 WRC. Therefore, Randy is advanced to Grade 3 progress-monitoring and his intervention materials are adjusted accordingly.

Recommendations for using this approach: Research norms for student performance and academic growth are the 'gold standard' in off-level goal-setting, as they provide fixed, external standards for proficiency that are not influenced by variable levels of student skill in local classrooms. When setting academic goals for struggling students, schools should use research norms whenever they are available. In particular, research norms should be used for high-stakes RTI cases that may be referred at some point to the Special Education Eligibility Team.

References

EasyCBM: (2010). *Interpreting the EasyCBM progress monitoring test results.* Retrieved from www.easycbm.com/static/files/pdfs/info/ProgMonScoreInterpretation.pdf

Hasbrouck, J. & Tindal, G. (2005).*Oral reading fluency: 90 years of measurement* [Technical report #33]. Eugene, OR: University of Oregon.

Shapiro, E. S. (2008). Best practices in setting progress-monitoring monitoring goals for academic skill improvement. In A. Thomas & J. Grimes (Eds.), *Best practices in school psychology V* (pp. 141-157). Bethesda, MD: National Association of School Psychologists.

Curriculum-Based Measurement: Reading

CBM-Oral Reading Fluency assesses general reading performance, as well as reading speed. In an oral reading fluency assessment, the student reads aloud from a passage for 1 minute. The reading sample is scored for words read correctly (WRC) and errors.

Grade	Percentile	Winter Oral Reading Fluency Norms (AIMSweb, 2007)	Weekly Growth Rates (AIMSweb, 2007)
2	50th%	79	1.1
	25th%	53	1.1
	10th%	25	0.8
3	50th%	98	0.9
	25th%	69	0.9
	10th%	42	0.6
4	50th%	114	0.8
	25th%	89	0.8
	10th%	62	0.7

Source: AimsWeb National Norms Table. (2007).

How To: Use Rubrics in Student Assessment

When a teacher attempts to judge whether a student has attained a particular Common Core State Standard, the instructor must evaluate some aspect of that student's *performance*. Such a performance may be observed directly or in the indirect form of work products or other artifacts. Some types of schoolwork easily lend themselves to a simple quantitative scoring approach: for example, a solution to a math computation problem is either correct ('1') or incorrect ('0'). Many types of academic performance, however, are more complex and require that the student master several domains that in sum create a quality product. A research paper, for example, can be judged of high quality only if the writer shows skill in such dimensions as word choice, organization, selection and summary of sources, and use of the writing-revising process-- among others.

Rubrics are a useful classroom method for evaluating complex, multi-dimensional tasks. In education, a widely used type of rubric is the *analytic* rubric (Moskal, 2000). To develop an analytic rubric, the teacher first describes the global performance task to be assessed. The teacher then defines the categories that make up the important dimensions of that task, develops exemplars representing mastery for each dimension, and creates a rating scale to be used in evaluating a particular student's work for each dimension (Schafer, Swanson, Bene', & Newberry, 2001).

Rubrics share similarities with checklists as observational instruments to measure academic performance. A checklist, though, is optimal for binary 'yes/no' situations when the instructor is simply confirming that an element of student performance or work product is either adequate or inadequate--e.g., the student's essay includes a title page/ contains at least 5 paragraphs/ includes 4 research sources. A rubric is the measure of choice when a dimension of academic performance can vary widely in quality from student to student--e.g., the organization of an essay or evidence of preparation for an oral presentation (Allen, 2004).

Rubrics have a number of advantages as a classroom assessment tool (Allen, 2004). They allow teachers to develop objective and consistent scoring criteria for complex student tasks, thus speeding assessment and improving the reliability of the evaluation. Rubrics can also provide clear guidance of work-expectations before the student begins the academic task, potentially eliminating confusion and increasing student self-confidence and motivation. Using a rubric, students can also evaluate their own work, helping them to internalize high standards of excellence and boosting motivation further via immediate performance feedback. As mentioned earlier, rubrics are also criterion-referenced: they set an absolute standard against which all students are to be assessed. In light of the fact that many schools have adopted the expectation that all learners will attain the Common Core State Standards, rubrics are a helpful classroom tool to evaluate on an ongoing basis whether specific students are on track to attain these ambitious learning goals.

Creating a Rubric in 4 Steps. Here are the steps to constructing a teacher-made analytic rubric (Allen, 2004; Moskal, 2000):

1. *Describe the task.* The teacher describes the academic performance task to be evaluated using the rubric. Examples might include an argumentative essay, oral presentation, participation in a discussion group, or conducting and documenting an in-class science experiment. The task description is a straightforward account of what the student is to do (and what product is to be created) but does not include quality indicators. NOTE: The Common Core State Standards contain summaries of academic expectations in English Language Arts and Mathematics tasks that can readily be turned into grade-appropriate rubric task descriptions.

2. *Define the dimensions that make up the task.* Next, the important component elements that make up the academic performance task are defined. This step is similar to a task analysis; the teacher lists the important component dimensions that are to be evaluated. For example, a teacher who wants to create a rubric to evaluate short research papers (task) may decide to divide the global writing task into 4 key dimensions: Word Choice, Details, Revision Process, and Use of Sources.

3. *Develop a rating scale.* The teacher develops a 3-5 level rating scale to evaluate student performance on each of the previously defined dimensions of the rubric. The teacher also devises a plain-English labeling system for the levels: e.g. "Needs work/competent/exemplary"; "Accomplished/average/developing/beginning".

   As an option, teachers can include point amounts or point ranges to accompany the rating scale. For example, an instructor may create a rating scale like the following: "Proficient (7-9 pts)/Intermediate (4-6 pts)/Beginning (1-3 pts)" In this rating scheme, each qualitative label is tied to a point range, allowing the instructor discretion regarding the number of points that can be awarded for each dimension.

4. *Provide descriptions of each dimension.* The teacher writes objective descriptions of student performance on each dimension that match the levels of the rating scale.

   A rubric for short research papers, for example, includes the dimension Word Choice. The teacher adopts a 3-level rating scale: 'Exemplary', 'Competent', and 'Needs Work'. At the high end of the scale, under 'Exemplary', the teacher describes Word Choice performance as: *The essay uses precise language throughout in descriptions and the presentation of ideas. It employs domain-specific vocabulary in most or all instances where appropriate.* In contrast, the same teacher describes Word Choice performance at the low end of the scale under 'Needs Work' as: *The essay uses general or vague language in descriptions and the presentation of ideas. It seldom or never employs examples of domain-specific vocabulary.*

Rubric Example: Student Discussion Group. A teacher is interested in assessing students' attainment of the Common Core ELA Speaking and Listening Standard for Grade 5 (CCSSELA.5.SL.1), which outlines expectations for participation in discussion groups. Using this Standard as a starting point, the teacher creates the following analytic rubric with a 3-item scale:

Analytic Rubric: 'Student Discussion Group' Example

Task: The student will take part in weekly in-class collaborative peer discussions of assigned readings, contributing ideas and responding appropriately to the ideas of others (from CCSSELA.5.SL.1).

Dimensions	Needs Work (1-3 pts)	Competent (4-6 pts)	Exemplary (7-9 pts)
Preparation	Has not completed the assigned readings and/or does not bring notes of the readings to the discussion..	Has completed the assigned reading(s) and brings notes of the readings to the discussion.	Has completed the assigned reading(s), brings notes of the readings to the discussion, and gives evidence of having done additional reading/research in the discussion topic.
Compliance With Discussion Rules/Roles	Fails to follow the rules set up for the discussion activity and/or does not adequately carry out the responsibilities of an assigned discussion role.	Follows the rules set up for the discussion activity. When assigned a role in discussion, adequately carries out the responsibilities of that role.	Follows the rules set up for the discussion activity. When needed, reminds others to adhere to discussion rules. When assigned a formal role

			(e.g., discussion leader), fully carries out the responsibilities of that role.
Contribution to Discussion	Does not actively sustain his or her part in the discussion. May pose questions of limited relevance to the discussion topic. May not respond appropriately to the comments of others.	Poses questions relevant to the discussion topic and responds appropriately to the comments of others. Remarks display a willingness to acknowledge the contributions of others in the discussion group,	Participates fully in the discussion. Poses questions relevant to the discussion topic and responds appropriately to the comments of others. Remarks display a good grasp of the topic and a willingness to acknowledge the contributions of others in the discussion group,

Rubrics: Additional Considerations. When developing and using rubrics for student assessment, teachers should keep these additional considerations in mind:

1. *Combine rubrics with quantitative academic information.* When feasible, consider pairing rubrics with quantitative data to have a more complete picture of academic performance. For example, a teacher working with a reluctant writer develops a rubric to track improvements in the quality of written expression. In addition, though, the instructor charts the word-count for each essay, with the goal of encouraging the student to write longer compositions.

2. *When using rubrics, ignore the curve.* Traditionally in schools, teachers have often graded on a curve, that is, they have plotted the range of student grade outcomes along a normal curve and awarded only a relative handful of high grades. Rubrics, however, do not fit on a curve, as they are a version of criterion-referenced performance goals that include clear, observable definitions of 'mastery' (Schafer, Swanson, Bene', & Newberry, 2001). It is possible, in fact highly desirable, that most or all students in a class might attain rubric ratings in the 'acceptable' or 'exceptional' range, because they are competing against specific, observable, attainable standards rather than against each other (Allen, 2004).

References

Allen, M. J. (2004). *Assessing academic programs in higher education.* Bolton, MA: Anker Publishing.

Moskal, Barbara M. (2000). Scoring rubrics: what, when and how?. *Practical Assessment, Research & Evaluation,* 7(3). Retrieved June 3, 2013 from http://PAREonline.net/getvn.asp?v=7&n=3

Schafer, W. D., Swanson, G., Bene', N., & Newberry, G. (2001). Effects of teacher knowledge of rubrics on student achievement in four content areas. *Applied Measurement in Education, 12*(2), 151-170.

How To: Use Checklists to Measure Academic Survival Skills

Students who hope to achieve success on the ambitious Common Core State Standards must first cultivate a set of general 'academic survival skills' that they can apply to any coursework (DiPerna, 2006). Examples of academic survival skills include the student's ability to study effectively, be organized, and manage time well.

When academic survival skills are described in global terms, though, it can be difficult to define them. For example, two teachers may have different understandings about what the term 'study skills' means. A solution is to complete a 'task analysis' of a given global academic-survival skill, dividing that larger skill into a checklist of component sub-skills (Kazdin, 1989). (Review the set of academic survival skills checklists appearing later in this article for examples of what these component-skills checklists look like.)

With a checklist in hand that breaks a global academic survival skill into components, a teacher can judge whether a student possesses those essential building-block strategies that make up a larger global 'survival skills' term. Teachers have access to good sources of information to verify what academic survival skills a student possesses, including direct observation; interviews (of the student, past teacher, or parent); and student work products.

> **TIP:** Teachers can access a free web application to create customized student-skill checklists. The Academic Survival Skills Checklist Maker provides a starter set of strategies to address homework, note-taking, organization, study, test-taking, and time management. Teachers can use the application to create and print customized checklists and can also save their checklists online. This application is available at: *http://www.interventioncentral.org/tools/academic-survival-skills-checklist-maker*

Schools can find a number of valuable uses for 'academic survival skills' checklists, including the following:

1. *Consistent expectations among teachers.* Teachers at a grade level, on an instructional team, or within an instructional department can work together to develop checklists for essential global academic-survival skills. As teachers collaborate to create these checklists, they reach agreement on the essential skills that students need for academic success and can then consistently promote those skills across their classrooms.

2. *Proactive student skills training.* One excellent use of these checklists is as a classwide student training tool. At the start of the school year, teachers can create checklists for those academic survival skills in which students are weak (e.g., study skills, time management) and use them as tools to train students in specific strategies to remediate these deficiencies. Several instructors working with the same group of students can even pool their efforts so that each teacher might be required to teach a checklist in only a single survival-skill area.

3. *Student skills self-check.* Teachers can use academic survival-skills checklists to promote student responsibility. Students are provided with master copies of checklists and encouraged to develop their own customized checklists by selecting and editing those strategies likely to work best for them. Instructors can then hold students accountable to consult and use these individualized checklists to expand their repertoire of strategies for managing their own learning.

4. *Monitoring progress of academic survival-skills interventions.* Often, intervention plans developed for middle and high school students include strategies to address academic survival-skill targets such as homework completion or organization. Checklists are a good way for teachers to

measure the student's baseline use of academic survival skills in a targeted area prior to the start of the intervention. Checklists can also be used to calculate a student outcome goal that will signify a successful intervention and to measure (e.g., weekly) the student's progress in using an expanded range of academic survival-skills during the intervention period.

For example, a teacher may develop a checklist (like any of those appearing later in this document) outlining 11 sub-skills that define her expectations for 'study skills'. Through interview, direct observation, and examination of student work products, the teacher ascertains that the student reliably used 7 of the 11 skills during baseline. She sets the outcome goal that—at the conclusion of a 5-week intervention period—the student will reliably use all 11 of those study sub-skills. Once per week during the intervention, the teacher meets with the student to review the checklist, record which additional study skills-if any—the student is now using, and chart this growth on a simple visual graph.

5. *Parent conferences.* When teachers meet with parents to discuss student academic concerns, academic survival-skills checklists can serve as a vehicle to define expected student competencies and also to decide what specific school and home supports will most benefit the student. In addition, parents often appreciate receiving copies of these checklists to review with their child at home.

When students struggle with global academic survival skills such as study, organization, or time management, those deficits can seem so all-encompassing as to inspire a sense of helplessness. In contrast, targeted and prescriptive checklists (such as those described here) that outline practical strategies to enhance school survival skills can serve as a tool to focus and empower teachers, parents, and students to accomplish the shared goal of turning every student into a effective, self-managing learner.

References

DiPerna, J. C. (2006). Academic enablers and student achievement: Implications for assessment and intervention services in the schools. *Psychology in the Schools, 43,* 7-17.

Kazdin, A. E. (1989). *Behavior modification in applied settings (4th ed.).* Pacific Gove, CA: Brooks/ Cole.

Academic Survival Skills Checklist: Study Skills

This form includes (1) your selected Academic Survival Skill Checklist items, (2) a column to verify whether the student possesses each survival skill (Y/N), and (3) a column to list the information used to verify each skill (Observation/Interview/Work Product).

Academic Survival-Skill Checklist	Student Displays Skill? (Y/N)	Data Source? (Observation/ Interview/ Work Product)
☐ MAINTAIN A STUDY SCHEDULE. Maintain a regular (e.g., daily) study schedule with sufficient time set aside to review course content and information.		
☐ AVOID DISTRACTERS. When studying, avoid distracters (e.g., cell phone, television, Internet) that can erode study time and divert attention.		
☐ CREATE AN ORGANIZED STUDY SPACE. Prepare the study environment by organizing a space and setting out all necessary work materials before beginning study.		
☐ SET STUDY GOALS. Prior to a study session, define one or more specific study goals to accomplish (e.g., to review information for an upcoming quiz; to locate key information to include in an essay).		
☐ MAKE A STUDY AGENDA. If studying multiple subjects in one session, create a study agenda for that session with a listing of the key information to be reviewed for each subject and the time allocated for that review.		
☐ DO THE TOUGH STUDY WORK FIRST. Tackle the most difficult or challenging study objectives first during study sessions, when energy levels and ability to concentrate are at their peak.		
☐ VARY ACTIVITIES. Mix up study activities during a study session (e.g., alternating between reading and writing) to maintain engagement and interest.		
☐ CHUNK A LARGE STUDY TASK INTO SMALLER UNITS. If studying a large amount of material in a single session, 'chunk' the material into smaller units and take short breaks between each unit to maintain focus.		
☐ TEACH CHALLENGING CONTENT. When studying complex or challenging material, assume the role of instructor and attempt to explain or describe the material to a real or imagined listener. Teaching study material is an efficient way to verify understanding.		
☐ HIGHLIGHT QUESTIONS. When reviewing notes or completing course readings, use highlighters, margin notes, sticky notes, or other notation methods to flag questions, unknown vocabulary terms, or areas of confusion for later review with teacher or tutor.		
☐ SEEK HELP WHEN NEEED. Approach the teacher or tutor for help as needed to answer questions or clear up areas of confusion identified during study sessions.		
☐ AVOID CRAM SESSIONS. Stay away from all-night cram sessions before major tests. Cram sessions are ineffective because they are inefficient and often leave students exhausted and unable to perform their best on exams. Instead, distribute study and test-review time across multiple days and consider allocating an upward limit of about 1 hour per study session to maintain focus and energy.		

Academic Survival Skills Checklist: Homework

This form includes (1) your selected Academic Survival Skill Checklist items, (2) a column to verify whether the student possesses each survival skill (Y/N), and (3) a column to list the information used to verify each skill (Observation/Interview/Work Product).

Academic Survival-Skill Checklist	Student Displays Skill? (Y/N)	Data Source? (Observation/ Interview/ Work Product)
☐ WRITE DOWN HOMEWORK ASSIGNMENTS CORRECTLY. Make sure that you have copied down your homework assignment(s) correctly and completely. If necessary, approach the instructor before leaving the classroom to seek clarification about the homework assignment.		
☐ ASSEMBLE ALL NECESSARY HOMEWORK MATERIALS. Make a list of those school work materials that you will need for that night's homework assignments and ensure that you have them before going home. School materials may include the course text, copies of additional assigned readings, your class notes, and partially completed assignments that are to be finished as homework. Additionally, monitor your work supplies at home (e.g., graph paper, pens, printer cartridges) and replenish them as needed.		
☐ USE AVAILABLE SCHOOL TIME TO GET A START ON HOMEWORK. Take advantage of open time in school (e.g., time given in class, study halls, etc) to get a start on your homework. Getting a head start on homework in school can reduce the amount of time needed to complete that work later in the day. Also, if you start homework in school and run into problems, you have a greater chance of being able to seek out a teacher or fellow student to resolve those problems proactively and thus successfully complete that assignment.		
☐ CREATE AN OPTIMAL HOMEWORK SPACE. Create an organized space at home for getting homework done. The space can be temporary (e.g., kitchen table) or permanent (e.g., a desk in your bedroom). It should be quiet, well-lit, and include a table or desk large enough to lay out your work materials and a comfortable chair.		
☐ SCHEDULE A REGULAR HOMEWORK TIME. Homework is easier to complete if you set aside sufficient time in your schedule to do it. If possible, your daily routine should include a standing time when any homework is to be done. In deciding when to schedule a homework period, consider such factors as when your energy level is highest, when surrounding distractions are less likely to occur, and when shared resources such as a computer or printer may be available for your use.		
☐ DEVELOP A DAILY HOMEWORK PLAN. Before beginning your homework each day, take a few minutes to review all of your homework assignments and to develop a work plan. Your plan should include a listing of each homework task and an estimate of how long it will take to complete that task. It is a good rule of thumb to select the most difficult homework task to complete first, when your energy and concentration levels are likely to be at their peak. At the conclusion of your homework session, review the plan, check off all completed tasks, and reflect on whether your time estimates were adequate for the various tasks.		

☐ DO NOT PROCRASTINATE ON LARGER HOMEWORK TASKS. Some homework assignments (e.g., term papers) require substantial work and successful completion of several related sub-tasks before attaining the final goal. It is a mistake to put off these larger assignments until the night before they are due. Instead, when first assigned a comprehensive task, break that task down into appropriate sub-tasks. Next to each sub-task, list a target date for completion. When compiling a daily homework plan, include any sub-tasks with upcoming due dates. Monitor your progress to ensure that you remain on schedule to complete the larger assignment on time.		
☐ USE HOMEWORK SUPPORTS SUPPLIED BY YOUR TEACHER. Make use of homework guides or resources of any kind offered by your teacher. For example, be sure to review the course syllabus for information about upcoming homework, as well as any print or online listings of homework assignments for the day or week. Take advantage of teacher office hours to drop in and get help with homework as needed.		
☐ GET YOUR HOMEWORK ORGANIZED. When several homework tasks are assigned daily from several courses, the total volume of work can quickly pile up. Adopt simple but effective organizational strategies to keep track of all the paperwork. For example, consider maintaining two file folders labeled 'Work in Progress' and 'Completed Work'. Make a point of emptying the 'Completed Work' folder each day by turning in the finished homework.		
☐ NOTE AREAS OF HOMEWORK CONFUSION. If you are stuck on a homework item, be sure to note the specific reason(s) that you are unable to complete it. For example, you may have difficulty with a homework item because you failed to comprehend a passage in your assigned reading (note the problem by highlighting the confusing passage), do not know the meaning of a term (note the problem by writing down the unknown term), or do not understand the teacher's assignment (note the problem by writing a comment on the assignment worksheet). By recording the reason(s) that you are unable successfully to complete a homework item, you demonstrate to your teacher both that you made a good-faith effort to do the work and that you are able to clearly explain where you encountered the problem and why.		
☐ CHECK HOMEWORK QUALITY. Students can improve homework performance by adopting quality self-checks. For example, before turning in any homework writing task, you might apply the SCOPE revision tool: check your composition for Spelling-Capitalization-Order of words-Punctuation-Expression of complete thoughts. If your teacher has given you rubrics or other rating forms to evaluate the quality of your work, these also may be useful for evaluating your homework.		

Academic Survival Skills Checklist: Note Taking

This form includes (1) your selected Academic Survival Skill Checklist items, (2) a column to verify whether the student possesses each survival skill (Y/N), and (3) a column to list the information used to verify each skill (Observation/Interview/Work Product).

Academic Survival-Skill Checklist	Student Displays Skill? (Y/N)	Data Source? (Observation/ Interview/ Work Product)
☐ SELECT AN OPTIMAL CLASSROOM LOCATION FOR NOTE-TAKING. Sit at a location in the classroom where you can hear the teacher clearly, see the board or overheads easily, and have few distractions.		
☐ ORGANIZE NOTES USING A LOGICAL FORMAT. Find an organizational format for your notes that works for you. Consider using visual cues such as indenting and text-based cues such as number or letter outline format to indicate the sequence and interrelationship of ideas.		
☐ MONITOR INSTRUCTOR CUES ABOUT IMPORTANT MATERIAL. When taking notes, pay attention to cues given by your instructor about what lecture content is important and should be included in your course notes. Cues signifying important lecture material include (1) information written on the blackboard or whiteboard; (2) instructor labeling of specific ideas or facts as important (e.g., "One crucial factor leading to the Civil War was..."); (3) instructor repetition of key points; (4) significant time devoted during lecture to particular points or concepts; (5) reviews of previously covered material given at the start of class; and (6) summaries of material given at the end of class.		
☐ BE PRECISE WHERE IT MATTERS. Much of your notes will be paraphrased in your own words. If you want to remember the exact wording of a key statement from your instructor, though, put the statement into quotation marks. Use abbreviations to save time--and be consistent in their use. Be careful and correct in writing down specific formulas, definitions, and important facts shared by the instructor.		
☐ KEEP NOTES BRIEF. Notes should be brief and to the point. During lecture, record notes in the form of key terms and phrases, rather than wordy sentences, to allow you both to keep up with the instructor and to have time to reflect on the content.		
☐ LABEL YOUR NOTES. Use a uniform header each day to label your notes, including the date, speaker, class, and topic. (Such a header is especially useful if you are taking notes on loose sheets of paper that will later be added to the appropriate notes-binder.) Number the pages for easy retrieval and referencing.		
☐ REVIEW YOUR NOTES FOR CONTENT. Leave space after each entry in your notes. Soon after class, review your notes and add additional comments or expand descriptions as needed to make your notes more intelligible.		

☐ DEVELOP STRATEGIES TO FILL IN MISSING CONTENT. All note-takers occasionally miss important content and must find ways to fill in those information gaps. If the instructor is moving so fast that you cannot fully capture the ideas presented, jot down key terms or phrases and then approach the teacher later to ask for help in filling in the missing content. Also, consider making an agreement with other students in the class to share notes with each other as needed to fill in gaps--and to borrow copies of each other's notes on days when one of you is absent.		
☐ USE INSTRUCTOR-SUPPLIED NOTES AS A HELP—NOT AS A CRUTCH. The act of note-taking requires that the student actively engage with and learn challenging course content. Therefore, if the course instructor supplies the class with copies of lecture notes, do not simply accept these notes passively. Instead, take your own notes during lecture and use the instructor's notes after class to fill in any gaps in your notes.		

Academic Survival Skills Checklist: Organization

This form includes (1) your selected Academic Survival Skill Checklist items, (2) a column to verify whether the student possesses each survival skill (Y/N), and (3) a column to list the information used to verify each skill (Observation/Interview/Work Product).

Academic Survival-Skill Checklist	Student Displays Skill? (Y/N)	Data Source? (Observation/ Interview/ Work Product)
☐ MAINTAIN AN ORDERLY WORKSPACE. Organize your home workspace so that you have a place for all of your materials and can quickly find what you need. (Organized does not mean super-neat. The goal is that you can locate an item when you need it.) Group similar items (e.g., reference books, writing materials) together for rapid access. Make a point of picking up after each work session.		
☐ MANAGE THE PAPERFLOW. Have a system for handling paper documents. For most students, this simple organizing system can effectively manage paper documents: (1) Work in Progress: Maintain a folder for current work-in-progress, including any pending assignments and related materials; (2) Reference Materials: For each course, reserve a section of your notebook to store those documents that you are saving for reference, including the course syllabus, past tests, and other review materials; (3) Trash/Recycle: Throw out any papers that you no longer need for pending work or future reference. Also, consider the OHIO rule for most paper documents: Only Handle It Once!		
☐ MAINTAIN A CURRENT 'TO DO' LIST. In paper or electronic format, maintain a running list of errands to complete or upcoming tasks to be accomplished. Place time in your schedule to carry out these miscellaneous jobs and check off each task as you complete it. Label those tasks that are high-priority to ensure that you accomplish the most urgent items first.		
☐ BACKPACKS AND LOCKERS: SCHEDULE REGULAR CLEANOUTS. Stuff accumulates. Make a point at the end of each week to clean out and straighten your backpack and school locker. Toss out documents that you no longer need. Put away in their rightful storage place clothing, food containers, electronics, and other objects that otherwise start to collect and clutter.		
☐ SCHOOL SUPPLIES: CREATE A GO BAG. Obtain a 'go bag' (zippable pouch or other container) large enough to hold a basic supply of school supplies, including pens, pencils, paper, a calculator, and other essential work materials. Keep the go bag in your backpack as a handy way to find work materials for any course. Check the go bag daily and restock as needed.		

☐ CREATE ROUTINES FOR RECURRING MULTI-STEP TASKS. Routines convert open-ended tasks into a structured, predictable, easy-to-follow sequence. The value of routines is that they allow us to complete tasks efficiently and almost without conscious thought--through force of habit. Examples of recurring tasks that could be turned into predictable routines are preparation for school, homework sessions, and exercise. To convert a task to a routine, (1) select a time in your schedule when you will carry out this recurring task, (2) write down the steps that make up the task, and (3) list any materials that you will need to carry out the task. For the first few times that you carry out a newly-scripted routine, make a point to monitor your performance (Did you do the task at the scheduled time, follow the steps, have all materials ready?). With practice, that task quickly turns into a comfortable routine.		
☐ REDUCE YOUR MEMORY LOAD: CREATE CHECKLISTS. For any recurring situation in which you are in danger of forgetting to bring materials or carry out important tasks, create and use checklists. For example, a student's checklist may list items often forgotten in the rush to leave for school in the morning: "Lunch, homework, sports clothes, calculator." Or a student may consult this simple checklist at the end of class: "Write down homework assignment, collect work materials for homework, make sure today's homework is turned in before leaving class."		
☐ CREATE MEETING LOGS FOR TEACHER CONFERENCES AND STUDENT WORK GROUPS. As a student, you may not attend many meetings. However, whenever you conference with a teacher or attend a student study or work group session, it is a good idea to write a brief 'log' entry summarizing the outcome. It is particularly helpful to write down meeting notes when you have committed to the teacher or your peers to do something: e.g., to email your summary of a research article to members of your study group or to turn in a missing assignment to your teacher by the end of the week. Jotting down a brief entry right after the meeting helps you to remember your obligations and encourages you to put those obligations into your schedule or onto your 'to do' list—where you know they will not be overlooked.		
☐ USE ELECTRONIC REMINDERS AND PROMPTS. As smartphones and other personal digital devices become more common, you can take advantage of their features to better organize your life. For example, set your cell phone alarm to remember important appointments or daily tasks. Or send yourself an email with a reminder of a task to be completed before you go to sleep.		

Academic Survival Skills Checklist: Time Management

This form includes (1) your selected Academic Survival Skill Checklist items, (2) a column to verify whether the student possesses each survival skill (Y/N), and (3) a column to list the information used to verify each skill (Observation/Interview/Work Product).

Academic Survival-Skill Checklist	Student Displays Skill? (Y/N)	Data Source? (Observation/ Interview/ Work Product)
☐ CREATE A MASTER SCHEDULE. Develop a Sunday-through-Saturday weekly master schedule for the quarter, semester, or school year. In that schedule, (1) fill in school classes and study periods, (2) include any regularly scheduled activities such as commuting, sports, clubs, lessons, or part-time jobs, (3) block out time for essential activities such as eating and sleeping, and (4) include adequate time for recreation. In the remaining blocks of open time in the schedule, reserve a minimum amount of time each day for study. Update this schedule whenever a significant schedule change occurs. TIP: Consider labeling several time-blocks as 'open' in the master schedule to accommodate occasional unforeseen study or other time requirements.		
☐ KEEP A DAILY CALENDAR. Whether you use a paper or electronic version, keep a calendar to track your changing daily schedule. When constructing each daily calendar schedule, it is most efficient to start with the structure of the master schedule and then add any additional events scheduled to occur on that day.		
☐ SCHEDULE PREVIEW AND REVIEW TIME FOR DEMANDING COURSES. When possible, reserve time before a challenging class to preview material to be covered and time soon after the class session to review lecture notes. Write these preview and review slots into your master schedule.		
☐ WHEN SCHEDULING, START WITH OUTCOME GOALS. When developing a daily or weekly schedule, first list any important goals to be accomplished by the end of that scheduled time-period (e.g., to produce a 5-paragraph essay; to complete a college application; to transcribe a set of paper notes into electronic format). After developing the schedule, double-check to ensure that you have incorporated sufficient time and the correct sequencing of activities into that schedule to attain those key goals.		
☐ USE UNEXPECTED POCKETS OF FREE TIME EFFICIENTLY. Have a plan to make efficient use of small amounts of unscheduled time that become available. Tasks suitable for brief pockets of open time could include reviewing and revising lecture notes, starting a homework assignment, studying note-cards to prepare for an upcoming test, and updating your study schedule for the following day.		

☐ ALLOCATE DOUBLE TIME FOR SIGNIFICANT ACADEMIC TASKS. When deciding how much time to schedule for a substantial academic task, predict the time required--and then double that estimate. People often reserve too little time for demanding tasks--so doubling your time estimates can correct for this over-optimistic bias.		
☐ TIME MANAGEMENT: REFLECT AND REVISE. At the end of each week, review your time-management planning efforts with a critical eye and note areas needing improvement. For example, investigate whether the amount of time that you typically set aside for study or other activities is sufficient, whether you are actually sticking to your general schedule, and whether there are important but overlooked activities or tasks that need to be added to your schedule.		

How To: Use the Cumulative Mastery Log to Record Progress in the Acquisition Stage of Learning

During academic interventions in which the student is newly learning a fixed set of academic items (e.g., math facts, spelling words, sight words, vocabulary terms), the instructor can conveniently track the impact of the intervention by recording and dating mastered items in a cumulative log.

First, the instructor defines the set of academic items to be taught or reviewed during the intervention (e.g., basic multiplication facts from 1-12; pre-primer sight-word list; vocabulary terms for a biology course). Next, the instructor sets criteria for judging when the student has mastered a particular item from the academic item set. (Example: *"A math fact is considered mastered when the student successfully answers that math-fact flashcard within 3 seconds on three successive occasions during a session and repeats this performance without error at the next session."*).

To collect baseline information, the instructor initially reviews all items from the academic-item set with the student--and records which items the student already knows. Then, throughout the intervention, the instructor logs and dates any additional items that the student masters.

The Cumulative Mastery Log that appears on the following pages structures the task of setting up and using a mastery log to track the cumulative results of an academic intervention.

Example: Mrs. Ostrowski, a 1st-grade teacher, decides to provide additional intervention support for Jonah, a student in her class who needs to work on sight-word recognition using a first-grade word list.

- **Definition of mastery.** Mrs. Ostrowski defines mastery for sight words as follows: *"When shown a sight word, the student will correctly read that word aloud within 3 seconds, will read the word correctly at least 3 times in a row with no errors in a single session, and will repeat this performance in the next session."*

- **Baseline data collection.** Before starting an intervention, the teacher inventories and records Jonah's baseline skills by reviewing the 41-item first-grade word list. As seen above, the teacher's definition of mastery of sight-words requires that a word cannot be counted as 'known' until the student reads it correctly multiple times across 2 sessions—so the baseline phase also takes 2 sessions to complete. The teacher finds that Jonah can read 21 of the 41 words correctly at baseline.

- **Intervention goal.** The teacher sets as an intervention goal that Jonah will master all remaining items—20 sight-words—within three weeks.

- **Cumulative progress-monitoring.** Mrs. Ostrowski then begins the daily intervention: incremental rehearsal of letters using flashcards (Joseph, 2006). Whenever Jonah is able to name a additional previously unknown word from the sight-word list, the teacher records and dates that item in her cumulative mastery log.

References

Joseph, L.M. (2006). Incremental rehearsal: A flashcard drill technique for increasing retention of reading words. *The Reading Teacher,* 59, 803-807.

Academic Skills: Cumulative Mastery Log

Student: _____ School Yr: _____ Classroom/Course: _____

Academic Item Set: Define the set of academic items to be measured (e.g., basic multiplication facts from 1-12; grade 1 sight-word list; vocabulary terms for biology course):

_____

_____

Criteria for Mastery: Describe the criteria for judging when the student has mastered a particular item from the academic item set. (Example: *"A math fact is considered mastered when the student successfully answers that math-fact flashcard within 3 seconds on three successive occasions during a session and repeats this performance without error at the next session."*):

_____

_____

Baseline Skills Inventory: Prior to beginning the intervention, inventory the student's current level of mastery of the skill being measured. (NOTE: Apply the 'criteria for mastery' guidelines written above when completing the baseline skills inventory.)

Person completing the inventory: _____ Date: ____/____/____

Item 1: _____	Item 11: _____	Item 21: _____
Item 2: _____	Item 12: _____	Item 22: _____
Item 3: _____	Item 13: _____	Item 23: _____
Item 4: _____	Item 14: _____	Item 24: _____
Item 5: _____	Item 15: _____	Item 25: _____
Item 6: _____	Item 16: _____	Item 26: _____
Item 7: _____	Item 17: _____	Item 27: _____
Item 8: _____	Item 18: _____	Item 28: _____
Item 9: _____	Item 19: _____	Item 29: _____
Item 10: _____	Item 20: _____	Item 30: _____

Academic Intervention: Cumulative Mastery Log

Student: _____ School Yr: _____ Classroom/Course: _____

Cumulative Mastery Log: During the intervention, log each mastered item below with date of mastery. NOTE: Be sure to use the 'criteria for mastery' defined on the first page of this form when judging whether the student has mastered a particular item.

Item 1: _____ Date: ___/___/___	Item 21: _____ Date: ___/___/___
Item 2: _____ Date: ___/___/___	Item 22: _____ Date: ___/___/___
Item 3: _____ Date: ___/___/___	Item 23: _____ Date: ___/___/___
Item 4: _____ Date: ___/___/___	Item 24: _____ Date: ___/___/___
Item 5: _____ Date: ___/___/___	Item 25: _____ Date: ___/___/___
Item 6: _____ Date: ___/___/___	Item 26: _____ Date: ___/___/___
Item 7: _____ Date: ___/___/___	Item 27: _____ Date: ___/___/___
Item 8: _____ Date: ___/___/___	Item 28: _____ Date: ___/___/___
Item 9: _____ Date: ___/___/___	Item 29: _____ Date: ___/___/___
Item 10: _____ Date: ___/___/___	Item 30: _____ Date: ___/___/___
Item 11: _____ Date: ___/___/___	Item 31: _____ Date: ___/___/___
Item 12: _____ Date: ___/___/___	Item 32: _____ Date: ___/___/___
Item 13: _____ Date: ___/___/___	Item 33: _____ Date: ___/___/___
Item 14: _____ Date: ___/___/___	Item 34: _____ Date: ___/___/___
Item 15: _____ Date: ___/___/___	Item 35: _____ Date: ___/___/___
Item 16: _____ Date: ___/___/___	Item 36: _____ Date: ___/___/___
Item 17: _____ Date: ___/___/___	Item 37: _____ Date: ___/___/___
Item 18: _____ Date: ___/___/___	Item 38: _____ Date: ___/___/___
Item 19: _____ Date: ___/___/___	Item 39: _____ Date: ___/___/___
Item 20: _____ Date: ___/___/___	Item 40: _____ Date: ___/___/___

How To: Enlist Students to Monitor Their Own Academic Goals

When a teacher discovers a large gap between a particular student's academic skills and the requirements of a reading or math Common Core State Standard, that instructor may decide to provide the student with a classroom academic intervention.

Research suggests that the teacher should also routinely include the *student* in the intervention plan by having that student set and self-monitor his or her own relevant academic performance goals. When students are able to set personal academic goals, take steps to meet those goals, and periodically reflect on their actual goal-attainment, they build important skills relating to self-regulation (Burnette et al., 2013). Self-regulated learners assume increasing responsibility for managing their own learning (Martin et al., 2003)--through the process of applying independent effort and adjusting learning goals over time to eventually bring their skills into alignment with grade-level expectations.

There is a wide range of academic behaviors and work-products that could be the focus of student-developed goals. For example, a student who seldom completes in-class writing assignments may set the goal of turning in an assignment after each work session. Or a student needing to develop reading vocabulary may set the goal of keeping a vocabulary journal and recording terms and definitions for at least 10 new vocabulary terms per week. (See the table *Student-Monitored Academic Goals* below for additional examples of common academic problems and corresponding student-friendly goals .)

Student-Monitored Academic Goals: Examples		
Academic Problem	>	**Student-Monitored Goal**
Limited fluency in basic math-facts	>	Number of correct digits on a timed (5-minute) math-fact worksheet
Lack of homework completion	>	Number of days per week when homework is turned in
Lack of independent reading	>	Number of pages or books read independently per week or month
Lack of time spent engaged in independent study	>	Number of minutes per week spent in study-time
Limited number of original sources cited in writing assignments	>	Number of research citations appearing in student composition

How to Set Up Student Academic Self-Monitoring: Initial Planning Conference & Periodic Check-Ins

The teacher who wants to start an academic self-monitoring plan will first meet with the student to assist in preparing the plan. Teachers can use the form *Academic Self-Monitoring: Teacher / Student Planner Sheet* appearing later in this document as an organizer to conduct an initial student conference and set up an academic self-monitoring plan.

For students who are younger, deficient in organizational skills, or poorly motivated, the teacher may also choose to check in at the beginning and end of each monitoring session-both to ensure that the student is setting goals and monitoring correctly and also to provide praise and encouragement.

Below are the stages for preparing and launching the student academic self- monitoring plan.

1. *Set up the self-monitoring plan.* In this initial planning meeting, the teacher facilitates the discussion but also prompts the student as much as possible to contribute to the plan. At this meeting, the teacher and student agree on the academic goal that the student is to track (e.g., 'multiplication math facts: 0-9'); select an objective measure to use in tracking progress on this task. (e.g., 'number of math-fact problems completed correctly on a 5-minute timed worksheet'); agree on how frequently the goal will be assessed (e.g., 'every day during math independent seatwork'); and set an initial performance goal (e.g., '25 digits correct'). Optionally, the student and instructor may also agree on a rate of expected improvement per session to help with updating goals (e.g., 'Ongoing goal: 1 additional digit correct than in the previous session').

2. *[Optional] Self-monitoring: Pre-session.* Before each self-monitoring session, the teacher meets briefly with the student to set a performance goal for that session.

3. *[Optional] Self-monitoring: Post-session.* After each self-monitoring session, the teacher and student meet again. The student compares the actual performance with the goal. If the student attains the goal, the teacher praises the student. If the student falls short of the goal, the teacher provides encouragement about the next session.

Student Self-Monitoring: Additional Advantages

While an important benefit of academic self-monitoring is the reinforcement of student responsibility and self-management skills, teachers may find several additional advantages:

- *Academic self-monitoring can increase on-task behavior.* Directing students with significant levels of classroom inattention to self-monitor their academic productivity is at least as effective in improving their focus as having them track their rate of on-task behavior. And measuring the amount of work completed has the added benefit of boosting student academic output (Maag, Reid & DiGangi, 1993). So a teacher might prompt a chronically inattentive student to set an academic performance goal at the start of each independent-work session (e.g., to write 200 words; to answer 20 math computation problems), then check in with the student at the end of the session to verify that he or she has attained the goal.

- *Academic self-monitoring is a useful way to track academic learning time.* The goal of instruction is to have students engaged in 'academic learning time', a state in which they are productively and successfully engaged in learning (Gettinger & Seibert, 2002). While it can be difficult for teachers to measure academic learning time (ALT) directly, student self-monitoring of academic productivity can serve as a useful proxy measure of ALT.

- *Data collected by the student helps to document the intervention.* With the increased emphasis on accountability in many schools, teachers are responsible for implementing, documenting, and monitoring classroom interventions. In some instances, the student's self-monitoring information can supplement data gathered by the teacher to more fully document the intervention's impact. As a product of the intervention, student-collected data can also be used to assess the integrity with which that intervention is carried out (Gansle & Noell, 2007).

References

Burnette J. L., O'Boyle, E. H., VanEpps, E. M., Pollack, J. M., & Finkel, E. J. (2013). Mind-sets matter: A meta-analytic review of implicit theories and self-regulation. *Psychological Bulletin, 139*, 655-701.

Gansle, K. A., & Noell, G. H. (2007). The fundamental role of intervention implementation in assessing response to intervention. In S. R. Jimerson, M. K. Burns, & A. M. VanDerHeyden (Eds.), *Response to intervention: The science and practice of assessment and intervention* (pp. 244-251).

Gettinger, M., & Seibert, J.K. (2002). Best practices in increasing academic learning time. In A. Thomas (Ed.*), Best practices in school psychology: Volume I* (4th ed., pp. 773-787). Bethesda, MD: National Association of School Psychologists.

Maag, J. W., Reid, R., & DiGangi, S. A. (1993). Differential effects of self-monitoring attention, accuracy, and productivity. *Journal of Applied Behavior Analysis, 26*, 329-344.

Martin, J. E., Mithaug, D. E., Cox, P., Peterson, L. Y., Van Dycke, J. L., & Cash, M.E. (2003). Increasing self-determination: Teaching students to plan, work, evaluate, and adjust. *Exceptional Children, 69*, 431-447.

Academic Self-Monitoring: Teacher / Student Planner Sheet

Student : _____ Teacher: _____ Classroom/Grade: _____ Date: _____

Directions to the Teacher: Meet with the student and use this Planner Sheet to put together an academic self-monitoring plan.

STEP 1: Define the academic target that will be the focus of the self-monitoring. Discuss with the student what academic area should be targeted for self-monitoring. Once you both agree on a monitoring target, write a problem-definition statement in the space provided (use the examples in the table on right as a guide):

Problem-Definition Statement: _____

_____

Academic Target Examples
• *Fluency in basic math-facts*
• *Homework completion*
• *Independent reading*
• *Time spent engaged in independent study*

STEP 2: Select a method for the student to self-monitor the academic problem. Decide with the student how the academic problem is to be monitored and write that monitoring method into the space provided (use the examples in the table on right as a guide):

Student Monitoring Method: _____

_____

_____

_____

Student-Monitoring Method Examples
• *Number of correct digits on a timed (5-minute) math-fact worksheet*
• *Number of days per week when homework is turned in*
• *Number of pages or books read independently per week or month*

STEP 3 [Optional]: Decide on a rate of improvement per monitoring session. You and the student can agree on a fixed rate of expected improvement per session--as a help in updating goals (e.g., 'Ongoing goal: To get 1 additional digit correct than in the previous session'; 'Ongoing goal: To write 5 additional words on the writing assignment than in the previous session').

Fixed rate of improvement per monitoring session: _____

_____

STEP 4: [Optional] Arrange for check-ins. You and the student can agree to meet for pre-session check-ins (to calculate self-monitoring goals) and/or post-session check-ins (to verify successful data collection and provide reinforcement and encouragement) for each self-monitoring session.

Will a pre-session check-in take place? ____ Y ____ N   Will a post-session check-in take place? ____ Y ____ N

STEP 5: Fill in the student self-monitoring form. Based on the decisions reached at this planning conference, fill in the *Academic Self-Monitoring: Student Recording Form* and direct the student to begin the self-monitoring plan.

Academic Self-Monitoring: Student Recording Form

Student Name: _____ Classroom/Grade: _____ School Year: _____

Academic Target

Student Self-Monitoring Method	Goal/Increase Per Session [Optional]

Directions to the Student: This form allows you to track your academic performance. Every time that you self-monitor, first record the date and set a goal that you hope to achieve, next perform the academic task, and finally record and evaluate your actual performance.

1	Date: _____	Goal: _____	Actual performance: _____	Goal achieved?: ___Y ___N
2	Date: _____	Goal: _____	Actual performance: _____	Goal achieved?: ___Y ___N
3	Date: _____	Goal: _____	Actual performance: _____	Goal achieved?: ___Y ___N
4	Date: _____	Goal: _____	Actual performance: _____	Goal achieved?: ___Y ___N
5	Date: _____	Goal: _____	Actual performance: _____	Goal achieved?: ___Y ___N
6	Date: _____	Goal: _____	Actual performance: _____	Goal achieved?: ___Y ___N
7	Date: _____	Goal: _____	Actual performance: _____	Goal achieved?: ___Y ___N

8	Date: _____	Goal: _____	Actual performance: _____	Goal achieved?: ___Y ___ N
9	Date: _____	Goal: _____	Actual performance: _____	Goal achieved?: ___Y ___ N
10	Date: _____	Goal: _____	Actual performance: _____	Goal achieved?: ___Y ___ N
11	Date: _____	Goal: _____	Actual performance: _____	Goal achieved?: ___Y ___ N
12	Date: _____	Goal: _____	Actual performance: _____	Goal achieved?: ___Y ___ N
13	Date: _____	Goal: _____	Actual performance: _____	Goal achieved?: ___Y ___ N
14	Date: _____	Goal: _____	Actual performance: _____	Goal achieved?: ___Y ___ N
15	Date: _____	Goal: _____	Actual performance: _____	Goal achieved?: ___Y ___ N
16	Date: _____	Goal: _____	Actual performance: _____	Goal achieved?: ___Y ___ N
17	Date: _____	Goal: _____	Actual performance: _____	Goal achieved?: ___Y ___ N
18	Date: _____	Goal: _____	Actual performance: _____	Goal achieved?: ___Y ___ N
19	Date: _____	Goal: _____	Actual performance: _____	Goal achieved?: ___Y ___ N
20	Date: _____	Goal: _____	Actual performance: _____	Goal achieved?: ___Y ___ N

Academic Self-Monitoring: Teacher / Student Planner Sheet

Student : _____Kevin H._____ Teacher: _Mrs. Staub_____ Classroom/Grade: _Science 9_ Date: _Oct 4_, 2013

Directions to the Teacher: Meet with the student and use this Planner Sheet to put together an academic self-monitoring plan.

STEP 1: Define the academic target that will be the focus of the self-monitoring. Discuss with the student what academic area should be targeted for self-monitoring. Once you both agree on a monitoring target, write a problem-definition statement in the space provided (use the examples in the table on right as a guide):

Problem-Definition Statement: _____Kevin needs to complete_____

_all assigned course readings in science on time._____

Academic Target Examples
• *Fluency in basic math-facts*
• *Homework completion*
• *Independent reading*
• *Time spent engaged in independent study*

STEP 2: Select a method for the student to self-monitor the academic problem. Decide with the student how the academic problem is to be monitored and write that monitoring method into the space provided (use the examples in the table on right as a guide):

Student Monitoring Method: _____Kevin will keep a daily log of_____

_pages read from assigned readings._____

_____

_____

Student-Monitoring Method Examples
• *Number of correct digits on a timed (5-minute) math-fact worksheet*
• *Number of days per week when homework is turned in*
• *Number of pages or books read independently per week or month*

STEP 3 [Optional]: Decide on a rate of improvement per monitoring session. You and the student can agree on a fixed rate of expected improvement per session--as a help in updating goals (e.g., 'Ongoing goal: To get 1 additional digit correct than in the previous session'; 'Ongoing goal: To write 5 additional words on the writing assignment than in the previous session').

Fixed rate of improvement per monitoring session: _____Not applicable._____

_____

STEP 4: [Optional] Arrange for check-ins. You and the student can agree to meet for pre-session check-ins (to calculate self-monitoring goals) and/or post-session check-ins (to verify successful data collection and provide reinforcement and encouragement) for each self-monitoring session.

Will a pre-session check-in take place? ____ Y ____ N   Will a post-session check-in take place? _X_ Y ____ N

STEP 5: Fill in the student self-monitoring form. Based on the decisions reached at this planning conference, fill in the *Academic Self-Monitoring: Student Recording Form* and direct the student to begin the self-monitoring plan.

Academic Self-Monitoring: Student Recording Form

Student Name: __Kevin H.__ Classroom/Grade: __Science 9__ School Year: __2013-2014__

Academic Target
My target is to complete all assigned course readings in science on time..

Student Self-Monitoring Method	Goal/Increase Per Session [Optional]
I will keep a daily log of pages read from assigned readings.	NA

Directions to the Student: This form allows you to track your academic performance. Every time that you self-monitor, first record the date and set a goal that you hope to achieve, next perform the academic task, and finally record and evaluate your actual performance.

1	Date: __Oct 7__	Goal: __11 pages assigned__	Actual performance: __8 pages read__	Goal achieved?: ___Y _X_ N
2	Date: __Oct 8__	Goal: __10 pages assigned__	Actual performance: __10 pages read__	Goal achieved?: _X_Y ___ N
3	Date: __Oct 9__	Goal: __8 pages assigned__	Actual performance: __8 pages read__	Goal achieved?: _X_Y ___ N
4	Date: _____	Goal: _____	Actual performance: _____	Goal achieved?: ___Y ___ N
5	Date: _____	Goal: _____	Actual performance: _____	Goal achieved?: ___Y ___ N
6	Date: _____	Goal: _____	Actual performance: _____	Goal achieved?: ___Y ___ N
7	Date: _____	Goal: _____	Actual performance: _____	Goal achieved?: ___Y ___ N

Chapter 6

Collecting Data to Track Interventions: Curriculum-Based Measures

Deficits in basic academic skills are a frequent source of problems with schoolwork. Students who do not know all of their letter sounds or are not fluent readers or cannot perform simple math operations are unlikely to attain the ambitious Common Core State Standards for their grade level. But when teachers attempt informally to assess the health of a student's basic academic skills, they often encounter significant barriers. Academic assessments can be time-consuming to administer and therefore difficult to fit into a busy classroom routine. Also, because informal assessments are often unstructured, their results can vary substantially with each observation, making it difficult to use cumulative data reliably to track student progress. And informal, teacher-made academic assessments typically lack performance norms, making it virtually impossible to quantify the skill-gap that separates a struggling student from typical peers.

Luckily, the classroom teacher can use curriculum-based measurement (CBM) as a convenient and reliable tool to monitor student growth in those basic math, reading, and writing skills that form the foundation for academic success (Reschly, Busch, Betts, Deno, & Long, 2009). The term 'curriculum-based measurement' describes a family of brief, timed assessments of basic academic skills. CBMs have been developed to cover a range of academic areas, including letter knowledge, oral reading, reading comprehension, number sense, math computation, and writing mechanics (Hosp, Hosp, & Howell, 2007).

Among advantages of using CBM for classroom assessment are that these measures are efficient to use in school settings; align with both the Common Core Standards and local curriculum-goals; are reliable and valid (possessing 'technical adequacy'); use standard procedures to prepare materials, administer, and score; give teachers objective and specific information about student academic performance; and include decision rules to help educators interpret student CBM data so that appropriate instructional decisions can be made (Hosp, Hosp & Howell, 2007).

Roadmap to This Chapter

The remainder of this chapter contains a series of 'How To' resources for administering curriculum-based measurements to track emerging student skills in early math fluency, math computation, letter sounds/names, reading fluency, reading comprehension, and written expression. Each resource includes a description of the measure as well as research-based grade-norms for evaluating student performance. Information is also included to allow readers to access online more complete directions for how to create materials, administer, and score the CBM. NOTE: This chapter is meant to serve as a continuation of the preceding chapter on classroom assessment. In particular, the discussion in the preceding chapter on student goal-setting will apply directly to goal-setting using CBMs. The resources related to the CBM materials include:

- *How To: Measure Letter Knowledge With CBM: Letter Name Fluency (LNF) & Letter Sound Fluency (LSF).* Automatic letter knowledge is an important foundation skill underlying both reading and writing. CBM letter-sound and letter-name assessments are included in this resource, with each type of assessment being administered individually and lasting 1 minute. Norms are included for grades K-1.

- *How To: Assess Reading Speed With CBM: Oral Reading Fluency Passages.* To assess reading fluency, the student is given a passage of controlled text to read aloud for 1 minute. Reading fluency is an important component of reading in its own right. It also correlates highly with reading comprehension through grade 3. Norms are included for grades 1-8.

- *How To: Assess Reading Comprehension With CBM: Maze Passages.* Maze passages are specially formatted selections of text that measure a student's reading comprehension. Because the student reads and responds to the Maze passage silently during independent reading, this assessment can be administered to a single student, small group, or an entire class. Typically, CBM-Maze administrations last 3 minutes. Norms are included for grades 2-6.

- *How To: Assess Early Math Difficulties in the Primary Grades With CBM.* In the early grades (kindergarten and grade 1), measures of early math fluency ('number sense') predict students' readiness for higher-level math operations. Three different methods for assessing early math fluency are presented with each type of assessment being administered individually and lasting 1 minute. Norms are included for grades K-1.

- *How To: Assess Mastery of Math Facts With CBM: Computation Fluency.* Speed in completing math computation problems is a good indicator of student proficiency in math facts. CBM math computation fluency probes are worksheets of math computation fluency problems. These CBMs can be group-administered and last 2 minutes. Norms are included for grades 1-6.

- *How To: Track Growth in Written Expression in the Elementary Grades With CBM.* Teachers can formatively assess a student's growth in the mechanics and conventions of writing through CBM-Written Expression. These CBMs can be group-administered, with a single administration lasting 4 minutes. Norms are included for grades 1-6.

References

Hosp, M.K., Hosp, J. L., & Howell, K. W. (2007). *The ABCs of CBM.* New York: Guilford.

Reschly, A. L., Busch, T. W., Betts, J., Deno, S. L., & Long, J. D. (2009). Curriculum-based measurement oral reading as an indicator of reading achievement: A meta-analysis of the correlational evidence. *Journal of School Psychology,* 47, 427-469.

How To: Measure Letter Knowledge with CBM—
Letter Name Fluency (LNF) & Letter Sound Fluency (LSF)

Teachers have always known that letter knowledge is a pre-requisite to the acquisition of reading skills. Before students can decode text, they must be fluent in recognizing both letters and their sounds. And recent research confirms that children's ability in primary grades to identify letter names and sounds is a strong predictor of reading readiness and future reading success (Ritchey & Speece, 2006).

Efficient, curriculum-based assessments to track student performance and growth in letter knowledge are Letter Name Fluency (LNF) and Letter Sound Fluency (LSF). In each assessment, the teacher administers timed 1-minute fluency probes (assessments) to children and compares the results to research norms to determine whether students are under-performing and therefore at risk for future academic problems. These two measures are time-efficient and the perfect means to track a student's progress in letter-skills instruction or intervention.

CBM-Letter Name Fluency/Letter Sound Fluency: How to Access Resources. Teachers seeking to screen their students in foundation letter-knowledge skills can obtain these free CBM-LNF/LSF assessment resources: (1) materials for assessment, (2) guidelines for administration and scoring, and (3) research-based norms.

- *Materials for assessment.* Schools can create free mixed-case random-letter lists by accessing the Letter Fluency Generator, an online application: *http://www.interventioncentral.org/teacher-resources/letter-name-fluency-generator*

- *Guidelines for administration and scoring.* Instructions for preparing, administering, and scoring CBM-Letter Name Fluency/Letter Sound Fluency assessments appear later in this document:

- *Research-based norms.* Two tables, *Curriculum Curriculum-Based Measurement: Letter Name Fluency (LNF)* and *Curriculum-Based Measurement: Letter Sound Fluency (LSF),* are included in this document. The norms include fluency benchmarks and growth norms for grades K-2 (EasyCBM, 2010).

References

Ritchey, K. D., & Speece, D. L. (2006). From letter names to word reading: The nascent role of sublexical fluency. *Contemporary Educational Psychology, 31,* 301-327.

Curriculum-Based Measurement-Letter Name Fluency (LNF)/Letter Sound Fluency (LSF): Guidelines for Use

CBM-LNF/LSF: Description

In the CBM-Letter Name Fluency (LNF) task, the student is given a random list of upper- and lower-case letters and has 1 minute to identify the names of as many letters as possible.

In the CBM-Letter Sound Fluency (LSF) task, the student is given a random list of upper- and lower-case letters and has 1 minute to identify as many letter sounds as possible.

Directions for Letter Name Fluency: LNF

CBM-Letter Name Fluency: Materials
The following materials are needed to administer CBM-LNF probes:
- Student and examiner copies of random list of upper- and lower-case letters
- Stopwatch

CBM-Letter Name Fluency: Preparation
Schools can create free mixed-case random-letter lists by accessing the Letter Fluency Generator, an online application:
http://www.interventioncentral.org/teacher-resources/letter-name-fluency-generator

CBM-Letter Name Fluency: Directions for Administration (adapted from Hosp, Hosp, & Howell, 2007; Ritchey & Speece, 2006)

1. The examiner sits at a table with the student and gives the student a copy of the randomized letter list.
2. The examiner says: "This list contains letters in mixed-up order. When I say 'begin', read the name of each letter aloud, starting from here [the examiner points to the top left of the page]. Read each letter as I point to it. Try your best and keep reading until I tell you to stop.
3. The examiner says: "Begin", starts the stop-watch, and points to the first letter.
4. As the student reads a letter correctly, the examiner immediately points to the next letter. If the student misreads a letter or hesitates for 3 seconds or longer, the examiner points to the next letter. The examiner does not correct student mistakes or provide the correct letter when the student hesitates.
5. At the end of 1 minute, the examiner stops the stop-watch, says: "Stop", and collects and scores the student letter list.
6. *Initial Assessment:* If the examiner is assessing the student for the first time, the examiner administers a total of 3 letter lists during the session using the above procedures and takes the median (middle) score as the best estimate of the student's letter naming speed.
   Progress-Monitoring: If the examiner is monitoring student growth in letter-naming (and has previously collected LNF data), only one letter list is given in the session.

CBM-Letter Name Fluency: Practice

If the student is not yet familiar with the LNF task, the teacher can administer one or more practice LNF probes (using the administration guidelines above) and provide coaching and feedback as needed until assured that the student fully understands the assessment.

CBM-Letter Name Fluency: Scoring Guidelines

The examiner adds up the total number of correct responses, giving the student credit for each correct letter name. The student does not receive credit for letter sounds or for giving correct letter-name responses after hesitations of 3 seconds or longer.

Directions for Letter Sound Fluency: LSF

CBM-Letter Sound Fluency: Materials
The following materials are needed to administer CBM-LSF probes:
- Student and examiner copies of random list of lower-case letters
- Stopwatch

CBM-Letter Sound Fluency: Preparation
Schools can create free lower-case random-letter lists by accessing the Letter Fluency Generator, an online application:
http://www.interventioncentral.org/teacher-resources/letter-name-fluency-generator

CBM-Letter Sound Fluency: Directions for Administration (adapted from Fuchs & Fuchs, n.d.; Hosp, Hosp, & Howell, 2007; Ritchey & Speece, 2006)

1. The examiner sits at a table with the student and gives the student a copy of the randomized letter list.
2. The examiner says: "This list contains letters in mixed-up order. When I say 'begin', say the sound of each letter aloud, starting from here [the examiner points to the top left of the page]. Give the sound of each letter as I point to it. Try your best and keep going until I tell you to stop.
3. The examiner says: "Begin", starts the stop-watch, and points to the first letter.
4. As the student gives a correct letter sound, the examiner immediately points to the next letter. If the student gives an incorrect letter sound or hesitates for 3 seconds or longer, the examiner points to the next letter. The examiner does not correct student mistakes or provide the correct letter sound when the student hesitates.
5. At the end of 1 minute, the examiner stops the stop-watch, says: "Stop", and collects and scores the student letter list.
6. *Initial Assessment:* If the examiner is assessing the student for the first time, the examiner administers a total of 3 letter lists using the above procedures and takes the median (middle) score as the best estimate of the student's letter sound fluency.
   Progress-Monitoring: If the examiner is monitoring student growth in letter-sound fluency (and has previously collected LSF data), only one letter list is given.

CBM-Letter Sound Fluency: Practice

If the student is not yet familiar with the LSF task, the teacher can administer one or more practice LSF probes (using the administration guidelines above) and provide coaching and feedback as needed until assured that the student fully understands the assessment.

CBM-Letter Sound Fluency: Scoring Guidelines

The examiner adds up the total number of correct responses, giving the student credit for each correct letter sound. Both hard and soft sounds for 'c' and 'g' are acceptable. Only the short version of vowel sounds are acceptable (Fuchs & Fuchs, n.d.).

References

Fuchs, L. S., & Fuchs, D. (n.d.). Using *CBM for progress monitoring.* National Center of Student Progress Monitoring. Retrieved from http://www.studentprogress.org/

Hosp, M. K., Hosp, J. L., & Howell, K. W. (2007). *The ABC's of CBM: A practical guide to curriculum-based measurement.* New York: Guilford Press.

Ritchey, K. D., & Speece, D. L. (2006). From letter names to word reading: The nascent role of sublexical fluency. *Contemporary Educational Psychology, 31,* 301-327.

Curriculum-Based Measurement: Letter Name Fluency (LNF) Norms
(EasyCBM, 2010)*

In the **CBM-Letter Name Fluency (LNF)** task, the student is given a random list of upper- and lower-case letters and has 1 minute to identify the names of as many letters as possible.

Grade	Percentile	Fall LNF (EasyCBM, 2010)	Winter LNF (EasyCBM, 2010)	Spring LNF (EasyCBM, 2010)	Weekly Growth (Calculated across 32 Instructional Wks)
K	50%ile	12	35	45	1.00
	20%ile	4	22	36	1.00
	10%ile	2	13	29	0.84
1	50%ile	40	56	68	0.88
	20%ile	28	42	49	0.66
	10%ile	20	34	42	0.69

Curriculum-Based Measurement: Letter Sound Fluency (LSF) Norms
(EasyCBM, 2010)*

In the **CBM-Letter Sound Fluency (LSF)** task, the student is given a random list of upper- and lower-case letters and has 1 minute to identify as many letter sounds as possible.

Grade	Percentile	Fall LSF (EasyCBM, 2010)	Winter LSF (EasyCBM, 2010)	Spring LSF (EasyCBM, 2010)	Weekly Growth
K	50%ile	2	18	34	1.00
	20%ile	1	8	23	0.69
	10%ile	0	4	18	0.56
1	50%ile	26	39	46	0.62
	20%ile	15	30	36	0.66
	10%ile	10	26	30	0.62

References:
- EasyCBM. (2010). *Interpreting the easyCBM progress monitoring test results.* Author. Retrieved from http://www.easycbm.com/static/files/pdfs/info/ProgMonScoreInterpretation.pdf

* Reported Characteristics of Student Sample(s) Used to Compile These Norms:
- **EasyCBM, 2010:** *Number of Students Assessed.* About 2000 students assessed for both LSF and LNF (EasyCBM, 2010; p.1)/*Geographical Location:* Washington & Oregon/ *Socioeconomic Status:* Not reported / *Ethnicity of Sample:* Not reported/*Limited English Proficiency in Sample:* Not reported.

Where to Find Materials: Schools can create free random-letter lists by accessing the Letter Fluency Generator. an online application: *http://www.interventioncentral.org/teacher-resources/letter-name-fluency-generator*

How To: Assess Reading Speed with CBM—
Oral Reading Fluency Passages

A student's accuracy and speed in reading aloud is an obvious and readily observable indicator of that student's reading ability. Reading fluency is an essential component of a student's global reading skills (National Institute of Child Health and Human Development, 2000). Furthermore, up through grade 3, reading fluency is arguably the best predictor of future reading success (Hosp, Hosp, & Howell, 2007).

The curriculum-based measure to track student reading speed is termed Oral Reading Fluency (ORF). In CBM-ORF, the student is given a grade-appropriate passage and asked to read aloud for one minute. The examiner marks as incorrect any words that the student misreads or hesitates on for 3 seconds or longer. The passage is then scored for Correctly Read Words (CRW). Although CBM-ORF is simple in format and quick to administer, its results are sensitive to short-term student gains in reading skills and predictive of long-term reading success, making this assessment an ideal progress-monitoring tool for classroom use.

CBM-ORF: How to Access Resources. Teachers can access a toolkit of resources for CBM-ORF, including: (1) materials for assessment, (2) guidelines for administration and scoring, and (3) research-based norms.

- *Materials for assessment.* DIBELS NEXT: Here are 3 sources for free CBM-ORF materials:

  DIBELS NEXT: Schools can obtain free ORF passages and ORF benchmarks for grades 1-6 from the DIBELS Next website: http://dibels.org/next.html

  EasyCBM: The easyCBM website (http://easycbm.com/) has collections of CBM-ORF passages (referred to as 'Passage Fluency') for grades 1-8. Teachers can create a free account on this website to access materials and benchmarks.

  Schools can also make their own CBM Oral Reading Fluency passages in PDF format based on text typed in by the user using the Reading Fluency Passages Generator, a free online application: *http://www.interventioncentral.org/teacher-resources/oral-reading-fluency-passages-generator*

- *Guidelines for administration and scoring.* Instructions for preparing, administering, and scoring CBM-ORF assessments appear later in this document:

- *Research-based norms.* A table, *Curriculum-Based Measurement: Oral Reading Fluency Norms*, is included in this document. The norms include fluency benchmarks for grades 1-8 and accompanying growth norms (Hasbrouck & Tindal, 2005).

References

Hasbrouck, J., & Tindal, G. (2005). Oral *reading fluency: 90 years of measurement.* Eugene, OR: Behavioral Research & Teaching/University of Oregon. Retrieved from http://brt.uoregon.edu

Hosp, M.K., Hosp, J. L., & Howell, K. W. (2007). *The ABCs of CBM.* New York: Guilford.

National Institute of Child Health and Human Development. (2000). *Report of the National Reading Panel. Teaching children to read: An evidence-based assessment of the scientific research literature on reading and its implications for reading instruction* (NIH Publication No. 00-4769). Washington, DC: U.S. Government Printing Office.

Curriculum-Based Measurement-Oral Reading Fluency (ORF): Guidelines for Use

CBM-ORF: Description
CBM-ORF measures a student's reading fluency by having that student read aloud for 1 minute from a prepared passage. During the student's reading, the examiner makes note of any reading errors in the passage. Then the examiner scores the passage by calculating the number of words read correctly.

CBM-ORF: Materials
The following materials are needed to administer a CBM-ORF passage:

- Student and examiner copies of a CBM-ORF passage (the process for creating ORF passages is described below)
- Stopwatch

CBM-ORF: Preparation
When assessing a student's Oral Reading Fluency skills, the examiner chooses 3 grade-appropriate passages. For children in the 1st and 2nd grades, each passage should be at least 150 words long, while passages of at least 250 words should be prepared for older students. Passages selected should not contain too much dialog and should avoid an excessive number of foreign words or phrases. In addition, only prose passages should be used in CBM assessments. Poetry and drama should be avoided because they tend to vary considerably and do not represent the kind of text typically encountered by students.

For ease of administration, the instructor will want to prepare examiner and student copies of each passage. Ideally, reading passages should be free of illustrations that may help a child to interpret the content of the text. The examiner copy should have a cumulative word total listed along the right margin of the passage for ease of scoring (see Figure 1).

It is strongly recommended that teachers use existing collections of well-constructed, reading passages organized by grade-level when conducting Oral Reading Fluency assessments. Here are 3 sources for free CBM-ORF materials:

DIBELS NEXT: Schools can obtain free ORF passages and ORF benchmark norms for grades 1-6 from the DIBELS Next website: *http://dibels.org/next.html*

Figure 1: Example of CBM Oral Reading Fluency Probe

Examiner Copy		Student Copy
Summertime! How lovely it was in the country, with	9	Summertime! How lovely it was in the country, with
the wheat standing yellow, the oats green, and the hay all	20	the wheat standing yellow, the oats green, and the hay all
stacked down in the grassy meadows! And there went the stork	31	stacked down in the grassy meadows! And there went the stork
on his long red legs, chattering away in Egyptian, for	41	on his long red legs, chattering away in Egyptian, for
he had learned that language from his mother. The fields and	52	he had learned that language from his mother. The fields and

---

EasyCBM: The easyCBM website (http://easycbm.com/) has collections of CBM-ORF passages (referred to as 'Passage Fluency') for grades 1-8. Teachers can create a free account on this website to access materials and benchmark norms.

Schools can also make their own CBM Oral Reading Fluency passages in PDF format based on text typed in by the user using the Reading Fluency Passages Generator, a free online application: *http://www.interventioncentral.org/teacher-resources/oral-reading-fluency-passages-generator*

CBM-ORF: Directions for Administration (Hosp, Hosp, & Howell, 2007; Wright, 2007)

1. The examiner and the student sit across the table from each other. The examiner hands the student the unnumbered copy of the CBM reading passage. The examiner takes the numbered copy of the passage, shielding it from the student's view.
2. The examiner says to the student: "When I say, 'begin', start reading aloud at the top of this page. Read across the page [demonstrate by pointing]. Try to read each word. If you come to a word you don't know, I'll tell it to you. Be sure to do your best reading. Are there any questions? [Pause] Begin."
3. The examiner starts the stopwatch when the student says the first word. If the student does not say the initial word within 3 seconds, the examiner says the word and starts the stopwatch.
4. As the student reads along in the text, the examiner records any errors by marking a slash (/) through the incorrectly read word. If the student hesitates for 3 seconds on any word, the examiner says the word and marks it as an error.
5. At the end of 1 minute, the examiner says, "Stop" and marks the student's concluding place in the text with a bracket ( ]).
6. *Initial Assessment:* If the examiner is assessing the student for the first time, the examiner administers a total of 3 reading passages during the session using the above procedures and takes the median (middle) score as the best estimate of the student's oral reading fluency.
    Progress-Monitoring: If the examiner is monitoring student growth in oral reading fluency (and has previously collected ORF data), only one reading passage is given in the session.

CBM-ORF: Directions for Practice

If the student is not yet familiar with CBM-Oral Reading Fluency probes, the teacher can administer one or more practice ORF probes (using the administration guidelines above) and provide coaching and feedback as needed until assured that the student fully understands the assessment.

CBM-ORF: Scoring Guidelines

Reading fluency is calculated by first determining the total words attempted within the timed reading probe and then deducting from that total the number of incorrectly read words.

The following scoring rules will aid the instructor in marking the reading probe:
- Words read correctly are scored as correct:
- Self-corrected words are counted as correct.
- Repetitions are counted as correct.
- Examples of dialectical speech are counted as correct.
- Inserted words are ignored.
- Words read to the student by the examiner after 3 seconds are counted as errors.
- Mispronunciations are counted as errors.
    Example

Text: The small gray fox ran to the cover of the trees.
Student: *"The smill gray fox ran to the cover of the trees."*

- Substitutions are counted as errors.
  Example
  Text: When she returned to the **house**, Grandmother called for Franchesca.
  Student: *"When she returned to the **home**, Grandmother called for Franchesca."*

- Omissions are counted as errors.
  Example
  Text: Anna could not compete in the last race.
  Student: *"Anna could not in the last race."*

- Transpositions of word-pairs are counted as a single error.
  Example
  Text: She looked at the bright, shining face of the sun.
  Student: *"She looked at the shining, bright face of the sun."*

Computing reading-fluency rate in a single passage

The scoring of a reading probe is straightforward. The examiner first determines how many words the reader actually attempted during the 1-minute reading sample. On the completed probe in Figure 2, for instance, the bracket near the end of the text indicates that the student attempted 48 words before his time expired. Next, the examiner counts up the number of errors made by the reader. On this probe, the student committed 4 errors. By deducting the number of errors from the total words attempted, the examiner arrives at the number of correctly read words per minute. This number serves as an estimate of reading fluency, combining as it does the student's speed and accuracy in reading. So by deducting the errors from total words attempted, we find that the child actually read 44 correct words in 1 minute.

Figure 2: Example of a scored reading probe

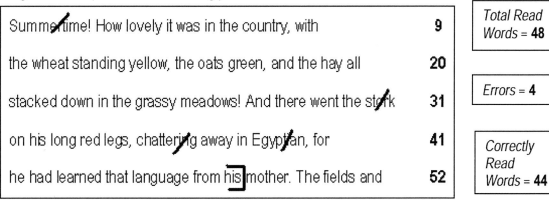

Accommodating omissions when scoring. . .

When a student skips several connected words or even an entire line during a reading probe, that omission creates a special scoring dilemma. An omission, after all, is considered to be a single error of tracking, no matter how many words were skipped at one time. However, if all words omitted in a line were individually counted as errors, the student's error rate would be greatly inflated. The solution is for the examiner to subtract all but one of the words in each omission before computing the total words attempted.

Let's see how that score adjustment would work. On the completed probe in Figure 3, the student omitted the text of an entire line while reading aloud. The examiner drew a line through all the connected words skipped by the child in that omitted line of text. Because a total of 11 words were omitted, the examiner drops 10 of those words before calculating the total words attempted.

When calculating the number of words the child attempted to read, the examiner notes that the child reached word 48 in the passage. Ten words are then deducted from the omitted lines to avoid inflating the error count. The adjusted figure for total words attempted is found to be 38 words. The child committed 5 errors (4 marked by slashes and 1 omission). These errors are subtracted from the revised figure of 38 total words attempted. Therefore, the number of correctly read words in this example would be 33.

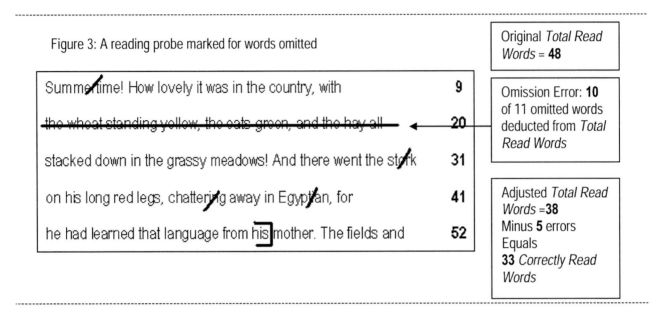

Figure 3: A reading probe marked for words omitted

Original *Total Read Words* = **48**

Omission Error: **10** of 11 omitted words deducted from *Total Read Words*

Adjusted *Total Read Words* =**38**
Minus **5** errors
Equals
33 *Correctly Read Words*

References

Hosp, M. K., Hosp, J. L., & Howell, K. W. (2007). *The ABC's of CBM: A practical guide to curriculum-based measurement.* New York: Guilford Press.

Wright, J. (2007). The *RTI toolkit: A practical guide for schools.* Port Chester, NY: National Professional Resources, Inc.

Curriculum-Based Measurement: Oral Reading Fluency Norms (Hasbrouck & Tindal, 2005)*

CBM-Oral Reading Fluency assesses general reading performance (Espin et al., 2010), as well as reading speed. In an oral reading fluency assessment, the student reads aloud from a passage for 1 minute. The reading sample is scored for words read correctly (WRC) and errors.

Grade	Percentile	Fall Oral Reading Fluency (Hasbrouck & Tindal, 2005)	Winter Oral Reading Fluency (Hasbrouck & Tindal, 2005)	Spring Oral Reading Fluency (Hasbrouck & Tindal, 2005)	Weekly Growth (Hasbrouck & Tindal, 2005)
1	50%ile		23	53	1.9
1	25%ile		12	28	1.0
1	10%ile		6	15	0.6
2	50%ile	51	72	89	1.2
2	25%ile	25	42	61	1.1
2	10%ile	11	18	31	0.6
3	50%ile	71	92	107	1.1
3	25%ile	44	62	78	1.1
3	10%ile	21	36	48	0.8
4	50%ile	94	112	123	0.9
4	25%ile	68	87	98	0.9
4	10%ile	45	61	72	0.8
5	50%ile	110	127	139	0.9
5	25%ile	85	99	109	0.8
5	10%ile	61	74	83	0.7
6	50%ile	127	140	150	0.7
6	25%ile	98	111	122	0.8
6	10%ile	68	82	93	0.8
7	50%ile	128	136	150	0.7
7	25%ile	102	109	123	0.7
7	10%ile	79	88	98	0.6
8	50%ile	133	146	151	0.6
8	25%ile	106	115	124	0.6
8	10%ile	77	84	97	0.6

References:

- Espin, C. Wallace, T., Lembke, E., Campbell, H., & Long, J. D. (2010). Creating a progress-monitoring system in reading for middle-school students: Tracking progress toward meeting high-stakes standards. *Learning Disabilities Research & Practice, 25*(2), 60-75.
- Hasbrouck, J., & Tindal, G. (2005). Oral *reading fluency: 90 years of measurement.* Eugene, OR: Behavioral Research & Teaching/University of Oregon. Retrieved from http://brt.uoregon.edu

*Reported Characteristics of Student Sample(s) Used to Compile These Norms:

- **Hasbrouck & Tindal, 2005:** *Number of Students Assessed:* 88167 students in fall norming;97237 students in winter norming; 112118 students in spring norming/*Geographical Location:* Nationwide/ *Socioeconomic Status:* Not reported / *Ethnicity of Sample:* Not reported/*Limited English Proficiency in Sample:* Not reported.

Where to Find Materials: Here are 3 sources for free CBM-Oral Reading Fluency materials:

DIBELS NEXT: Schools can obtain free ORF passages and ORF benchmarks for grades 1-6 from the DIBELS Next website: http://dibels.org/next.html

EasyCBM: The easyCBM website (http://easycbm.com/) has collections of CBM-ORF passages (referred to as 'Passage Fluency') for grades 1-8. Teachers can create a free account on this website to access materials and benchmarks.

Schools can also make their own CBM Oral Reading Fluency passages in PDF format based on text typed in by the user using the Reading Fluency Passages Generator, a free online application:
http://www.interventioncentral.org/teacher-resources/oral-reading-fluency-passages-generator

How To: Assess Reading Comprehension with CBM—Maze Passages

A student's ability to comprehend text requires the presence of a bundle of component reading skills, including strong reading vocabulary, fluent decoding, and use of efficient and effective 'fix-up' strategies when encountering unknown words (National Institute of Child Health and Human Development, 2000). Motivation and attentiveness also play important roles in reading comprehension. While a student's understanding of text depends on many factors, however, teachers need a simple, time-efficient method both to screen students for reading-comprehension problems and to monitor the progress of any student who is receiving an academic intervention to improve text comprehension.

Curriculum-Based Measurement-Maze is a tool ideally suited to assess student reading comprehension (Parker, Hasbrouck, & Tindal, 1992). The student is given a specially formatted sample of text. The first sentence of the Maze passage is left intact. In the remainder of the passage, every seventh word is selected to be incorporated into a response item that consists of the original word plus two foils (words that would not make sense if substituted in the passage in place of the original, correct word). These three choices are randomly arranged and inserted back into the text. When reading the Maze passage, the reader reviews each response item and circles the word from the three choices that best restores the meaning of that segment of the passage.

Maze passages have been found to be better predictors of future reading performance than CBM oral reading fluency probes for students in grades 4 and higher (Hosp, Hosp & Howell, 2007).

CBM-Maze: How to Access Resources. Teachers can access a toolkit of resources for CBM-Maze, including: (1) materials for assessment, (2) guidelines for administration and scoring, and (3) research-based norms.

- *Materials for assessment.* Schools can access free Maze assessments with accompanying benchmarks for grades 2-6 at the DIBELS Next website: *http://dibels.org/next.html* Note: Users must create an account before they can download materials.

  Using the Maze Passage Generator, a free online application, teachers can generate their own CBM maze passages in PDF format from text typed in by the user:

  http://www.interventioncentral.org/teacher-resources/test-of-reading-comprehension

- *Guidelines for administration and scoring.* Instructions for preparing, administering, and scoring CBM-Maze assessments appear later in this document:

- *Research-based norms.* A table, *Curriculum-Based Measurement: Maze Passage Fluency Norms,* is included in this document. The norms include fluency benchmarks for grades 2-6 (Jenkins & Jewell, 1993; Graney, Missall, Martinez, & Bergstrom, 2009) and accompanying weekly growth norms (Fuchs et al., 1993).

References

Hosp, M.K., Hosp, J. L., & Howell, K. W. (2007). *The ABCs of CBM.* New York: Guilford.

National Institute of Child Health and Human Development. (2000). *Report of the National Reading Panel. Teaching children to read: An evidence-based assessment of the scientific research literature on reading and its implications for reading instruction* (NIH Publication No. 00-4769). Washington, DC: U.S. Government Printing Office.

Parker, R., Hasbrouck, J. E., & Tindal, G. (1992). The maze as a classroom-based reading measure: Construction methods, reliability, and validity. Journal of Special Education, 26 (2), 195-218.

Curriculum-Based Measurement-Maze: Guidelines for Use

CBM-Maze: Description

CBM-Maze passages are timed (3-minute) reading comprehension assessments with a multiple-choice response format. The student reads and completes the passage silently. CBM-Maze can be administered to a single student, a small group, or an entire class (Espin et al., 2010).

CBM-Maze: Materials
The following materials are needed to administer CBM-Maze passages:

- Student and examiner copies of CBM Maze passage (the process for creating Maze passages is described below)
- Stopwatch
- Pencils for students

CBM-Maze: Preparation
Before administering CBM-Maze, the teacher creates or obtains a Maze passage, using these guidelines (Espin et al., 2010):
- Passages used for Maze should provide sufficient reading material to occupy students for 3 minutes of silent reading. Samples should be at least 300 words in length.
- The first sentence of the Maze passage is left intact.
- In the text following the first sentence, every seventh word is selected to be incorporated into a response item that consists of the original word plus two foils (words that would not make sense if substituted in the passage in place of the original, correct word). These three choices are randomly arranged and inserted back into the text. Here is a sample of a Maze response item: *The rain (sang, cement, fell) on the garden.*

Schools can obtain free Maze passages and Maze benchmarks for grades 2-6 from the DIBELS Next website: *http://dibels.org/next.html*

Schools can also obtain their own CBM Maze passages in PDF format based on text typed in by the user by accessing the Maze Passage Generator, a free online application: *http://www.interventioncentral.org/teacher-resources/test-of-reading-comprehension*

CBM-Maze: Directions for Administration (adapted from Sarasti, 2009)

1. The examiner distributes copies of CBM Maze probes to all the students in the group.
2. The examiner says: "When I say 'begin', start reading the story silently. Wherever you come to a group of 3 word-choices, circle the word that makes sense. Work as fast as you can but do your best work. If you finish the first page, go to the next page and continue working until I tell you to stop."
3. The examiner says: "Ready? Begin" and starts the stopwatch.
4. After 3 minutes, the examiner stops the stopwatch and says:"Stop. Pencils down".
5. These directions are repeated for each Maze passage administered in a session. The examiner then collects and scores the passages.
6. *Initial Assessment:* If the examiner is assessing the student for the first time, the examiner administers a total of 3 Maze probes during the session, using the above procedures and takes the median (middle) score as the best estimate of the student's reading-comprehension skills.
Progress-Monitoring: If the examiner is monitoring student growth in computation (and has previously collected Maze data), only one Maze probe is given in the session.

CBM-Maze: Directions for Practice

If students are not yet familiar with the Maze, use the Maze practice page and accompanying examiner directions appearing later in this document to ensure student understanding of the activity before administering the assessment.

CBM-Maze: Scoring Guidelines

The examiner adds up the total number of correct responses, giving the student credit for each Maze choice-item in which the correct word is circled.

References

Espin, C. Wallace, T., Lembke, E., Campbell, H., & Long, J. D. (2010). Creating a progress-monitoring system in reading for middle-school students: Tracking progress toward meeting high-stakes standards. *Learning Disabilities Research & Practice, 25*(2), 60-75.

Sarasti, I. A. (2009). *An investigation of the reliability and validity of curriculum-based measurement maze probes: A comparison of 1-minute, 2-minute, and 3-minute time frames.* Unpublished doctoral dissertation, Temple University, Philadelphia, PA.

CBM-Maze: Directions for Practice (adapted from Sarasti, 2009)

If students are not yet familiar with the Maze, use the Maze practice page and these examiner directions to ensure student understanding of the assessment activity:

1. The examiner hands out copies of the Maze practice page to students.

2. The examiner says: "We will practice a story together. Look at the practice page. Read the first sentence to yourself while I read it aloud: *The rain (sang, cement, fell) on the garden.* The three choices are sang, cement, fell.

   The rain sang on the garden. That sentence does not make sense.
   The rain cement on the garden. That sentence does not make sense.
   So the correct word to circle is *fell.*"

   [The examiner scans the group to ensure that all students circle the correct word before continuing.]

3. The examiner says: "Now go to the next sentence on the practice page. Read it to yourself while I read it aloud: *The teacher walked (quickly, blue, trust) down the hall.* Which word is the correct choice to complete the sentence?

   [Ensure that students chorally give the correct response before continuing.]

   That's right: *The teacher walked quickly down the hall* is correct, so circle the word *quickly.*"

4. The examiner says: "Now read the next sentence on your practice page to yourself. Raise your hand when you have the answer.

   [When students are ready, the examiner reads the practice sentence with correct answer: *The ship sailed (blank, toward, eight) the port.*]

   Yes, the correct sentence is *The ship sailed toward the port.* Now that you have chosen the correct word, what do you do?"

   [The students should say "Circle it." The examiner ensures that all students fully understand the Maze response task.]

   Yes, you circle the correct word. You are ready to do the next story on your own."

CBM-Maze: Practice Page

1. The rain (sang, cement, fell) on the garden.

2. The teacher walked (quickly, blue, trust) down the hall.

3. The ship sailed (blank, toward, eight) the port.

Curriculum-Based Measurement: Maze Passage Fluency Norms
(Fuchs, Fuchs, Hamlett, Waltz, & Germann, 1993; Graney, Missall, Martinez, & Bergstrom, 2009; Jenkins & Jewell, 1993)*

CBM-Maze assesses basic student reading comprehension. In a Maze assessment, the student is given a passage in which every seventh word has been selected as a choice item. The student reads the passage silently. Each time the student comes to a choice item, the student chooses from among 3 replacement words: the correct word and two distractors. The student circles the replacement word that he or she believes best restores the meaning of the text. The Maze is timed: while the length of Maze assessments can vary, the most common time-standard is 3 minutes (Graney et al., 2009).

Grade	Fall Maze (Jenkins & Jewell, 1993)	Fall:+/-1 SD (≈16th%ile to 84th%ile)	Spring Maze (Jenkins & Jewell, 1993)	Spring: +/-1 SD (≈16th%ile to 84th%ile)	Weekly Growth (Fuchs et al., 1993)
2	6	1↔11	15	7↔23	0.40

Grade	Fall Maze (Graney et al., 2009)	Fall:+/-1 SD (≈16th%ile to 84th%ile)	Winter Maze (Graney et al., 2009)	Winter: +/-1 SD (≈16th%ile to 84th%ile)	Spring Maze (Graney et al., 2009)	Spring: +/-1 SD (≈16th%ile to 84th%ile)	Weekly Growth (Fuchs et al., 1993)
3	13	7↔19	14	8↔20	15	9↔21	0.40
4	14	9↔19	21	12↔30	20	12↔28	0.40
5	18	11↔25	22	14↔30	26	18↔34	0.40

Grade	Fall Maze (Jenkins & Jewell, 1993)	Fall:+/-1 SD (≈16th%ile to 84th%ile)	Spring Maze (Jenkins & Jewell, 1993)	Spring: +/-1 SD (≈16th%ile to 84th%ile)	Weekly Growth (Fuchs et al., 1993)
6	33	22↔44	39	26↔52	0.40

References:

- Fuchs, L. S., Fuchs, D., Hamlett, C. L., Waltz, L., & Germann, G. (1993). Formative evaluation of academic progress: How much growth can we expect? *School Psychology Review, 22,* 27–48.
- Graney, S. B., Missall, K. N., Martinez, R. S., & Bergstrom, M. (2009). A preliminary investigation of within-year growth patterns in reading and mathematics curriculum-based measures. *Journal of School Psychology, 47,* 121-142.
- Jenkins, J. R., & Jewell, M. (1993). Examining the validity of two measures for formative teaching: Read aloud and maze. *Exceptional Children, 59,* 421-432.

*Reported Characteristics of Student Sample(s) Used to Compile These Norms:

- **Fuchs et al., 1993:** *Number of Students Assessed:* 257 students across grades 2-6/ *Geographical Location:* Upper Midwest: Sample drawn from 5 elementary schools/ *Socioeconomic Status:* 33%-55% rate of Free & Reduced Lunch across participating schools/ *Ethnicity of Sample:* Not reported/ *Limited English Proficiency in Sample:* Not reported.

- **Graney, 2009:** *Number of Students Assessed:* Average of 444 students in each year of this 2-year study.; Grade 3: 151; Grade 4: 149; Grade 5: 144/ *Geographical Location:* Midwest: Sample drawn from grades 3-5 in one rural school: 8 classrooms in grade 3; 7 classrooms in grade 4; 7 classrooms in grade 5/ *Socioeconomic Status:* 31% Free & Reduced Lunch/ *Ethnicity of Sample:* 93% White; 4% Multiracial; 2% African-American; 1% Latino/ *Limited English Proficiency in Sample:* Not reported.

- **Jenkins & Jewell, 1993:** *Number of Students Assessed:* Grade 2: 47; Grade 6: 125/ *Geographical Location:* Pacific Northwest: Sample drawn from grades 2 & 6 in two elementary schools/ *Socioeconomic Status:* 33% Free & Reduced Lunch/ *Ethnicity of Sample:* Not reported/ *Limited English Proficiency in Sample:* Not reported.

Where to Find Materials: Schools can access free Maze assessments with accompanying benchmarks for grades 2-6 at the DIBELS Next website: *http://dibels.org/next.html* Note: Users must create an account before they can download materials.

Teachers can also create their own CBM Maze passages in PDF format based on text typed in by the user using the Maze Passage Generator, a free online application:
http://www.interventioncentral.org/teacher-resources/test-of-reading-comprehension

Limitations of These Research Norms: Norms generated from small-scale research studies--like those used here--provide estimates of student academic performance based on a sampling from only one or two points in time, rather than a more comprehensive sampling across separate fall, winter, and spring screenings. These norms also have been compiled from a relatively small student sample that is not fully representative of a diverse 'national' population. Nonetheless, norms such as these are often the best information that is publically available for basic academic skills and therefore do have a definite place in classroom instruction decision-making.

These norms can be useful in general education for setting student performance outcome goals for core instruction and/or any level of academic intervention. Similarly, these norms can be used to set performance goals for students with special needs. In both cases, however, single-sample norms would be used only if more comprehensive fall/winter/spring academic performance norms are not available.

How To: Assess Early Math Difficulties in the Primary Grades with CBM

In the early elementary grades, students' success in mathematics can be predicted by assessing their acquisition and use of foundation numeracy skills (Gersten, Jordan, & Flojo, 2005). The term *number sense* is often used as short-hand to describe a child's emerging grasp of fundamental mathematical concepts such as what numbers mean, how sets of objects can be described in numerical terms, counting, and simple operations of mental arithmetic (Chard et al, 2005). *Number sense* is difficult to define with precision because the descriptor encompasses a wide range of early math skills (Clarke & Shinn, 2004). By the time a student has entered kindergarten or 1st grade, however, this term can be framed more concretely as a student's ability to access and use a mental number-line.

In the primary grades, the Common Core State Standards in Mathematics are built on the assumption that the successful math student can rapidly access a mental number line for use in such applied mathematical tasks as counting, making accurate comparisons between number, and estimating amounts. For example, a Kindergarten Counting & Cardinality standard (CCSM.K.CC.2) states that a student will "count forward beginning from a given number within the known sequence (instead of having to begin at 1)." (National Governors Association Center for Best Practices et al., 2010; p. 11). Similarly, a Grade 1 standard for Number & Operations in Base 10 (CCSM.1.NBT.1) sets as a student goal to "count to 120, starting at any number less than 120. " (National Governors Association Center for Best Practices et al., 2010; p. 15). Clearly, these and other math standards for the early grades must depend on students' ability to envision and mentally manipulate an internal number-line.

Early Math Fluency Measures: What They Are. Teachers at the primary level have a pressing need for screening tools that can quickly identify those students who require additional instructional support to address deficient number-sense skills. Early Math Fluency measures are one useful means to assess the strength of a young student's 'number sense' (Chard, et al., 2005) and serve as good predictors of mathematical readiness at Kindergarten and Grade 1. Early Math Fluency measures are examples of Curriculum-Based Measurement (Hosp, Hosp, & Howell, 2007) and include Quantity Discrimination, Missing Number, and Number Identification. All Early Math Fluency assessments have an administration time of 1 minute. Here are brief descriptions for three of these measures:

- *Quantity Discrimination:* The student is presented with pairs of numbers randomly sampled from 1-20 and must identify the larger number in each pair.

- *Missing Number:* The student is presented with response items consisting of 3 sequential numbers with one of those numbers randomly left blank. (Each 3-number series is randomly generated from the pool of numbers 1-20.) The student attempts to name the missing number in each series.

- *Number Identification:* The student is presented with a randomly generated series of numbers ranging from 1-20 and names as many of those numbers aloud as time allows.

Early Math Fluency Measures: How to Access Resources. Teachers who would like to screen their Kindergarten and Grade 1 students for possible number-sense delays can obtain these free Early Math Fluency assessment resources: (1) materials for assessment, (2) guidelines for administration and scoring, and (3) research-based norms.

- *Materials for assessment.* Schools can create their own CBM Early Math Fluency assessment materials at no cost, using NumberFly, a free online application:

  http://www.interventioncentral.org/tools/early-math-fluency-generator

- *Guidelines for administration and scoring.* The following sets of instructions for preparing, administering, and scoring Early Math Fluency assessments appear later in this document:

  - *Early Math Fluency/Quantity Discrimination: Guidelines for Use*
  - *Math Fluency/Missing Number: Guidelines for Use*
  - *Math Fluency/Number Identification: Guidelines for Use*

- *Research-based norms.* A table, *Curriculum-Based Measurement: Early Mathematics Fluency Norms*, is included in this document. These fluency benchmarks were researched by Chard et al. (2005) and provide Fall/Winter/Spring screening norms for Quantity Discrimination, Missing Number, and Number Identification.

References

Chard, D. J., Clarke, B., Baker, S., Otterstedt, J., Braun, D., & Katz, R. (2005). Using measures of number sense to screen for difficulties in mathematics: Preliminary findings. *Assessment for Effective Intervention, 30*(3), 3-14.

Clarke, B., & Shinn, M. (2004). A preliminary investigation into the identification and development of early mathematics curriculum-based measurement. *School Psychology Review, 33*, 234–248.

Gersten, R., Jordan, N. C., & Flojo, J. R. (2005). Early identification and interventions for students with mathematics difficulties. *Journal of Learning Disabilities, 38*, 293-304.

Hosp, M.K., Hosp, J. L., & Howell, K. W. (2007). *The ABCs of CBM.* New York: Guilford.

National Governors Association Center for Best Practices & Council of Chief State School Officers. (2010). *Common core state standards for mathematics.* Washington, DC: Authors. Retrieved from http://www.corestandards.org/

Early Math Fluency/Quantity Discrimination: Guidelines for Use

This introduction to the Quantity Discrimination probe provides information about the preparation, administration, and scoring of this Early Math CBM measure. Additionally, it offers brief guidelines for integrating this assessment into a school-wide 'Response-to-Intervention' model.

Quantity Discrimination: Description (Clarke & Shinn, 2004; Gersten, Jordan & Flojo, 2005)
The student is given a sheet containing pairs of numbers. In each number pair, one number is larger than the other. The numbers in each pair are selected from within a predefined range (e.g., no lower than 1 and no higher than 20). During a one-minute timed assessment, the student identifies the larger number in each pair, completing as many items as possible while the examiner records any Quantity Discrimination errors.

Quantity Discrimination: Preparation
The following materials are needed to administer Quantity Discrimination (QD) Early Math CBM probes:

- Student and examiner copies of a QD assessment probe. (**Note:** Customized QD probes can be created conveniently and at no cost using Numberfly, a web-based application. Visit Numberfly at *http://www.interventioncentral.org/php/numberfly/numberfly.php*).

- A pencil, pen, or marker

- A stopwatch

Quantity Discrimination: Directions for Administration
1. The examiner sits with the student in a quiet area without distractions. The examiner sits at a table across from the student.

2. The examiner says to the student:

   "The sheet on your desk has pairs of numbers. In each set, one number is bigger than the other."

   "When I say, 'start,' tell me the name of the number that is larger in each pair. Start at the top of this page and work across the page [demonstrate by pointing]. *Try to figure out the larger number for each example.. When you come to the end of a row, go to the next row. Are there any questions?* [Pause] *Start."*

   NOTE: If the student has difficulties with speech production, the examiner can use this alternate wording for directions: *"When I say, 'start,' point to the number that is larger in each pair"*

3. The examiner begins the stopwatch when the student responds aloud to the first item. If the student hesitates on a number for 3 seconds or longer on a Quantity Discrimination item, the examiner says, *"Go to the next one."* (If necessary, the examiner points to the next number as a student prompt.)

4. The examiner marks each Quantity Discrimination error by marking a slash (/) through the incorrect response item on the examiner form.

5. At the end of one minute, the examiner says, *"Stop"* and writes in a right-bracket symbol ( ]) on the examiner form after the last item that the student had attempted when the time expired. The examiner then collects the student Quantity Discrimination sheet.

6. *Initial Assessment:* If the examiner is assessing the student for the first time, the examiner administers a total of 3 QD probes during the session using the above procedures and takes the median (middle) score as the best estimate of the student's QD skills.

   Progress-Monitoring: If the examiner is monitoring student growth in QD (and has previously collected QD data), only one QD probe is given in the session.

Quantity Discrimination: Directions for Practice

If the student is not yet familiar with QD probes, the teacher can administer one or more practice assessments (using the administration guidelines above) and provide coaching and feedback as needed until assured that the student fully understands the assessment.

Quantity Discrimination: Scoring Guidelines

Correct QD responses include:

- Quantity Discriminations read correctly
- Quantity Discriminations read incorrectly but corrected by the student within 3 seconds

Incorrect QD responses include:

- The student's reading the smaller number in the QD number pair
- Correct QD responses given after hesitations of 3 seconds or longer
- The student's calling out a number other than appears in the QD number pair
- Response items skipped by the student

To calculate a Quantity Discrimination fluency score, the examiner:

1. counts up all QD items that the student attempted to answer and
2. subtracts the number of QD errors from the total number attempted.
3. The resulting figure is the number of correct Quantity Discrimination items completed.(QD fluency score).

Quantity Discrimination Probes as Part of a Response to Intervention Model

- Universal Screening: To proactively identify children who may have deficiencies in development of foundation math concepts, or 'number sense' (Berch, 2005), schools may choose to screen all kindergarten and first grade students using Quantity Discrimination probes. Those screenings would take place in fall, winter, and spring. Students who fall below the 'cutpoint' of the 35th percentile (e.g., Gersten, Jordan & Flojo, 2005).of the grade norms on the QD task would be identified as having moderate deficiencies and given additional interventions to build their 'number sense' skills.

- Tier I (Classroom-Based) Interventions: Teachers can create Quantity Discrimination probes and use them independently to track the progress of students who show modest delays in their math foundation skills.

- Tier II (Individualized) Interventions. Students with more extreme academic delays may be referred to a school-based problem-solving team, which will develop more intensive, specialized interventions to target the student's academic deficits (Wright, 2007). Quantity Discrimination probes can be used as one formative measure to track student progress with Tier II interventions to build foundation math skills.

Quantity Discrimination: Measurement Statistics

Test-Retest Reliability Correlations for Quantity Discrimination Probes		
Time Span	*Correlation*	*Reference*
13-week interval	**0.85**	Clarke & Shinn (2004)
26-week interval	**0.86**	Clarke & Shinn (2004)

Predictive Validity Correlations for Quantity Discrimination Probes		
Predictive Validity Measure	*Correlation*	*Reference*
Curriculum-Based Measurement Math Computation Fluency Probes: Grade 1 Addition & Subtraction (Fall Administration of QD Probe and Spring Administration of Math Computation Probe)	**0.67**	Clarke & Shinn (2004)
Woodcock-Johnson Tests of Achievement: Applied Problems subtest (Fall Administration of QD Probe and Spring Administration of WJ-ACH subtest)	**0.79**	Clarke & Shinn (2004)
Number Knowledge Test	**0.53**	Chard, Clarke, Baker, Otterstedt, Braun & Katz.(2005) cited in Gersten, Jordan & Flojo (2005)

References

Chard, D. J., Clarke, B., Baker, S., Otterstedt, J., Braun, D., & Katz, R. (2005). Using measures of number sense to screen for difficulties in mathematics: Preliminary findings. *Assessment For Effective Intervention, 30*(2), 3-14.

Clarke, B., & Shinn, M. (2004). A preliminary investigation into the identification and development of early mathematics curriculum-based measurement. *School Psychology Review, 33*, 234–248.

Gersten, R., Jordan, N.C., & Flojo, J.R. (2005). Early identification and interventions for students with mathematics difficulties. *Journal of Learning Disabilities, 38*, 293-304.

Berch, D. B. (2005). Making sense of number sense: Implications for children with mathematical disabilities. *Journal of Learning Disabilities, 38*, 333-339..

Wright, J. (2007). *The RTI toolkit: A practical guide for schools.* Port Chester, NY: National Professional Resources, Inc.

Early Math Fluency/Missing Number: Guidelines for Use

This introduction to the Missing Number probe provides information about the preparation, administration, and scoring of this Early Math CBM measure. Additionally, it offers brief guidelines for integrating this assessment into a school-wide 'Response-to-Intervention' model.

Missing Number: Description (Clarke & Shinn, 2004; Gersten, Jordan & Flojo, 2005)
The student is given a sheet containing multiple number series. Each series consists of 3-4 numbers that appear in sequential order. The numbers in each short series are selected to fall within a predefined range (e.g., no lower than 1 and no higher than 20). In each series, one number is left blank (e.g., '1 2 _ 4').During a one-minute timed assessment, the student states aloud the missing number in as many response items as possible while the examiner records any Missing Number errors.

Missing Number: Preparation
The following materials are needed to administer Missing Number (MN) Early Math CBM probes:

- Student and examiner copies of a MN assessment probe. (**Note:** Customized MN probes can be created conveniently and at no cost using Numberfly, a web-based application. Visit Numberfly at *http://www.interventioncentral.org/php/numberfly/numberfly.php*).

- A pencil, pen, or marker

- A stopwatch

Missing Number: Directions for Administration
1. The examiner sits with the student in a quiet area without distractions. The examiner sits at a table across from the student.

2. The examiner says to the student:

    "The sheet on your desk has sets of numbers. In each set, a number is missing."

    "When I say, 'start,' tell me the name of the number that is missing from each set of numbers. Start at the top of this page and work across the page [demonstrate by pointing]. *Try to figure out the missing number for each example.. When you come to the end of a row, go to the next row. Are there any questions?* [Pause] *Start. "*

    NOTE: If the student has difficulties with speech production, the examiner can give the student a pencil and use this alternate wording for directions: *"When I say, 'start, write in the number that is missing from each set of numbers."*

3. The examiner begins the stopwatch when the student reads the first number aloud. If the student hesitates on a number for 3 seconds or longer on a Missing Number item, the examiner says the correct number aloud and says, *"Go to the next one."* (If necessary, the examiner points to the next number as a student prompt.)

4. The examiner marks each Missing Number error by marking a slash (/) through the incorrect response item on the examiner form.

5. At the end of one minute, the examiner says, *"Stop"* and writes in a right-bracket symbol ( ]) on the examiner form after the last item that the student had attempted when the time expired. The examiner then collects the student Missing Number sheet.

6. *Initial Assessment:* If the examiner is assessing the student for the first time, the examiner administers a total of 3 MN probes during the session using the above procedures and takes the median (middle) score as the best estimate of the student's MN skills.
   Progress-Monitoring: If the examiner is monitoring student growth in MN (and has previously collected MN data), only one MN probe is given in the session.

Missing Number: Directions for Practice

If the student is not yet familiar with MN assessments, the teacher can administer one or more practice MN probes (using the administration guidelines above) and provide coaching and feedback as needed until assured that the student fully understands the assessment.

Missing Number: Scoring Guidelines
Correct MN responses include:

- Missing numbers read correctly
- Missing numbers read incorrectly but corrected by the student within 3 seconds

Incorrect MN responses include:

- Missing numbers read incorrectly
- Missing numbers read correctly after hesitations of 3 seconds or longer
- Response items skipped by the student

To calculate a Missing Number fluency score, the examiner:

1. counts up all MN items that the student attempted to read aloud and
2. subtracts the number of MN errors from the total number attempted.
3. The resulting figure is the number of correct Missing Number items completed.(MN fluency score).

Missing Number Probes as Part of a Response to Intervention Model
- Universal Screening: To proactively identify children who may have deficiencies in development of foundation math concepts, or 'number sense' (Berch, 2005), schools may choose to screen all kindergarten and first grade students using Missing Number probes. Those screenings would take place in fall, winter, and spring. Students who fall below the 'cutpoint' of the 35th percentile (e.g., Gersten, Jordan & Flojo, 2005).of the grade norms on the MN task would be identified as having moderate deficiencies and given additional interventions to build their 'number sense' skills.

- Tier I (Classroom-Based) Interventions: Teachers can create Missing Number probes and use them independently to track the progress of students who show modest delays in their math foundation skills.

- Tier II (Individualized) Interventions. Students with more extreme academic delays may be referred to a school-based problem-solving team, which will develop more intensive, specialized interventions to target the student's academic deficits (Wright, 2007). Missing Number probes can be used as one formative measure to track student progress with Tier II interventions to build foundation math skills.

Missing Number: Measurement Statistics

Test-Retest Reliability Correlations for Missing Number Probes		
Time Span	*Correlation*	*Reference*
13-week interval	**0.79**	Clarke & Shinn (2004)
26-week interval	**0.81**	Clarke & Shinn (2004)

Predictive Validity Correlations for Missing Number Probes		
Predictive Validity Measure	*Correlation*	*Reference*
Curriculum-Based Measurement Math Computation Fluency Probes: Grade 1 Addition & Subtraction (Fall Administration of MN Probe and Spring Administration of Math Computation Probe)	**0.67**	Clarke & Shinn (2004)
Woodcock-Johnson Tests of Achievement: Applied Problems subtest (Fall Administration of MNF Probe and Spring Administration of WJ-ACH subtest)	**0.72**	Clarke & Shinn (2004)
Number Knowledge Test	**0.61**	Chard, Clarke, Baker, Otterstedt, Braun & Katz.(2005) cited in Gersten, Jordan & Flojo (2005)

References

Chard, D. J., Clarke, B., Baker, S., Otterstedt, J., Braun, D., & Katz, R. (2005). Using measures of number sense to screen for difficulties in mathematics: Preliminary findings. *Assessment For Effective Intervention, 30*(2), 3-14.

Clarke, B., & Shinn, M. (2004). A preliminary investigation into the identification and development of early mathematics curriculum-based measurement. *School Psychology Review, 33*, 234–248.

Gersten, R., Jordan, N.C., & Flojo, J.R. (2005). Early identification and interventions for students with mathematics difficulties. *Journal of Learning Disabilities, 38*, 293-304.

Berch, D. B. (2005). Making sense of number sense: Implications for children with mathematical disabilities. *Journal of Learning Disabilities, 38*, 333-339..

Wright, J. (2007). *The RTI toolkit: A practical guide for schools.* Port Chester, NY: National Professional Resources, Inc.

Early Math Fluency/Number Identification: Guidelines for Use

This introduction to the Number Identification probe provides information about the preparation, administration, and scoring of this Early Math CBM measure. Additionally, it offers brief guidelines for integrating this assessment into a school-wide 'Response-to-Intervention' model.

Number Identification: Description (Clarke & Shinn, 2004; Gersten, Jordan & Flojo, 2005)
The student is given a sheet containing rows of randomly generated numbers (e.g., ranging from 1 to 20). During a one-minute timed assessment, the student reads aloud as many numbers as possible while the examiner records any Number Identification errors.

Number Identification: Preparation
The following materials are needed to administer Number Identification (NID) Early Math CBM probes:

- Student and examiner copies of a NID assessment probe. (**Note:** Customized NID probes can be created conveniently and at no cost using Numberfly, a web-based application. Visit Numberfly at *http://www.interventioncentral.org/php/numberfly/numberfly.php*).

- A pencil, pen, or marker

- A stopwatch

Number Identification: Directions for Administration
1. The examiner sits with the student in a quiet area without distractions. The examiner sits at a table across from the student.

2. The examiner says to the student:

   "The sheet on your desk has rows of numbers."

   "When I say, 'start,' begin reading the numbers aloud. Start at the top of this page and read across the page [demonstrate by pointing]. *Try to read each number. When you come to the end of a row, go to the next row. Are there any questions?* [Pause] *Start. "*

3. The examiner begins the stopwatch when the student reads the first number aloud. If the student hesitates on a number for 3 seconds or longer, the examiner says, *"Go to the next one."* (If necessary, the examiner points to the next number as a student prompt.)

4. The examiner marks each Number Identification error by marking a slash (/) through the incorrectly read number on the examiner form.

5. At the end of one minute, the examiner says, *"Stop"* and writes in a right-bracket symbol ( ]) on the examiner form from the point in the number series that the student had reached when the time expired. The examiner then collects the student Number Identification sheet.

6. *Initial Assessment:* If the examiner is assessing the student for the first time, the examiner administers a total of 3 NID probes during the session using the above procedures and takes the median (middle) score as the best estimate of the student's NID skills.
   Progress-Monitoring: If the examiner is monitoring student growth in NID (and has previously collected NID data), only one NID probe is given in the session.

Number Identification: Directions for Practice

If the student is not yet familiar with NID assessments, the teacher can administer one or more practice NID probes (using the administration guidelines above) and provide coaching and feedback as needed until assured that the student fully understands the assessment.

Number Identification: Scoring Guidelines
Correct NID responses include:

- Numbers read correctly
- Numbers read incorrectly but corrected by the student within 3 seconds

Incorrect NID responses include:

- Numbers read incorrectly
- Numbers read correctly after hesitations of 3 seconds or longer
- Numbers skipped by the student

To calculate a Number Identification fluency score, the examiner:

1. counts up all numbers that the student attempted to read aloud and
2. subtracts the number of errors from the total of numbers attempted.
3. The resulting figure is the number of correct numbers identified.(NID fluency score).

Number Identification Probes as Part of a Response to Intervention Model
- Universal Screening: To proactively identify children who may have deficiencies in development of foundation math concepts, or 'number sense' (Berch, 2005), schools may choose to screen all kindergarten and first grade students using Number Identification probes. Those screenings would take place in fall, winter, and spring. Students who fall below the 'cutpoint' of the 35th percentile (e.g., Jordan & Hanich, 2003).of the grade norms on the NID task would be identified as having moderate deficiencies and given additional interventions to build their 'number sense' skills.

- Tier I (Classroom-Based) Interventions: Teachers can create Number Identification probes and use them independently to track the progress of students who show modest delays in their math foundation skills.

- Tier II (Individualized) Interventions. Students with more extreme academic delays may be referred to a school-based problem-solving team, which will develop more intensive, specialized interventions to target the student's academic deficits (Wright, 2007). Number Identification probes can be used as one formative measure to track student progress with Tier II interventions to build foundation math skills.

Number identification: Measurement Statistics

Test-Retest Reliability Correlations for Number Identification Probes		
Time Span	*Correlation*	*Reference*
13-week interval	**0.85**	Clarke & Shinn (2004)
26-week interval	**0.76**	Clarke & Shinn (2004)

Predictive Validity Correlations for Number Identification Probes		
Predictive Validity Measure	*Correlation*	*Reference*
Curriculum-Based Measurement Math Computation Fluency Probes: Grade 1 Addition & Subtraction (Fall Administration of MN Probe and Spring Administration of Math Computation Probe)	**0.60**	Clarke & Shinn (2004)
Woodcock-Johnson Tests of Achievement: Applied Problems subtest (Fall Administration of NID Probe and Spring Administration of WJ-ACH subtest)	**0.72**	Clarke & Shinn (2004)
Number Knowledge Test	**0.58**	Chard, Clarke, Baker, Otterstedt, Braun & Katz.(2005) cited in Gersten, Jordan & Flojo (2005)

References

Chard, D. J., Clarke, B., Baker, S., Otterstedt, J., Braun, D., & Katz, R. (2005). Using measures of number sense to screen for difficulties in mathematics: Preliminary findings. *Assessment For Effective Intervention, 30*(2), 3-14.

Clarke, B., & Shinn, M. (2004). A preliminary investigation into the identification and development of early mathematics curriculum-based measurement. *School Psychology Review, 33*, 234–248.

Gersten, R., Jordan, N.C., & Flojo, J.R. (2005). Early identification and interventions for students with mathematics difficulties. *Journal of Learning Disabilities, 38*, 293-304.

Jordan, N. C. & Hanich, L. B. (2003). Characteristics of children with moderate mathematics deficiencies: A longitudinal perspective. *Learning Disabilities Research and Practice, 18*(4), 213-221.

Berch, D. B. (2005). Making sense of number sense: Implications for children with mathematical disabilities. *Journal of Learning Disabilities, 38*, 333-339..

Wright, J. (2007). *The RTI toolkit: A practical guide for schools.* Port Chester, NY: National Professional Resources, Inc.

Curriculum-Based Measurement: Early Mathematics Fluency Norms (Chard, Clarke, Baker, Otterstedt, Braun, & Katz, 2005)*

CBM-Early Mathematics Fluency measures assess the strength of a student's 'number sense' (Chard, et al., 2005) and are good predictors of mathematical readiness at Kindergarten and Grade 1. Early Math Fluency measures include Quantity Discrimination, Missing Number, and Number Identification. All Early Math Fluency assessments have an administration time of 1 minute.

Quantity Discrimination (QD): 1 Minute: The student is presented with pairs of numbers randomly sampled from 1-20 and must identify the larger number in each pair.

Grade	Fall QD (Chard et al., 2005)	Fall:+/-1 SD (≈16th%ile to 84th%ile)	Winter QD (Chard et al., 2005)	Winter: +/-1 SD (≈16th%ile to 84th%ile)	Spring QD (Chard et al., 2005)	Spring: +/-1 SD (≈16th%ile to 84th%ile)	Weekly Growth
K	15	8↔22	20	8↔32	23	12↔34	0.25
1	23	16↔30	30	21↔39	37	28↔46	0.44

Missing Number (MN): 1 Minute: The student is presented with response items consisting of 3 sequential numbers with one of those numbers randomly left blank. (Each 3-number series is randomly generated from the pool of numbers 1-20.) The student attempts to name the missing number in each series.

Grade	Fall MN (Chard et al., 2005)	Fall: +/-1 SD (≈16th%ile to 84th%ile)	Winter MN (Chard et al., 2005)	Winter: +/-1 SD (≈16th%ile to 84th%ile)	Spring MN (Chard et al., 2005)	Spring: +/-1 SD (≈16th%ile to 84th%ile)	Weekly Growth
K	3	0↔7	10	3↔17	14	7↔21	0.34
1	9	3↔15	17	11↔23	20	14↔26	0.34

Number Identification (NID): 1 Minute: The student is presented with a randomly generated series of numbers ranging from 1-20 and names as many of those numbers aloud as time allows.

Grade	Fall NID (Chard et al., 2005)	Fall: +/-1 SD (≈16th%ile to 84th%ile)	Winter NID (Chard et al., 2005)	Winter: +/-1 SD (≈16th%ile to 84th%ile)	Spring NID (Chard et al., 2005)	Spring: +/-1 SD (≈16th%ile to 84th%ile)	Weekly Growth
K	14	0↔28	45	27↔63	56	38↔74	1.31
1	34	18↔50	53	36↔70	62	46↔78	0.88

Reference: Chard, D. J., Clarke, B., Baker, S., Otterstedt, J., Braun, D., & Katz, R. (2005). Using measures of number sense to screen for difficulties in mathematics: Preliminary findings. *Assessment for Effective Intervention, 30*(3), 3-14.

*Reported Characteristics of Student Sample(s) Used to Compile These Norms: *Number of Students Assessed:* Kindergarten: 168; Grade 1: 207/*Geographical Location:* Pacific Northwest: Sample drawn from 7 elementary schools in one district of 5500 students/ *Socioeconomic Status:* Students qualifying for free and reduced lunch: Range of 27% to 69% across 7 participating schools/*Ethnicity:* District population: 13% minorities/*ELLs:* District Population: 4% English Language Learners

Where to Find Materials: Schools can create their own CBM Early Math Fluency assessment materials at no cost, using NumberFly, a free online application:*http://www.interventioncentral.org/tools/early-math-fluency-generator* This program generates printable student and examiner assessment sheets for CBM Quantity Discrimination, Missing Number, and Number Identification. From this site, the user can also download guidelines for administering and scoring these Early Math Fluency measures.

How To: Assess Mastery of Math Facts with CBM— Computation Fluency

Computation Fluency measures a student's accuracy and speed in completing 'math facts' using the basic number operations of addition, subtraction, multiplication, and division. Computation fluency in the elementary grades is a strong predictor of later success in higher-level math coursework (Gersten, Jordan, & Flojo, 2005).

For students to attain 'computational fluency', however, they must be both accurate and speedy in solving basic math facts--ideally through automatic recall (VanDerHeyden & Burns, 2008). In an influential report, the National Mathematics Advisory Panel (2008) stressed the need for students to become proficient in math facts, calling on schools to make it a priority to "develop automatic recall of addition and related subtraction facts, and of multiplication and related division facts." (p. xix).

The Common Core Standards also recognize the importance of computation fluency. For example, a 4th-grade math standard in Number and Operations in Base Ten (CCSM.4.NBT.4) states that the student will "fluently add and subtract multi-digit whole numbers using the standard algorithm" (National Governors Association Center for Best Practices et al., 2010; p. 29). However, the challenge for teachers is to define specifically what level of performance is required to identify a student as fluent in compuation.

CBM-Computation Fluency is a brief, timed assessment that can indicate to teachers whether a student is developing computation fluency and is thus on track to master grade-appropriate math facts (basic computation problems). This assessment can be administered to an individual student or to larger groups. The student is given a worksheet containing math facts and is given 2 minutes to answer as many problems as possible. The worksheet is then collected and scored, with the student receiving credit for each correct digit in his or her answers. Teachers can then compare any student's performance to research norms to determine whether that student is at risk because of delayed computational skills (Burns, VanDerHeyden, & Jiban, 2006).

Computation Fluency Measures: How to Access Resources. Teachers who would like to screen their students in grades 1 through 6 for possible delays in computation skills can obtain these free Computation Fluency assessment resources: (1) materials for assessment, (2) guidelines for administration and scoring, and (3) research-based norms.

- *Materials for assessment.* Schools can customize their own CBM Computation Fluency assessment materials at no cost, using the Math Worksheet Generator, a free online application: *http://www.interventioncentral.org/teacher-resources/math-work-sheet-generator*

  This program generates printable student and examiner assessment sheets for CBM Computation Fluency.

- *Guidelines for administration and scoring.* Instructions for preparing, administering, and scoring CBM-Computation Fluency assessments appear later in this document:

- *Research-based norms.* A table, *Curriculum-Based Measurement: Computation Fluency Norms* is included in this document. The table contains fluency benchmarks for grades 1-6, drawn from several research studies (e.g., Burns, VanDerHeyden, & Jiban, 2006).

References

Burns, M. K., VanDerHeyden, A. M., & Jiban, C. L. (2006). Assessing the instructional level for mathematics: A comparison of methods. *School Psychology Review, 35*, 401-418.

Gersten, R., Jordan, N. C., & Flojo, J. R. (2005). Early identification and interventions for students with mathematics difficulties. *Journal of Learning Disabilities, 38*, 293-304.

Hosp, M.K., Hosp, J. L., & Howell, K. W. (2007). *The ABCs of CBM.* New York: Guilford.

National Governors Association Center for Best Practices & Council of Chief State School Officers. (2010). *Common core state standards for mathematics.* Washington, DC: Authors. Retrieved from http://www.corestandards.org/

National Mathematics Advisory Panel. (2008*). Foundations for success: The final report of the National Mathematics Advisory Panel.* Washington, DC. U.S. Department of Education. Retrieved from http://www2.ed.gov/about/bdscomm/list/mathpanel/index.html

VanDerHeyden, A. M., & Burns, M. K. (2008). Examination of the utility of various measures of mathematics proficiency. Assessment for Effective Intervention, 33, 215-224.

Curriculum-Based Measurement-Computation Fluency: Guidelines for Use

CBM-Computation Fluency: Description

CBM-Computation Fluency measures a student's accuracy and speed in completing 'math facts' using the basic number operations of addition, subtraction, multiplication, and division. CBM-Computation Fluency probes are 2-minute assessments of basic math facts that are scored for number of 'correct digits'.

There are 2 types of CBM math probes, single-skill worksheets (those containing like problems) and multiple-skill worksheets (those containing a mix of problems requiring different math operations). Single-skill probes give instructors good information about students' mastery of particular problem-types, while multiple-skill probes allow the teacher to test children's math competencies on a range of computational objectives during a single CBM session.

Both types of math probes can be administered either individually or to groups of students. The examiner hands the worksheet(s) out to those students selected for assessment. Next, the examiner reads aloud the directions for the worksheet. Then the signal is given to start, and students proceed to complete as many items as possible within 2 minutes. The examiner collects the worksheets at the end of the assessment for scoring.

CBM-Computation Fluency: Materials

The following materials are needed to administer CBM-Computation Fluency:

- Student and examiner copies of CBM Computation Fluency Probes
- Stopwatch
- Pencils for students

CBM-Computation Fluency: Preparation

After computational objectives have been selected, the instructor is ready to prepare math probes. The teacher may want to create single-skills probes, multiple-skill probes, or both types of CBM math worksheets. The teacher will probably want to consult the Common Core State Standards for Mathematics or district math curriculum when selecting the kinds of problems to include in the single- or multiple-skill probe.

Creating the single-skill math probe. As the first step in putting together a single-skill math probe, the teacher will select one computational objective as a guide. The worksheet, then, will consist of problems randomly constructed that conform to the computational objective chosen.

Figure 1: A Sampling of Math Computational Goals for Addition, Subtraction, Multiplication, and Division (from Wright, 2002).

Addition
Two 1-digit numbers: sums to 10
Two 3-digit numbers: no regrouping
1- to 2-digit number plus 1- to 2-digit number: regrouping

Subtraction
Two 1-digit numbers: 0 to 9
2-digit number from a 2-digit number: no regrouping
2-digit number from a 2-digit number: regrouping

Multiplication
Multiplication facts: 0 to 9
2-digit number times 1-digit number: no regrouping
3-digit number times 1-digit number: regrouping

Division
Division facts: 0 to 9
2-digit number divided by 1-digit number: no remainder
2-digit number divided by 1-digit number: remainder

Wright, J. (2002) *Curriculum-Based Assessment Math Computation Probe Generator: Multiple-Skill Worksheets in Mixed Skills.* Retrieved from *http://www.interventioncentral.org/teacher-resources/math-work-sheet-generator*

For example, the instructor may select any of the computational objectives in Figure 1 as the basis for a math probe. The teacher would then construct a series of problems that match the computational goal, as in Figure 2. In general, single-skill math probes should contain between 80 and 200 problems, and worksheets should have items on both the front and back of the page. Adequate space should also be left for the student to show his or her work, especially with more complex problems such as long division.

Figure 2: Example of a single-skill math probe: Three to five 3- and 4-digit numbers: no regrouping

```
     105    |      2031   |      111   |       634   |
 +   600    |   +   531   |   +  717   |   +  8240   |
 +   293    |   +  2322   |   +  260   |   +   203   |
            |             |            |             |
```

Creating the Multiple-skill Math Probe. To assemble a multiple-skill math probe, the instructor will first select the range of math operations and of problem-types that will make up the probe. Once the computational objectives have been

Figure 3: Example of a multiple-skill math probe:
- *Division: 3-digit number divided by 1-digit number: no remainder*
- *Subtraction: 2-digit number from a 2-digit number: regrouping*
- *Multiplication" 3-digit number times 1-digit number: no regrouping*
- *Division: Two 3-digit numbers: no regrouping*

```
  _____    |      20    |      113   |       106   |
 9/431      |    -18     |   x    2   |   +   172   |
            |            |            |   +   200   |
            |            |            |   +   600   |
            |            |            |             |
```

chosen, the teacher can make up a worksheet of mixed math facts conforming to those objectives. Using our earlier example, the teacher who wishes to estimate the proficiency of his 4th-grade math group may decide to create a multiple-skills CBM probe. He could choose to sample only those problem-types that his students have either mastered or are presently being taught. Figure 3 shows four computation skills with matching sample problems that might appear on a worksheet of mixed math facts.

NOTE: Schools can customize their own CBM Computation Fluency assessment materials at no cost, using the Math Worksheet Generator, a free online application:
http://www.interventioncentral.org/teacher-resources/math-work-sheet-generator

CBM-Computation Fluency: Directions for Administration

1. The examiner distributes copies of math probes to all the students in the group, face down. (Note: These probes may also be administered individually). The examiner says to the students: "The sheets on your desk are math facts."
2. If the students are to complete a single-skill probe, the examiner says: "All the problems are [addition or subtraction or multiplication or division] facts."

If the students are to complete a multiple-skill probe, the examiner then says: "There are several types of problems on the sheet. Some are addition, some are subtraction, some are multiplication, and some are division [as appropriate]. Look at each problem carefully before you answer it."

3. The examiner then says: "When I say 'begin', turn the worksheet over and begin answering the problems. Start on the first problem on the left on the top row [point]. Work across and then go to the next row. If you can't answer a problem, make an 'X' on it and go to the next one. If you finish one side, go to the back. Are there any questions? ".
4. The examiner says 'Start' and starts the stopwatch. While the students are completing worksheets, the examiner and any other adults assisting in the assessment circulate around the room to ensure that students are working on the correct sheet and that they are completing problems in the correct order (rather than picking out only the easy items)..
5. After 2 minutes have passed, the examiner says, "Stop" and collects the CBM computation probes for scoring.
6. *Initial Assessment:* If the examiner is assessing the student for the first time, the examiner administers a total of 3 computation probes during the session using the above procedures and takes the median (middle) score as the best estimate of the student's computation fluency.
   Progress-Monitoring: If the examiner is monitoring student growth in computation (and has previously collected CBM-Computation Fluency data), only one computation probe is given in the session.

CBM-Computation Fluency: Directions for Practice

If the student is not yet familiar with CBM-Computation Fluency probes, the teacher can administer one or more practice computation probes (using the administration guidelines above) and provide coaching and feedback as needed until assured that the student fully understands the assessment.

CBM-Computation Fluency: Scoring Guidelines

Traditional approaches to computational assessment usually give credit for the total number of correct answers appearing on a worksheet. If the answer to a problem is found to contain one or more incorrect digits, that problem is marked wrong and receives no credit. In contrast to this all-or-nothing marking system, CBM assigns credit to each individual correct digit appearing in the solution to a math fact.

On the face of it, a math scoring system that awards points according to the number of correct digits may appear unusual, but this alternative approach is grounded in good academic-assessment research and practice. By separately scoring each digit in the answer of a computation problem, the instructor is better able to recognize and to give credit for a student's partial math competencies. Scoring computation problems by the digit rather than as a single answer also allows for a more minute analysis of a child's number skills.

Imagine, for instance, that a student was given a CBM math probe consisting of addition problems, sums less than or equal to 19 (incorrect digits appear in boldface and italics):

Figure 4: Example of completed problems from a single-skill math probe

```
    105    |     2031   |     111    |      634
+   600    |  +   531   |  +  717    |  +  8240
+   293    |  +  2322   |  +  260    |  +   203
    98 8   |     4884   |    108 7   |     9 0 77
```

If the answers in Figure 4 were scored as either correct or wrong, the child would receive a score of 1 correct answer out of 4 possible answers (25 percent). However, when each individual digit is scored, it becomes clear that the student actually correctly computed 12 of 15 possible digits (80 percent). Thus, the CBM procedure of assigning credit to each correct digit demonstrates itself to be quite sensitive to a student's emerging, partial competencies in math computation.

The following scoring rules will aid the instructor in marking single- and multiple-skill math probes:

- Individual correct digits are counted as correct.
  Reversed or rotated digits are not counted as errors unless their change in position makes them appear to be another digit (e.g., 9 and 6).

- Incorrect digits are counted as errors.
  Digits that appear in the wrong place value, even if otherwise correct, are scored as errors.
  Example

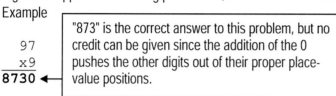

```
    97
   x 9
  8730 ◄──
```
"873" is the correct answer to this problem, but no credit can be given since the addition of the 0 pushes the other digits out of their proper place-value positions.

- The student is given credit for "place-holder" numerals that are included simply to correctly align the problem. As long as the student includes the correct space, credit is given whether or not a "0" has actually been inserted.

  Example

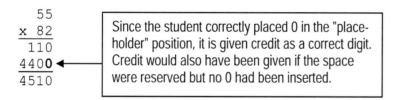

```
     55
   x  82
    110
   4400 ◄──
   4510
```
Since the student correctly placed 0 in the "place-holder" position, it is given credit as a correct digit. Credit would also have been given if the space were reserved but no 0 had been inserted.

- In more complex problems such as advanced multiplication, the student is given credit for all correct numbers that appear below the line.

  Example

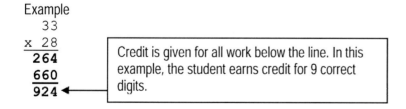

```
     33
   x 28
    264
    660
    924 ◄──
```
Credit is given for all work below the line. In this example, the student earns credit for 9 correct digits.

- Credit is not given for any numbers appearing above the line (e.g., numbers marked at the top of number columns to signify regrouping).

  Example

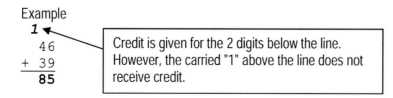

```
    1 ◄──
    46
  + 39
    85
```
Credit is given for the 2 digits below the line. However, the carried "1" above the line does not receive credit.

Curriculum-Based Measurement: Computation Fluency Norms
(Burns, VanDerHeyden, & Jiban, 2006; Deno & Mirkin, 1977; Fuchs & Fuchs, 1993; Fuchs & Fuchs, n.d.)*

CBM-Computation Fluency measures a student's accuracy and speed in completing 'math facts' using the basic number operations: addition, subtraction, multiplication, and division. CBM-Computation Fluency probes are 2-minute assessments of basic math facts that are scored for number of 'correct digits'.

NOTE: The norms for grades 2-5 presented below are for 1 minute, while the norms for grades 1 and 6 are for 2 minutes. To use any of the 1-minute norms, (1) administer and score a standard 2-minute Computation Fluency probe; (2) divide that student score by 2; and then (3) compare that converted student score to the appropriate 1-minute norm within grades 2-5 (Burns, VanDerHeyden, & Jiban, 2006).

Grade	End of Year Benchmark: Correct Digits per 2 Mins (Fuchs & Fuchs, n.d.)	Weekly Growth: 'Realistic' (Fuchs & Fuchs, 1993)	Weekly Growth: 'Ambitious' (Fuchs & Fuchs, 1993)
1	20	0.3	0.5

Grade	Performance Level	Correct Digits per 1 Min (Burns, VanDerHeyden, & Jiban, 2006)	Weekly Growth: 'Realistic' (Fuchs & Fuchs, 1993)	Weekly Growth: 'Ambitious' (Fuchs & Fuchs, 1993)
2	Mastery	More than 31	0.3	0.5
	Instructional	14-31		
	Frustration	Less than 14		
3	Mastery	More than 31	0.3	0.5
	Instructional	14-31		
	Frustration	Less than 14		
4	Mastery	More than 49	0.75	1.2
	Instructional	24-49		
	Frustration	Less than 24		
5	Mastery	More than 49	0.75	1.2
	Instructional	24-49		
	Frustration	Less than 24		

Grade	Performance Level	Correct Digits per 2 Mins (Deno & Mirkin, 1977)	Weekly Growth: 'Realistic' (Fuchs & Fuchs, 1993)	Weekly Growth: 'Ambitious' (Fuchs & Fuchs, 1993)
6	Mastery	More than 79	0.45	1.0
	Instructional	40-79		
	Frustration	Less than 40		

References:

- Burns, M. K., VanDerHeyden, A. M., & Jiban, C. L. (2006). Assessing the instructional level for mathematics: A comparison of methods. *School Psychology Review, 35*, 401-418.
- Deno, S. L., & Mirkin, P. K. (1977). *Data-based program modification: A manual.* Reston, VA: Council for Exceptional Children.
- Fuchs, L. S., & Fuchs, D. (n.d.). *Using curriculum-based measurement for progress monitoring in math.* National Center on Student Progress Monitoring. Retrieved from http://www.studentprogress.org
- Fuchs, L. S., & Fuchs, D. (1993). Formative evaluation of academic progress: How much growth can we expect? *School Psychology Review, 22*, 27-49.
- Gersten, R., Jordan, N. C., & Flojo, J. R. (2005). Early identification and interventions for students with mathematics difficulties. *Journal of Learning Disabilities, 38*, 293-304.

*Reported Characteristics of Student Sample(s) Used to Compile These Norms:

- **Burns, VanDerHeyden, & Jiban, 2006:** *Number of Students Assessed:* 434 students across grades 2-5/*Geographical Location:* Southwest: Sample drawn from 1 elementary school/ *Socioeconomic Status:* 15% rate of Free & Reduced Lunch/ *Ethnicity of Sample:* 74% Caucasian-non-Hispanic; 17% Hispanic or Latino; 6% African-American; 3% Asian-American; 1% Native American/*Limited English Proficiency in Sample:* 2% of students.
- **Deno & Mirkin, 1977:** *Number of Students Assessed:* Not reported/*Geographical Location:* Sample drawn from 1 elementary school; location not reported/ *Socioeconomic Status:* Not reported/ *Ethnicity of Sample:* Not reported/*Limited English Proficiency in Sample:* Not reported.
- **Fuchs & Fuchs, n.d.:** *Number of Students Assessed:* Not reported/*Geographical Location:* Not reported/ *Socioeconomic Status:* Not reported/ *Ethnicity of Sample:* Not reported/*Limited English Proficiency in Sample:* Not reported.
- **Fuchs & Fuchs, 1993:** *Number of Students Assessed:* Year 1: 177 students in grades 1-6; Year 2:1208 students across grades 1-6/*Geographical Location:* Upper Midwest: Sample drawn from 5 elementary schools/ *Socioeconomic Status:* 33%-55% rate of Free & Reduced Lunch across participating schools/ *Ethnicity of Sample:* Not reported/*Limited English Proficiency in Sample:* Not reported.

Where to Find Materials: Schools can create their own CBM Computation Fluency assessment materials at no cost, using the Math Worksheet Generator, a free online application:
http://www.interventioncentral.org/teacher-resources/math-work-sheet-generator

This program generates printable student and examiner assessment sheets for CBM Computation Fluency.

Limitations of These Research Norms: Norms generated from small-scale research studies--like those used here--provide estimates of student academic performance based on a sampling from only one or two points in time, rather than a more comprehensive sampling across separate fall, winter, and spring screenings. These norms also have been compiled from a relatively small student sample that is not fully representative of a diverse 'national' population. Nonetheless, norms such as these are often the best information that is publically available for basic academic skills and therefore do have a definite place in classroom instruction decision-making.

These norms can be useful in general education for setting student performance outcome goals for core instruction and/or any level of academic intervention. Similarly, these norms can be used to set performance goals for students with special needs. In both cases, however, single-sample norms would be used only if more comprehensive fall/winter/spring academic performance norms are not available.

How To: Track Growth in Written Expression in the Elementary Grades with CBM

The act of writing is complex. Translating thought into written expression requires that the student master a host of foundation writing skills, including the physical production of text; and mastery of rules of capitalization, spelling, punctuation, and syntax (Robinson & Howell, 2008).

Tracking student growth in emerging writing skills can be confusing and time-consuming for teachers. However, Curriculum-Based Measurement-Written Expression (CBM-WE) is an efficient, reliable method of formative student assessment that yields numeric indicators that are instructionally useful--such as total words written, correctly spelled words, and correct writing sequences (Gansle et al., 2006). CBM-WE probes are group-administered writing samples with an administration time of about 4 minutes. CBM-Written Expression is therefore a powerful means to monitor a student's progress in the mechanics and conventions of writing.

CBM-Written Expression: What It Measures. Teachers have several assessment options to choose from when using CBM-Written Expression (Gansle et al., 2006; Wright, 1992):

- *Total Words Written (TWW):* This measure is a count of the total words written during the CBM-WE assessment. Teachers might select Total Words Written as a progress-monitoring target if the student needs to focus on writing fluency (getting more words onto the page).

- *Correctly Spelled Words (CSW):* This measure is a count of correctly spelled words written during the CBM-WE assessment. If poor spelling is a blocker to student writing, the teacher may select this monitoring target.

- *Correct Writing Sequences (CWS):* This measure is a tabulation of correct 'writing sequences' written during the CBM-WE assessment. One Correct Writing Sequence is scored whenever two adjacent units of writing (e.g., two words appearing next to each other) are found to be correct in their punctuation, capitalization, spelling, and syntactical and semantic usage. When the student is expected to have mastered the basic mechanics and conventions of writing, Correct Writing Sequences are a useful method to track this group of interrelated skills.

CBM-Written Expression Fluency Measures: How to Access Resources. Teachers who wish to screen their students in basic writing skills can obtain these free CBM-Written Expression assessment resources: (1) materials for assessment, (2) guidelines for administration and scoring, and (3) research-based norms.

- *Materials for assessment.* Schools can create their own CBM Written Expression Fluency assessment materials at no cost, using the Written Expression Probe Generator, a free online application: *http://www.interventioncentral.org/tools/writing-probe-generator*

  This program allows the user to customize and to generate printable story-starter worksheets in PDF format.

- *Guidelines for administration and scoring.* Instructions for preparing, administering, and scoring CBM-Written Expression assessments appear later in this document:

- *Research-based norms.* A table, *Curriculum-Based Measurement: Written Expression Fluency Norms*, is included in this document. The norms include fluency benchmarks for grades 1-6 (Malecki & Jewell, 2003) and growth norms for grades 1-4 (Tadatada, 2011).

References

Gansle, K. A., VanDerHeyden, A. M., Noell, G. H., Resetar, J. L., & Williams, K. L. (2006). The technical adequacy of curriculum-based and rating-based measures of written expression for elementary school students. *School Psychology Review, 35*, 435-450.

Malecki, C. K., & Jewell, J. (2003). Developmental, gender, and practical considerations in scoring curriculum-based measurement writing probes. *Psychology in the Schools, 40*, 379-390.

McMaster, K., & Espin, C. (2007). Technical features of curriculum-based measurement in writing: A literature review. *Journal of Special Education, 41*(2), 68-84.

Robinson, L. K., & Howell, K. W. (2008). Best practices in curriculum-based evaluation & written expression. In A. Thomas & J. Grimes (Eds.), *Best practices in school psychology V* (pp. 439-452). Bethesda, MD: National Association of School Psychologists.

Tadatada, A. (2011). *Growth rates of curriculum-based measurement-written expression at the elementary school level.* Unpublished master's thesis, Western Kentucky University, Bowling Green.

Wright, J. (1992). *Curriculum-based measurement: A manual for teachers. Retrieved* September 23, 20011, from http://www.jimwrightonline.com/pdfdocs/cbaManual.pdf

Curriculum-Based Measurement-Written Expression: Guidelines for Use

CB-Written Expression: Description (McMaster & Espin, 2007)
CBM-Written Expression probes are simple to administer and offer several scoring options. Written-expression probes may be given individually or to groups of students. The examiner prepares a lined composition sheet with a story-starter sentence or partial sentence at the top. The student thinks for 1 minute about a possible story to be written from the story-starter, then spends 3 minutes writing the story. The examiner collects the writing sample for scoring. Depending on the preferences of the teacher, the writing probe can be scored in several ways, as explained below (from Wright, 1992).

CBM-Written Expression: Materials
The following materials are needed to administer CBM-Written Expression probes:

- Student copy of CBM writing probe with story-starter (the process for creating story-starters is described below)
- Stopwatch
- Pencils for students

CBM-Written Expression: Preparation
Before administering CBM-Written Expression, the teacher selects a 'story starter' (a brief introductory sentence or partial sentence) to serve as a prompt to elicit student story writing. The teacher selects a story-starter and places it at the top of a lined composition sheet. The story-starter should avoid wording that encourages students to generate lists. It should also be open-ended, requiring the writer to build a narrative rather than simply to write down a "Yes" or "No" response.

Schools can create their own CBM Written Expression Fluency assessment materials at no cost, using the Written Expression Probe Generator, a free online application: *http://www.interventioncentral.org/tools/writing-probe-generator*
This program allows the user to customize and to generate printable story-starter worksheets in PDF format.

The CBM writing probe in Figure 1 is an example of how a such a probe might be formatted. (This particular probe was used in a 5th-grade classroom.):

Figure 1: Example of a CBM writing probe

CBM Writing Probe

Name: _____ Grade: _____ Date: _____

One day, I was out sailing. A storm carried me far out to sea and wrecked

my boat on a desert island. _____

_____

_____

CBM-Written Expression: Directions for Administration

1. The examiner distributes copies of CBM writing probes to all the students in the group. (Note: These probes may also be administered individually).
2. The examiner says to the students: *I want you to write a story. I am going to read a sentence to you first, and then I want you to write a short story about what happens. You will have 1 minute to think about the story you will write and then have 3 minutes to write it. Do your best work. If you don't know how to spell a word, you should guess. Are there any questions? For the next minute, think about . . .* [insert story-starter].
3. The examiner starts the stopwatch. At the end of 1 minute, the examiner says, *Start writing.*
4. While the students are writing, the examiner and any other adults helping in the assessment circulate around the room. If students stop writing before the 3-minute timing period has ended, monitors encourage them to continue writing.
5. After 3 additional minutes, the examiner says, *Stop writing.* CBM writing probes are collected for scoring.

CBM-Written Expression: Scoring Guidelines

The instructor has several options when scoring CBM writing probes. Student writing samples may be scored according to the:

1. Total Words Written (TWW),
2. Correctly Spelled Words (CSW), or
3. Correct Writing Sequences (One Correct Writing Sequence is scored whenever two adjacent units of writing (e.g., two words appearing next to each other) are found to be correct in their punctuation, capitalization, spelling, and syntactical and semantic usage.)

Scoring methods differ both in the amount of time that they require of the instructor and in the type of information that they provide about a student's writing skills. Advantages and potential limitations of each scoring system are presented below.

Total Words Written (TWW). The examiner counts up and records the total number of words written during the 3-minute writing probe. Misspelled words are included in the tally, although numbers written in numeral form (e.g., 5, 17) are not counted. Calculating total words is the quickest of scoring methods. A drawback, however, is that it yields only a rough estimate of writing fluency (that is, of how quickly the student can put words on paper) without examining the accuracy of spelling, punctuation, and other writing conventions. A 6th-grade student wrote the CBM writing sample in Figure 2. Using the total-words scoring formula, this sample is found to contain 45 words, including misspellings.

Figure 2: CBM writing sample scored for Total Words Written:

I woud drink water from the ocean	**7 words**
and I woud eat the fruit off of	**8 words**
the trees. Then I woud bilit a	**7 words**
house out of trees, and I woud	**7 words**
gather firewood to stay warm. I	**6 words**
woud try and fix my boat in my	**8 words**
spare time.	**2 words**
	Total=45 words

Correctly Spelled Words. The examiner counts up only those words in the writing sample that are spelled correctly. Words are considered separately, not within the context of a sentence. When scoring a good rule of thumb is to determine whether--in isolation--the word represents a correctly spelled term in English. If it does, the word is included in the tally. Assessing the number of correctly spelled words has the advantage of being quick. Also, by examining the accuracy of the student's spelling, this approach monitors to some degree a student's mastery of written language. As seen in figure 3, our writing sample is contains 39 correctly spelled words.

Figure 3: CBM writing sample scored for Correctly Spelled Words

I woud drink water from the ocean	**6 correctly spelled words**
and I woud eat the fruit off of	**7 correctly spelled words**
the trees. Then I woud bilit a	**5 correctly spelled words**
house out of trees, and I woud	**6 correctly spelled words**
gather firewood to stay warm. I	**6 correctly spelled words**
woud try and fix my boat in my	**7 correctly spelled words**
spare time.	**2 correctly spelled words**
	Total=39 correctly spelled words

Correct Writing Sequences. When scoring correct writing sequences, the examiner goes beyond the confines of the isolated word to consider units of writing and their relation to one another. Using this approach, the examiner starts at the beginning of the writing sample and looks at each successive pair of writing units (writing sequence). Words are considered separate writing units, as are essential marks of punctuation. To receive credit, writing sequences must be correctly spelled and be grammatically correct. The words in each writing sequence must also make sense within the context of the sentence. In effect, the student's writing is judged according to the standards of informal standard American English. A caret (^) is used to mark the presence of a correct writing sequence.

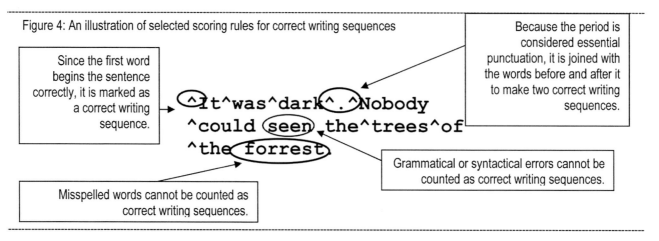

Figure 4: An illustration of selected scoring rules for correct writing sequences

Since the first word begins the sentence correctly, it is marked as a correct writing sequence.

Because the period is considered essential punctuation, it is joined with the words before and after it to make two correct writing sequences.

Misspelled words cannot be counted as correct writing sequences.

Grammatical or syntactical errors cannot be counted as correct writing sequences.

The following scoring rules will aid the instructor in determining correct writing sequences:

- Correctly spelled words make up a correct writing sequence (reversed letters are acceptable, so long as they do not lead to a misspelling):
Example

    ^Is^that^a^red^car^?

- Necessary marks of punctuation (excluding commas) are included in correct writing sequences:
Example

    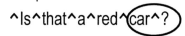

- Syntactically correct words make up a correct writing sequence:
Example

    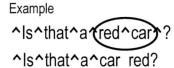
    ^Is^that^a^car red?

- Semantically correct words make up a correct writing sequence:
Example

    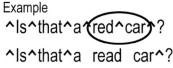
    ^Is^that^a read car^?

- If correct, the initial word of a writing sample is counted as a correct writing sequence:
Example

    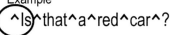

- Titles are included in the correct writing sequence count:
Example

    ^The^Terrible^Day

Not surprisingly, evaluating a writing probe according to correct writing sequences is the most time-consuming of the scoring methods presented here. It is also the scoring approach, however, that yields the most comprehensive information about a student's writing competencies. While further research is needed to clarify the point, it also seems plausible that the correct writing sequence method is most sensitive to short-term student improvements in writing. Presumably, advances in writing skills in virtually any area (e.g., spelling, punctuation) could quickly register as higher writing sequence scores. Our writing sample in Figure 5 is found to contain 37 correct writing sequences.

Figure 5: CBM Writing sample scored for Correct Writing Sequence (Each correct writing sequence is marked with a caret(^)).

```
^I woud drink^water^from^the^ocean          5 correct writing sequences

^and^I woud eat^the^fruit^off^of            6 correct writing sequences

^the^trees^.^Then^I woud bilit a            5 correct writing sequences

^house^out^of^trees, ^and^I woud            6 correct writing sequences

gather^firewood^to^stay^warm^.^I            6 correct writing sequences

woud try^and^fix^my^boat^in^my              6 correct writing sequences

^spare^time^.                               3 correct writing sequences
```

Total = 37 correct writing sequences

References

McMaster, K., & Espin, C. (2007). Technical features of curriculum-based measurement in writing: A literature review. *Journal of Special Education, 41*(2), 68-84.

Wright, J. (1992). *Curriculum-based measurement: A manual for teachers. Retrieved* September 23, 20011, from http://www.jimwrightonline.com/pdfdocs/cbaManual.pdf

Curriculum-Based Measurement: Written-Expression Fluency Norms

CBM-Written Expression measures assess the mechanics and conventions of writing and can yield numeric indicators such as total words written, correctly spelled words, and correct writing sequences (Gansle et al., 2006). CBM-Written Expression probes are group-administered writing samples with an administration time of about 4 minutes.

Total Words Written (TWW): This measure is a count of the total words written during the CBM-WE assessment.

Grade	Fall TWW (Malecki & Jewell, 2003)	Fall:+/-1 SD (≈16th%ile to 84th%ile)	Spring TWW (Malecki & Jewell, 2003)	Spring: +/-1 SD (≈16th%ile to 84th%ile)	Weekly Growth (Tadatada, 2011)
1	8	3↔13	14	7↔21	0.45
2	24	14↔34	31	19↔43	0.43
3	36	23↔49	36	24↔48	0.35
4	41	30↔52	46	30↔62	0.25
5	51	34↔68	67	43↔91	--
6	44	31↔57	58	44↔72	--

Correctly Spelled Words (CSW): This measure is a count of correctly spelled words written during the CBM-WE assessment.

Grade	Fall CSW (Malecki & Jewell, 2003)	Fall:+/-1 SD (≈16th%ile to 84th%ile)	Spring CSW (Malecki & Jewell, 2003)	Spring: +/-1 SD (≈16th%ile to 84th%ile)	Weekly Growth (Tadatada, 2011)
1	5	1↔9	10	3↔17	0.45
2	20	10↔30	27	15↔39	0.46
3	32	19↔45	33	21↔45	0.37
4	38	26↔50	44	29↔59	0.26
5	48	31↔65	65	42↔88	--
6	42	29↔55	56	41↔71	--

Correct Writing Sequences (CWS): This measure is a tabulation of correct 'writing sequences' written during the CBM-WE assessment. One Correct Writing Sequence is scored whenever two adjacent units of writing (e.g., two words appearing next to each other) are found to be correct in their punctuation, capitalization, spelling, and syntactical and semantic usage.

Grade	Fall CWS (Malecki & Jewell, 2003)	Fall:+/-1 SD (≈16th%ile to 84th%ile)	Spring CWS (Malecki & Jewell, 2003)	Spring: +/-1 SD (≈16th%ile to 84th%ile)	Weekly Growth (Tadatada, 2011)
1	2	0↔4	7	1↔13	0.36
2	15	5↔25	24	11↔37	0.44
3	28	14↔42	31	18↔44	0.35
4	38	25↔51	42	26↔58	0.22
5	46	28↔64	63	40↔86	--
6	41	27↔55	54	37↔71	--

References:

- Gansle, K. A., VanDerHeyden, A. M., Noell, G. H., Resetar, J. L., & Williams, K. L. (2006). The technical adequacy of curriculum-based and rating-based measures of written expression for elementary school students. *School Psychology Review, 35*, 435-450.
- Malecki, C. K., & Jewell, J. (2003). Developmental, gender, and practical considerations in scoring curriculum-based measurement writing probes. *Psychology in the Schools, 40*, 379-390.
- Tadatada, A. (2011*). Growth rates of curriculum-based measurement-written expression at the elementary school level.* Unpublished master's thesis, Western Kentucky University, Bowling Green.

Reported Characteristics of Student Sample(s) Used to Compile These Norms:

Malecki & Jewell, 2003: *Number of Students Assessed:* 946 Total; Grade 1: Fall:133 -Spring:123; Grade 2: Fall:200 -Spring:156; Grade 3: Fall:168 -Spring:109; Grade 4: Fall:192 -Spring:182; Grade 5: Fall:127 -Spring:120; Grade 6: Fall:57 -Spring:54/*Geographical Location:* Northern Illinois: Sample drawn from 5 suburban and rural schools across three districts/ *Socioeconomic Status:* Not reported/*Ethnicity of Sample:* Not reported/*English Language Learners in Sample:* Not reported.

Tadatada, 2011: *Number of Students Assessed:* 1,004 Total; Grade 1: 207; Grade 2: 208; Grade 3: 204; Grade 4: 220; Grade 5: 165/*Geographical Location:* Bowling Green, KY: Sample drawn from 5 elementary schools in single district/ *Socioeconomic Status:* Not reported/*Ethnicity of Sample:* 64% White; 18% African-American; 13% Hispanic; 3% Asian; 3% Other/*Limited English Proficiency in Sample:* 19%.

Where to Find Materials: Schools can create their own CBM Written Expression Fluency assessment materials at no cost, using the Written Expression Probe Generator, a free online application:

http://www.interventioncentral.org/tools/writing-probe-generator

This program allows the user to customize and to generate printable story-starter worksheets in PDF format.

Limitations of These Research Norms: Norms generated from small-scale research studies--like those used here-- provide estimates of student academic performance based on a sampling from only one or two points in time, rather than a more comprehensive sampling across separate fall, winter, and spring screenings. These norms also have been compiled from a relatively small student sample that is not fully representative of a diverse 'national' population. Nonetheless, norms such as these are often the best information that is publically available for basic academic skills and therefore do have a definite place in classroom instruction decision-making.

These norms can be useful in general education for setting student performance outcome goals for core instruction and/or any level of academic intervention. Similarly, these norms can be used to set performance goals for students with special needs. In both cases, however, single-sample norms would be used only if more comprehensive fall/winter/spring academic performance norms are not available.

Chapter 7

Increasing Student Responsibility Through Self-Management

One of the missions of schools is to help students take greater responsibility for managing their own learning as they advance through the grades. This fact is obvious even to the casual observer. Children in second grade, for example, have their instruction planned out almost entirely by the teacher, typically move about the school in groups under the watchful supervision of adults, and have few expectations placed upon them about completing schoolwork outside of the classroom. In contrast, 6th grade students in many schools are expected to be productive participants in collaborative learning with peers, to move efficiently and quickly to locations throughout the building with little supervision, to complete substantial amounts of homework independently, to plan and carry out complex academic tasks such as research papers and multi-step science experiments, and to articulate clearly to staff what additional academic help and support they may need.

The Common Core State Standards, too, convey the message that, from an early age, students must embrace the role of active, engaged, motivated learners. Consider, for example, this Reading Standard for Information Text for grade 6 (CCSSELA. RI.6.2), which states that students will "determine a central idea of a text and how it is conveyed through particular details; provide a summary of the text distinct from personal opinions or judgments." (National Governors Association, 2010; p. 39). Even a superficial analysis of this sample standard reveals a cluster of demanding academic expectations: the student must have the skill-set to extract main ideas and supporting details from assigned readings and summarize the gist of the text while filtering out bias and opinion. But also implied in this standard are important assumptions about the student's capacity for *self-management:* for example, the ability to plan the sequential steps of the activity, self-monitor whether the task is being correctly completed, and recognize when teacher assistance is needed.

Roadmap to This Chapter

No single set of skills are universally accepted as defining student 'self-management.' At minimum, however, most teachers would agree that self-managing students are able to engage in work-planning and goal-setting (Martin et al., 2003), monitor their own learning and behaviors (Rafferty, 2010), and negotiate with teachers and advocate for their learning needs (Peterson, Young, West, & Peterson, 1999). The resources that follow provide teachers with the tools to begin instilling within the struggling student those self-management skills that will serve them for a lifetime.

- *How To: Teach Students to Manage Behaviors Through Self-Monitoring.* This resource shows teachers how to put together a student self-monitoring program in 7 steps. Several ready-made self-monitoring forms are included: Behavior Rating Scale, Behavior Checklist, and Frequency Count.

- *How To: Improve Student Self-Management Through Work-Planning Skills: Plan, Work, Evaluate, Adjust.* This resource gives teachers a structured meeting agenda and documentation form to walk students through the process of creating realistic work plans for simple or complex academic tasks. The teacher and student first meet in a 'work-planning' conference to create the work plan and set a performance goal. They then meet again after the work is completed for a 'self-evaluation' conference in which the student reflects on whether he or she attained the work goal and adjusts future expectations based on the experience.

• *How To: Model Student Responsibility and Self-Advocacy Through the Student Problem-Solving Conference.* A key way that students learn to accept academic responsibility and to advocate for their learning needs is to work through these issues in successful negotiations with teachers. This resource includes a 'safe' meeting structure and accompanying forms that teachers can use when meeting with students to assemble an academic intervention. Products resulting from the problem-solving conference are a written plan to provide academic help and a clear delineation of both teacher and student responsibilities to support the plan. This meeting structure is flexible and can be used with students alone and in student-parent conferences.

The reader is also reminded that additional student self-management resources appear elsewhere in this book. For instance, a description of Cover-Copy-Compare, a student-managed intervention to learn spelling words or math facts, can be found in chapter 3 (academic interventions). Additionally, a guide for having students select and self-monitor academic goals appears in chapter 5 (classroom data collection). Also, Academic Survival Skills Checklists (also in chapter 5) are designed for students to use in monitoring their own academic support skills.

References

Martin, J. E., Mithaug, D. E., Cox, P., Peterson, L. Y., Van Dycke, J. L., & Cash, M.E. (2003). Increasing self-determination: Teaching students to plan, work, evaluate, and adjust. *Exceptional Children, 69,* 431-447.

National Governors Association Center for Best Practices & Council of Chief State School Officers. (2010). *Common core state standards for English language arts and literacy in history/social studies, science, and technical subjects.* Washington, DC: Authors.

Peterson, L. D., Young, K. R., West, R. P., & Peterson, M. H. (1999). Effects of student self-management on generalization of student performance to regular classrooms. *Education and Treatment of Children,* 22, 357-372.

Rafferty, L. A. (2010). Step-by-step: Teaching students to self-monitor. *Teaching Exceptional Children,* 43(2), 50-58.

How To: Teach Students to Change Behaviors Through Self-Monitoring

Student self-monitoring is an effective tool for behavior change. Self-monitoring has two components, measurement and evaluation (Loftin, Gibb, & Skiba, 2005): That is, the student (1) measures and records his or her own behavior (measurement), and then (2) compares that recorded behavior to a pre-determined standard (evaluation). Self-monitoring can take many forms. One student may use a paper form to rate her study skills at the end of each class period, for example, while another student might verbally rate his social behaviors when approached by his teacher at random times across the school day.

Self-monitoring takes advantage of a behavioral principle: the simple acts of measuring one's target behavior and comparing it to an external standard or goal can result in lasting improvements to that behavior. Self-monitoring is sometimes described as having 'reactive' effects (Kazdin, 1989), because students who measure and pay close attention to selected behaviors often react to this monitoring information by changing those target behaviors in the desired direction.

In classroom settings, self-monitoring offers several advantages. Self-monitoring requires that the student be an active participant in the intervention, with responsibility for measuring and evaluating his or her behaviors. Also, in order to accurately self-evaluate behaviors, the student must first learn the teacher's behavioral expectations. That ability of a child or youth to understand and internalize the behavioral expectations of others is a milestone in the development of social skills. Finally, student self-monitoring data is typically economical to collect, even in a busy classroom, and can often be used to document the success of a behavioral intervention.

There are many possible variations to student self-monitoring programs. In order to be most effective, however, self-monitoring programs will usually include the following 7 steps:

1. Define Behavior Target(s) to Self-Monitor

The teacher and student select and carefully define one or more behaviors that the student will monitor.

Targets for self-monitoring can include behaviors to *increase* (Webber et al., 1993), such as:
- Focusing on the task or assignment (on-task).
- Making positive statements to peers.
- Completing work.
- Complying with teacher requests.
- Reading pages of text read during study periods.
- Completing math computation problems.

Self-monitoring can also focus on behaviors to *decrease* (Dunlap, Clarke, Jackson, Ramos, & Brinson, 1995), such as:
- Calling out.
- Leaving one's seat.
- Requesting teacher assistance.

The teacher should meet privately with the student to discuss the behavior(s to be monitored. For each goal behavior, the teacher and student write a clear, specific behavioral definition that provides observable 'look-fors' to indicate when the behavior is displayed. For example, 'on-task' can be made observable by defining it as "eyes on the teacher or desk-work".

2. Choose a Method for Recording Self-Monitoring Data

Student self-monitoring does not necessarily require that monitoring data be written down. For example, a student who regularly consults a self-correction checklist before turning in math assignments or keeps a mental count of call-outs during large-group instruction may see behavioral improvements even if she does not commit her self-monitoring information to writing. However, creating a written record of self-monitoring data will allow the student to collect data over time to look for trends of improvement and to share self-monitoring information with teachers and/or parents.

Reviewed here are three convenient formats to structure the collection of self-monitoring data and to record the resulting behavioral data--rating scale, checklist, and frequency count (Chafouleas, Riley-Tillman, & Sugai, 2007):

- *Rating scale.* A rating scale consists of one or more items that a student can use to complete a global rating of a corresponding number of behaviors (e.g., "How well did I: (1) stay in my seat?; (2) participate?; (3) avoid distracting others?; (4) follow directions?"). The rating scale usually has a qualitative, sliding-scale rating format (e.g., "poor...fair...good"). Rating scales are typically completed at the conclusion of a fixed observation period (e.g., after a class period; at the end of the school day). See the sample *Behavior Rating Scale* later in this article for an example of how to set up a rating scale to measure student behaviors.

- *Checklist.* A checklist is a listing of behaviors (to be increased or decreased) that the student periodically reviews, checking off those behaviors actually displayed during the monitoring period. For example, a student may have a checklist for independent assignments that contains these 3 work-readiness items: *(1) I have all work materials needed, (2) My desk workspace is organized, (3) I understand the directions of this assignment.* Before beginning independent work, that student reviews and verifies that these preparatory actions have been carried out. Checklists are helpful for monitoring multi-step behaviors (e.g., the plan-write-revise-edit stages of the writing process) or for monitoring clusters of several related behaviors (e.g., as illustrated in the work-readiness example cited above). Investigate the sample *Behavior Checklist* elsewhere in this article as a guide for setting up a behavior checklist.

- *Frequency count.* In a frequency count, the student keeps a running tally of the number of times that he or she displays a target behavior (e.g., number of call-outs or requests for teacher assistance) during an observation period. Check out the example, *Frequency Count,* further on in this article for advice on monitoring the frequency of student behaviors.

3. Choose a Self-Monitoring Schedule

Because self-monitoring requires that the student periodically measure his or her behavior, the teacher and student must decide on what schedule the monitoring will occur (Rafferty, 2010; Webber et al. 1993). Here are options:

- *Start of period or day.* The student monitors at the start of the class period or school day. Sample behaviors suitable for 'start' intervals include arriving to class on time and having all required work materials.

- *End of period or day.* The student monitors at the end of the class period or school day. Sample behaviors suitable for 'end' intervals include copying homework assignments from the board and global ratings of the student's behavior during that classroom period or school day.

- *Scheduled transition points through period or day.* The student monitors periodically during the class period or school day, with each monitoring episode tied to a scheduled, easily identified 'transition point' that naturally occurs in that classroom setting. A common transition point would be the student's moving from one learning activity to another (e.g., from independent seatwork to whole-class lecture). Sample behaviors suitable for 'transition point' intervals include the speed of the student's transition between activities and the student's general behavior during transition periods.

- *Start or end of assignments.* As student academic work is often the focus of self-monitoring, a logical time-point for doing that monitoring is when beginning or finishing assignments. Sample behaviors suitable for 'start of assignments' include checking for the presence of all work materials and clearing the desk to create an uncluttered work space. Sample behaviors suitable for 'end of assignments' include ensuring that a writing assignment is legible and correctly formatted and applying a self-correction checklist to a math assignment to catch and correct common mistakes.

- *Fixed intervals through period or day.* The student monitors at fixed periods during the class period or school day (e.g., every 15 minutes; at the top of each hour). Sample behaviors suitable for 'fixed' intervals include overall classroom behaviors, attention and focus, social interactions with other students, and compliance with adult requests.

4. Decide on a Monitoring Cue.

Once the teacher and student have determined a monitoring schedule, they should decide on a cue to trigger student monitoring (Rafferty, 2010). Below are some options. (Note that most of these cuing methods can either be self-administered by the student or used by the teacher to cue one student, a small group, or even an entire class):

- *'Beep tape'.* The student is given an audio tape (or electronic audio file) with beeps spaced at fixed intervals whose rate matches the student's self-monitoring schedule. For example, a student monitors his on-task behavior every 5 minutes on a self-rating scale using an MP3 player with an audio-file beep tape with tones at 5 minute intervals. NOTE: Schools can download free fixed-interval beep tapes in MP3 format and in a range of interval-lengths from: *http://www.interventioncentral.org/free-audio-monitoring-tapes*

- *Timer.* The student or teacher sets a timer (e.g., kitchen timer, cell-phone timer, stopwatch) for a pre-set interval. When the timer rings, the student self-monitors behavior and then the timer is reset. For example, a student in a math class sets a cell-phone timer with vibration setting for 3-minute intervals during independent work. When the timer rings, the student counts up the number of math-computation problems completed during the interval.

- *Teacher-delivered cue.* The teacher delivers a cue to the student to remind him or her to self-monitor. For example, at the end of an in-class writing assignment, an English instructor prompts the class to review their compositions using self-correction checklists before turning in their work.

- *Student-delivered cue.* The student is given responsibility to initiate self-monitoring informally without use of a timer, beep tape, or other external cue. For example, a student monitoring her understanding of assigned texts during in-class independent reading is directed to use a rating scale at least 3 times during the activity to rate and record her comprehension of the text --with the student determining how to space those self-checks.

5. [Optional] Choose Rewards for Successful Behavior Change.

The teacher may want to choose suitable rewards to further motivate students to use self-monitoring to move toward positive behavior change (Loftin, Gibb, & Skiba, 2005). Teachers can increase the power of a self-monitoring program by rewarding students when they consistently achieve positive ratings. Remember, though, that students differ in what experiences, privileges, or objects they find positively reinforcing. Here are 3 ideas for figuring out what rewards will motivate a particular student:

- *Watch the student in action.* Teachers can often get a very good idea of a student's preferred rewards, or reinforces, simply by observing the student across the school day. The locations where a student chooses to spend time, the people he or she chooses to interact with, and the activities the student engages in all provide hints about what the student finds rewarding. For example, one student may have a friend that he enjoys spending time with, suggesting that the student would view 'free time with a friend of your choice' as a motivating reward. Another student might frequently beg the teacher to be allowed to care for the class mascot, a pet rabbit—presenting the possible reward idea of 'five minutes petting the rabbit'.

- *Ask people who know the student well.* Adults such as parents or past teachers who have interacted with the student regularly for months or years may be able to supply a list of ideas about rewards that will really motivate him or her.

- *Administer a reinforcer survey.* Reinforcer surveys contain a list of possible rewards acceptable for use in a classroom. The teacher meets with the student to review each reinforcer item on the survey, and the student rates whether he or she finds the item to be a motivating reward. The teacher can then create a menu of possible rewards for the student using those reinforcers that the student rated as most motivating. (HINT: Teachers can conveniently create their own customized reinforcer surveys online at this web address: *http://www.interventioncentral.org/teacher-resources/student-rewards-finder.*)

6. Conduct Periodic Accuracy Checks.

Periodically, the teacher should check the student's self-monitoring data and procedures--particularly at the start of the monitoring--to ensure that the student is recording accurately (Webber et al., 1993). Random spot-checks tend to result in higher-quality student self-recording data.

7. Fade the Self-Monitoring Plan.

As the student attains his or her behavioral goals, self-monitoring procedures should be faded--that is, gradually simplified or discontinued (Loftin, Gibb, & Skiba, 2005; Rafferty, 2010). The goals in fading are (1) to streamline self-monitoring so that it becomes sustainable over the long term, while (2) maintaining the student's behavioral gains. Specific methods used in fading will vary, depending on the elements that make up the self-monitoring plan. Fading strategies might include condensing the monitoring format (e.g., distilling a 6-item checklist for monitoring classwork-readiness into a single question: "Am I ready to work?"), changing the monitoring cue (e.g., moving from use of an external beep-tape to student-delivered cues); and monitoring less frequently (e.g., having the student shift down from a daily monitoring schedule to monitoring twice per week on randomly selected days).

References

Chafouleas, S., Riley-Tillman, C., & Sugai, G. (2007). *School-based behavioral assessment: Informing intervention and instruction.* New York: Guilford Press.

Dunlap, G., Clarke, S., Jackson, M., Ramos, E., & Brinson, S. (1995). Self-monitoring of classroom behaviors with students exhibiting emotional and behavioral challenges. *School Psychology Quarterly, 10,* 165-177.

Kazdin, A. E. (1989). *Behavior modification in applied settings* (4th ed.). Pacific Gove, CA: Brooks/Cole.

Loftin, R. L., Gibb, A. C., & Skiba, R. (2005). Using self-monitoring strategies to address behavior and academic issues. *Impact, 18*(2), 12-13. Retrieved from the Web site of the Institute on Community Integration, University of Minnesota (http://ici.umn.edu).

Rafferty, L. A. (2010). Step-by-step: Teaching students to self-monitor. *Teaching Exceptional Children, 43*(2), 50-58.

Webber, J., Scheuermann, B., McCall, C., & Coleman, M. (1993). Research on self-monitoring as a behavior management technique in special education classrooms: A descriptive review. *Remedial & Special Education, 14*(2), 38-56.

Student Name: ____________ Grade/Classroom: ____________

Student Self-Monitoring: **Behavior Rating Scale**

This self-rating scale allows you to rate how well you carry out selected behaviors.

How to Use This Behavior Rating Scale. This scale is to be used to rate your selected behaviors at the end of a pre-determined period (e.g., after independent work; at the end of the school day; at the end of math class.)

How to Set Up the Behavior Rating Scale: Follow these steps to prepare the rating scale:

- *Select Behaviors.* In the left column of the table below, write down up to 6 behavior goals that you plan to rate (e.g., stay in seat, complete seatwork, work well with others, participate in the activity, keep workspace clear).
- *Choose a Schedule for Completing the Rating Scale.* Decide when you will fill out this self-rating scale (e.g., after independent work; at the end of the school day; at the end of math class; just before lunch and again at school dismissal).

  I plan to complete this rating scale on the following schedule:

  ____.

Behaviors: How well did I...	1 Date __/__/__	2 Date __/__/__	3 Date __/__/__	4 Date __/__/__	5 Date __/__/__
•	☐ Good ☐ Fair ☐ Poor	☐ Good ☐ Fair ☐ Poor	☐ Good ☐ Fair ☐ Poor	☐ Good ☐ Fair ☐ Poor	☐ Good ☐ Fair ☐ Poor
•	☐ Good ☐ Fair ☐ Poor	☐ Good ☐ Fair ☐ Poor	☐ Good ☐ Fair ☐ Poor	☐ Good ☐ Fair ☐ Poor	☐ Good ☐ Fair ☐ Poor
•	☐ Good ☐ Fair ☐ Poor	☐ Good ☐ Fair ☐ Poor	☐ Good ☐ Fair ☐ Poor	☐ Good ☐ Fair ☐ Poor	☐ Good ☐ Fair ☐ Poor
•	☐ Good ☐ Fair ☐ Poor	☐ Good ☐ Fair ☐ Poor	☐ Good ☐ Fair ☐ Poor	☐ Good ☐ Fair ☐ Poor	☐ Good ☐ Fair ☐ Poor
•	☐ Good ☐ Fair ☐ Poor	☐ Good ☐ Fair ☐ Poor	☐ Good ☐ Fair ☐ Poor	☐ Good ☐ Fair ☐ Poor	☐ Good ☐ Fair ☐ Poor

Student Name: ______________ Grade/Classroom: ______________

Student Self-Monitoring: **Behavior Checklist**

Behavior checklists are simple way to 'check off' whether or not you carry out selected behaviors.

How to Use This Behavior Checklist. This behavior checklist can be used before starting an activity to ensure that you are prepared (e.g., before beginning independent work) or after the activity (e.g., at the completion of independent work) to track whether you displayed target behaviors. This behavior checklist form allows you to list up to 6 different behaviors. NOTE: Checklists are an excellent tool at the end of an assignment for you to use to check your work.

How to Set Up the Behavior Checklist: Follow these steps to prepare the checklist:

- *List Behaviors to Be Tracked.* In the left column of the table below, write down up to 6 behaviors to make up your checklist. Good checklist items are those that can be easily verified as 'done' or 'not done' (e.g., arrived to class on time; brought all work materials to class; avoided chatting with classmates during independent work time).
- *Choose a Schedule for Completing the Behavior Checklist.* Decide when you will fill out this checklist (e.g., before or after independent work; at the start or end of the school day; before or after math class).

  I plan to complete this behavior checklist on the following schedule:

  ____.

Behaviors: I engaged in these behaviors...	1 Date __/__/__	2 Date __/__/__	3 Date __/__/__	4 Date __/__/__	5 Date __/__/__
•	☐ Yes ☐ No	☐ Yes ☐ No	☐ Yes ☐ No	☐ Yes ☐ No	☐ Yes ☐ No
•	☐ Yes ☐ No	☐ Yes ☐ No	☐ Yes ☐ No	☐ Yes ☐ No	☐ Yes ☐ No
•	☐ Yes ☐ No	☐ Yes ☐ No	☐ Yes ☐ No	☐ Yes ☐ No	☐ Yes ☐ No
•	☐ Yes ☐ No	☐ Yes ☐ No	☐ Yes ☐ No	☐ Yes ☐ No	☐ Yes ☐ No
•	☐ Yes ☐ No	☐ Yes ☐ No	☐ Yes ☐ No	☐ Yes ☐ No	☐ Yes ☐ No

Student Self-Monitoring: **Frequency Count**

A frequency count is a recording of the number of times that a you engaged in a behavior during a specific time-period (e. g., during a class period). Frequency counts can be used to track behaviors that you want to increase or decrease.

How to Use This Frequency-Count Form. With this frequency count form, you record each occurrence of the behavior with a tally-mark ('/'). At the end of the time-period, you add up the tally-marks to get a total sum of behaviors for that observation session.

How to Set Up the Frequency-Count Form: Follow these steps to prepare the frequency-count form:

- *Define the Target Frequency-Count Behavior.* In the space below, describe the behavior that you will measure using a frequency count. (Here are some examples: "leaving my seat without teacher permission", "completing a math problem", "requesting teacher help", "talking with other students about off-task topics"):

  Target Behavior to Measure: _____

- *Choose a Schedule for Conducting the Frequency Count.* Decide when you will use the frequency-count form to track the target behavior:

  I plan to conduct the frequency count at the following time(s) and/or during the following activitie(s):

  _____

1	**Tally Box:** Write a mark ('/') in this box each time the target behavior occurs:		Total Behaviors for Session
Date: ___/___/___		>	

2	**Tally Box:** Write a mark ('/') in this box each time the target behavior occurs:		Total Behaviors for Session
Date: ___/___/___		>	

3	**Tally Box:** Write a mark ('/') in this box each time the target behavior occurs:		Total Behaviors for Session
Date: ___/___/___		>	

4	**Tally Box:** Write a mark ('/') in this box each time the target behavior occurs:		Total Behaviors for Session
Date: ___/___/___		>	

5	**Tally Box:** Write a mark ('/') in this box each time the target behavior occurs:		Total Behaviors for Session
Date: ___/___/___		>	

Grade/Classroom:

Student Name:

How To: Improve Student Self-Management Through Work-Planning Skills—Plan, Work, Evaluate, Adjust

It is no surprise to teachers that, when students have poor work-planning skills, their academic performance often suffers. Work-planning is the student's ability to inventory a collection of related sub-tasks to be done, set specific outcome goals that signify success on each sub-task, allocate time sufficient to carry out each sub-task, evaluate actual work performance, and make necessary adjustments in future work-planning as needed (Martin, Mithaug, Cox, Peterson, Van Dycke & Cash, 2003).. When students are deficient as work planners, the negative impact can be seen on in-class and homework assignments as well as on longer-term projects such as research papers. Teachers can develop students' work-planning skills by training them in a simple but effective sequence: to plan upcoming work, complete the work, evaluate their work performance, and adjust their future work plans based on experience (Martin et al., 2003).

The vehicle for teachers to train students to develop strong work-planning skills is through conferencing: the teacher and student meet for a pre-work *planning* conference and then meet again after the work is completed at a *self-evaluation* conference. NOTE: The *Student Independent Work: Planning Tool* that appears later in this document is a graphic organizer that can be used to structure and record these 2-part teacher-student conferences.

Phase 1: Work-Planning Conference

Before the student begins the assigned academic work, the teacher meets with the student to develop the work plan. (While the teacher often initially assumes a guiding role in the work-planning conference, the instructor gradually transfers responsibility for developing the plan to the student as that student's capacity for planning grows.)

There are 3 sections in the work-planning conference: (1) inventory the sub-tasks to be done, (2) assign an estimated time for completion, and (3) set a performance goal for each item on the task list:

1. *Inventory the sub-tasks to be done.* The student describes each academic task in clear and specific terms (e.g., "Complete first 10 problems on page 48 of math book", "write an outline from notes for history essay"). For this part of the work plan, the teacher may need to model for the student how to divide larger global assignments into component tasks.

2. *Assign an estimated time for completion.* The student decides how much time should be reserved to complete each task (e.g., For a math workbook assignment: "20 minutes" or "11:20 to 11:40"). Because students with limited planning skills can make unrealistic time projections for task completion, the teacher may need to provide additional guidance and modeling in time estimation during the first few planning sessions.

3. *Set a performance goal.* The student sets a performance goal to be achieved for each sub-task. Performance goals are dependent on the student and may reference the amount, accuracy, and/or qualitative ratings of the work: (e.g., for a reading assignment: "To read at least 5 pages from assigned text, and to take notes of the content"; for a math assignment: "At least 80% of problems correct"; for a writing assignment: "Rating of 4 or higher on class writing rubric"). The teacher can assist the student to set specific, achievable goals based on that student's current abilities and classroom curriculum expectations.

Phase 2: Self-Evaluation Conference

When the work has been completed, the teacher and student meet again to evaluate the student's performance. There are 2 sections to this conference: (1) Compare the student's actual performance to the original student goal; and (2) adjust future expectations and performance in light of the experience gained from the recently completed work.

1. *Compare the student's actual performance to the original student goal.* For each sub-task on the plan, the student compares his or her actual work performance to the original performance goal and notes whether the goal was achieved. In addition to noting whether the performance goal was attained, the student evaluates whether the sub-task was completed within the time allocated.

2. *Adjust future expectations and performance.* For each sub-task that the student failed to reach the performance goal within the time allocated, the student reflects on the experience and decides what adjustments to make on future assignments. For example, a student reviewing a homework work-plan who discovers that she reserved insufficient time to complete math word problems may state that, in future, she should allocate at least 30 minutes for similar sub-tasks. Or a student who exceeds his performance goal of no more than 4 misspellings in a writing assignment may decide in future to keep a dictionary handy to check the spelling of questionable words before turning in writing assignments.

References

Martin, J. E., Mithaug, D. E., Cox, P., Peterson, L. Y., Van Dycke, J. L., & Cash, M.E. (2003). Increasing self-determination: Teaching students to plan, work, evaluate, and adjust. *Exceptional Children, 69*, 431-447.

Student Independent Work: Planning Tool

Student: _____ **Teacher/Staff Member:** _____ **Date:** ___/___/___

		Planning	Planning	Planning	Self-Evaluation	Self-Evaluation
	Date:	**Sub-Task:** Describe each assignment sub-task to be completed.	**Time Allocated:** Estimate the time required for this task. E.g., "20 mins"; "11:20-11:40"	**Performance Goal:** Write your goal for the amount, accuracy, and/or quality of work to be completed.	**Actual Performance:** After the assignment, record the amount, accuracy, and/or quality of the work *actually completed.*	**Goal Met?:** Did you achieve the goal within the time allocated?
1	___/___/___					☐ YES ☐ NO
2	___/___/___					☐ YES ☐ NO
3	___/___/___					☐ YES ☐ NO
4	___/___/___					☐ YES ☐ NO

Adjustment: Find any 'NO' responses in the **Goal Met?** column. In the space below, write the number of that goal and your plan to improve on that goal next time.

Number of Goal Not Met & Action Plan to Fix: _____

Number of Goal Not Met & Action Plan to Fix: _____

Number of Goal Not Met & Action Plan to Fix: _____

How To: Model Student Responsibility and Self-Advocacy Through the Student Problem-Solving Conference

Conferences between a student and teacher (or counselor or other educator) are a perfect opportunity for that student to learn how to communicate effectively with school staff, advocate for his or her own educational needs, and assume responsibility for study and schoolwork. Ideally, student conferences should result in an action-plan to fix whatever problems led to the conference.

This worksheet is an organizer that teachers, counselors, and other educators can use to structure a meeting with the student and to develop a student-directed intervention. The framework is flexible. A single teacher, or guidance counselor, or entire instructional team can use the form when conferencing with a student. This form can also be very helpful to structure parent-teacher-student meetings to make them more productive and to document the intervention plans developed there. The meeting agenda puts the focus on the student, who is prompted to define his or her own intervention-outcome goals, and take ownership of some of the ideas selected for the intervention plan.

Below are educator guidelines for helping the student complete 5 sections of the Student Self-Directed Interventions: Planning Sheet (attached). The purpose of each section is explained, with tips for the educator on how to manage that segment of the problem-solving meeting:

Section 1: Defining Your Goals

Student Directions: *Define 1-2 intervention goals that you would like to work on:*

The student is likely to need your assistance to select 1-2 specific goals to be the focus of the intervention. The defined goal(s) may include basic academic skills, cognitive strategies, and/or more general 'academic enabling' skills. NOTE: If the presenting student problem stems from deficits in basic academic skills or cognitive strategies, you may want to review the appropriate reading or math Common Core State Standards for ideas on how to word the goal statement in standards-based form.

Section 2: Selecting Student-Directed Interventions

Student Directions: *List up to 4 strategies that you will take on your own to reach your goal(s).*

The goal is for the student to take initiative in selecting several strategies that he or she is responsible for doing to reach the goal. As you assist the student in selecting and writing down self-help strategies, specify how frequently or under what conditions the student will use each strategy (e.g., "At the start of each class period, the student will review a checklist to ensure that she has all work materials."). The student form also allows you to meet with the student for follow-up sessions and to check off whether he or she is consistently using the self-help strategies. NOTE: The student may need training before he or she can use some strategies independently. Several sample student-directed solutions appear below:

- ☐ Self-monitor preparation for class using a student-created checklist
- ☐ Bring all work materials to class
- ☐ Write complete lecture notes
- ☐ Maintain a clear, uncluttered work space
- ☐ Create a structured work plan before completing larger assignments
- ☐ Complete additional readings to reinforce understanding of course concepts, content
- ☐ Take practice tests to prepare for actual class or state tests

- ☐ Write down homework assignment and double-check for accuracy and completeness before leaving class
- ☐ Ensure that all work materials for homework go home
- ☐ Study course material on a regular review schedule
- ☐ Prepare nightly homework plans, check off completed tasks
- ☐ Use 'self-help' Internet sites (e.g., algebrahelp.com) to find answers to questions

Section 3: Selecting Interventions Supported by Others

Student Directions: *List up to 4 types of assistance that you will obtain from others to reach your goal(s):*

In this section are listed those student supports that require assistance from others. As you help the student to choose and document strategies involving others, specify how frequently or under what conditions the student will use each strategy (e.g., "When the student has a question about lecture content or an assignment, he will bring that question to the teacher during her free period."). The student form also allows you to meet with the student for follow-up sessions and to check off whether he or she is continuing to use these 'other-assisted' strategies. Several sample 'interventions supported by others' appear below:

- ☐ Use teacher-supplied guided notes in class
- ☐ Seek instructor help during free periods
- ☐ Receive tutoring services from peer or adult
- ☐ Be assigned an adult mentor
- ☐ Set up regular 'check-in' sessions with a school staff member to monitor student's intervention follow-through
- ☐ Have the teacher review and sign off on homework assignments written in the student's notebook/course agenda

- ☐ Create a study group with other students
- ☐ Have parent(s) assist as 'homework coaches' to help the student to organize, get started with, and complete homework
- ☐ Meet with the teacher for brief weekly conferences to review course performance (e.g., grades, missing work, etc.)

Section 4: Measuring Progress Toward Your Goals

Student Directions: *Select up to 2 ways that you will measure progress toward your intervention goal(s):*

The task in this section is to select one or more ways that you and the student can track whether the intervention(s) being tried are actually effective in helping the student to achieve his or her goal(s). As you help the student to choose each method for monitoring progress, specify how frequently the data is to be collected (e.g., 'daily', 'weekly', 'after each tutoring session'). The student form also allows you to meet with the student for follow-up sessions and to check off whether the data is being collected consistently. Several sample methods for tracking student progress on intervention appear below:

☐ 'Academic Enabler' Skills Checklist	☐ Homework Log
☐ Behavior Report Card: To be completed by the teacher and/or student	☐ School/Home Note
	☐ Evaluation of Work Products

Section 5: Setting an Intervention 'Check-Up' Date

Directions: *Decide how many instructional weeks your intervention will last. Write in the intervention 'end date' (the calendar date when you will review progress to see if your current intervention plan is effective):*

The student must allocate sufficient time for the intervention to accurately judge whether it is a success. Generally, student interventions should last between 4 and 8 instructional weeks. You can assist the student in both setting a reasonable timespan for the intervention and (by consulting a school calendar) writing down the end-date to mark the conclusion of the intervention.

Student Self-Directed Interventions: Planning Sheet

Student: _____ Date: _____ Teacher/Course: _____

Section 1: Defining Your Goals

Directions: Define 1-2 intervention goals that you would like to work on. Try to be specific.

1	
2	

Section 2: Selecting Student-Directed Interventions

Directions: List up to 4 strategies that you will use on your own to reach your goal(s).	Check-in Date: _____	Check-in Date: _____	Check-in Date: _____
1	Strategy still in use? ☐ Y ☐ N	Strategy still in use? ☐ Y ☐ N	Strategy still in use? ☐ Y ☐ N
2	Strategy still in use? ☐ Y ☐ N	Strategy still in use? ☐ Y ☐ N	Strategy still in use? ☐ Y ☐ N
3	Strategy still in use? ☐ Y ☐ N	Strategy still in use? ☐ Y ☐ N	Strategy still in use? ☐ Y ☐ N
4	Strategy still in use? ☐ Y ☐ N	Strategy still in use? ☐ Y ☐ N	Strategy still in use? ☐ Y ☐ N

Section 3: Selecting Interventions Supported by Others

Directions: List up to 3 types of assistance that you plan to obtain from others to reach your goal(s):	Check-in Date: _____	Check-in Date: _____	Check-in Date: _____
1	Strategy still in use? ☐ Y ☐ N	Strategy still in use? ☐ Y ☐ N	Strategy still in use? ☐ Y ☐ N
2	Strategy still in use? ☐ Y ☐ N	Strategy still in use? ☐ Y ☐ N	Strategy still in use? ☐ Y ☐ N
3	Strategy still in use? ☐ Y ☐ N	Strategy still in use? ☐ Y ☐ N	Strategy still in use? ☐ Y ☐ N

Section 4: Measuring Progress Toward Your Goals

Directions: Select up to 2 ways that you will measure progress toward your intervention goal(s).	Check-in Date: _____	Check-in Date: _____	Check-in Date: _____
1	Monitoring still in use? ☐ Y ☐ N	Monitoring still in use? ☐ Y ☐ N	Monitoring still in use? ☐ Y ☐ N
2	Monitoring still in use? ☐ Y ☐ N	Monitoring still in use? ☐ Y ☐ N	Monitoring still in use? ☐ Y ☐ N

Section 5: Setting an Intervention 'Check-Up' Date

Directions: Decide how many instructional weeks your intervention will last. Write in the intervention 'end date' (the calendar date when you will review progress to see if your current intervention plan is effective):

Number of instructional weeks the intervention will last: _____   End Date: _____/_____/_____

Chapter 8

Using Techniques to Help Teachers Succeed as Change-Agents

The philosopher Lao Tzu once said, "A journey of a thousand miles begins with a single step." He meant, of course, that an undertaking can reach a successful end only if it is actually started. This book has presented a toolkit of procedures and strategies that teachers can use in their classrooms to help students make real academic and behavioral improvements. It is a simple fact, however, that students do not fix themselves; teachers are the catalyst in accomplishing student gains. Teachers must therefore alter their own instructional or behavior-management practices before student behaviors can change or learning can improve.

Yet even well-intentioned teachers frequently fail to make the kinds of changes in their own practice that are necessary to significantly benefit students. This lapse between intention and action is not a problem just in education; examples can be found in other professions and indeed throughout society. The behavioral economist Sendhil Mullainathan calls this the 'last mile' problem: the failure to get the best research-based solutions into the hands of people who can make a difference--and then to have those people use them effectively (Mullainathan, 2010).

There are plenty of good explanations for why teachers may fall short in the quest to become classroom interventionists. And many of the obstacles that they must navigate past to transform themselves into effective change-agents reflect the current reality of schools. For example, a lack of time is often a significant concern. With many students potentially requiring interventions, the teacher may wonder how to manage all of those individual plans. Resources to support interventions (e.g., funds to purchase materials) can also be quite limited. As teachers adopt the role of interventionist, they may also feel the need for additional training in intervention or assessment. While obstacles such as these that reside in the school system can pose a significant challenge, they can usually be managed or overcome with imagination, and collegial and administrative support.

However, the most important factor contributing to the success of classroom interventions is teacher motivation. Simply put, teachers who believe that they can be effective interventionists and are energized to do so are far more likely to attain success than their reluctant colleagues who lack confidence in their ability to carry out that role. The good news for teachers who want to close that last mile and to expand their ability to provide in-class interventions is that they can move from positive intentions to purposeful action by following these 6 motivation-building ideas:

1. *Commit to the mission of classroom intervention.* The initial step in building motivation is to wholly embrace a unifying, energizing principle or belief (Oettingen & Gollwitzer, 2010). The core belief supported by this book is that the teacher can and should assume the role of classroom interventionist. Committing to a core belief does not imply that the teacher ignores obvious obstacles to implementation. For example, there can be commitment to the interventionist role even as there is recognition that scheduling interventions will be a difficult task. Rather, committing to a core belief means that the educator reflects on that belief and explicitly accepts it as a guiding and motivating principle.

2. *Add interventionists to your social network.* The attitudes and actions of the people with whom we regularly interact (our social networks) tend to influence our own behaviors—often profoundly. Research indicates, for example, that individuals' weight and smoking status can be predicted based on the characteristics of other

members of their social networks (Bahr, Browning, Wyatt, & Hill, 2009; Christakis & Fowler, 2008). There is evidence that, like most people, teachers tend to form natural social networks with professional colleagues based primarily on proximity and perceived personal similarities such as age or family characteristics (Coburn, Mata & Choi, 2013; McPherson, Smith-Lovin, & Cook, 2001). However, teachers can access motivating social support to help them transition into an interventionist role by making a point to find and regularly network with other teachers who share their interest in classroom intervention. In an Internet age, of course, such connections can occur through email or social media sites as well as in person.

3. *Set manageable starting goals.* The role of classroom interventionist has many components. A teacher must be able, for example, to clearly define student academic and behavioral problems, to develop a bank of research-based intervention ideas to address common classroom concerns, to document student intervention plans, and so forth. Educators who try to roll out all elements of classroom intervention at once run the risk of finding themselves quickly overwhelmed. One motivational strategy, then, is to set more modest, manageable initial goals for changing one's classroom practice and then to build on that success (Oettingen & Gollwitzer, 2010).

   For example, a 6th-grade teacher, Ms. Foster, selects as a goal that she will conduct a classroom reading-fluency intervention for a single student over the next two months, to include documentation and the collection of progress-monitoring data. She is able to integrate this pilot intervention easily into her instructional routine— and she also gains valuable insight into how to set up and implement interventions that will allow her then to set incrementally more ambitious goals to provide interventions to multiple students.

4. *Envision success—and contrast with the present situation.* Teachers can boost their motivation to make a specific change to their professional practice by envisioning

the future benefits that would result from such a change, contrasting those benefits with the current situation, and then enumerating the steps or actions needed to move from the status quo to the proposed change-state (Oettingen & Gollwitzer, 2010). This 'mental contrasting' of future and present states provides the teacher with a roadmap for implementation. Just as important, the very act of concretely imagining the steps required to reach the desired goal is motivational as it makes that goal appear more attainable.

For example, a 4th-grade teacher, Mr. Sterlitz, wishes to institute a classwide peer tutoring program for math computation with constant time delay (one of the academic intervention resources discussed in chapter 3). He first envisions having the program fully in place and imagines the following benefits: students will drill more intensively on math facts; will be fully engaged in the collaborative activity; and will make accelerated progress in math computation skills. The teacher next contrasts the future program with drawbacks of the present situation: students currently get little practice on math facts; often appear unmotivated to work on math activities; and make only marginal progress to build math computation skills. Mr. Sterlitz then contemplates each of the steps needed to transform the present situation into the future desired state: e.g., prepare student tutoring folders; create student tutor pairs; train students in the tutoring procedures, etc.

5. *Create implementation work-plans.* Once an appropriate starter goal has been defined and a scenario for successful implementation has been envisioned, the teacher is ready to break that more general goal into a work-plan that includes a listing of specific sub-tasks along with associated timelines and expected outcomes. After implementation, the teacher can review the plan, evaluate outcomes and make future adjustments as necessary to strengthen the intervention process. If the work-plan process described here appears familiar, this may be because it was first presented as a student self-regulation strategy (Martin et al., 2003) in chapter 7 of

this book: *How To: Improve Student Self-Management Through Work-Planning Skills: Plan, Work, Evaluate, Adjust.* Readers may find that section's work-planning form to be a useful tool for structuring their own implementation plans.

6. *Anticipate obstacles and generate solutions.* As teachers tinker with their instructional and behavior-management practices to take on the role of classroom interventionist, they are almost sure to encounter some degree of difficulty. When unexpected, such hindrances have the potential to drain motivation and momentum. However, teachers who anticipate potential roadblocks and generate responses to handle them are more likely both to maintain motivation and to weather the inevitable setbacks in reaching their eventual goal (Oettingen & Gollwitzer, 2010). A convenient format for anticipating obstacles and describing their solutions is through use of "if/then" statements (i.e., **if** a particular problem arises, **then** the teacher will adopt a particular solution).

Returning to the earlier implementation example to illustrate, Mr. Sterlitz generates a list of several difficulties that could arise in starting a math tutoring program in his 4th-grade classroom. A particular concern is that students will not take the program seriously but will instead use the tutoring time to interact socially. Mr. Sterlitz generates possible solutions by framing that concern as an "If/then" statement: "**If** students start to socialize during tutoring sessions, **then** I will reteach the rules of tutoring, remind students of expected behaviors before each tutoring session, publicly praise students who are engaged in tutoring, promptly redirect off-task students back to task, and reshuffle tutoring pairs if necessary."

When Mahatma Gandhi said, "You must be the change you wish to see in the world," he could well have been describing teachers. Educators who are able to 'be the change'—to positively shift their professional behaviors in ways suggested in this book—can expect to be rewarded by seeing improvements in their own practice passed along as gains in student learning and behavior.

References

Bahr, D. B. Browning, R. C., Wyatt, H. R., & Hill, J. O. (2009). Exploiting social networks to mitigate the obesity epidemic. *Obesity*, 17, 723-728.

Coburn, C. E., Mata, W. S., & Choi, L. (2013). The embeddedness of teachers' social networks: Evidence from a study of mathematics reform. *Sociology of Education,* 86, 311-342.

Christakis, N. A., & Fowler, J. H. (2008). The collective dynamics of smoking in a large social network. *The New England Journal of Medicine,* 358(21), 2249-2258.

Martin, J. E., Mithaug, D. E., Cox, P., Peterson, L. Y., Van Dycke, J. L., & Cash, M.E. (2003). Increasing self-determination: Teaching students to plan, work, evaluate, and adjust. *Exceptional Children,* 69, 431-447.

McPherson, M., Smith-Lovin, L., & Cook, J. M. (2001). Birds of a feather: Homophily in social networks. *Annual Review of Sociology,* 27, 415-444.

Mullainathan, S. (2010, February). *Solving social problems with a nudge* [Video file]. Retrieved from http://www.ted.com/talks/sendhil_mullainathan.html

Oettingen, G., & Gollwitzer, P. M. (2010). Strategies of setting and implementing goals. In J. E. Maddux & J. P. Tangney (Eds.), *Social psychological foundations of clinical psychology.* (pp. 114-135). New York: The Guilford Press.

RESOURCES

For current books related to both *Common Core State Standards (CCSS)* and *Response To Intervention (RTI)*, please go to the National Professional Resources, Inc. web site at: www.NPRinc.com

Any of the books on this site as well as an array of the ***Laminated Reference Guides*** listed below may be ordered through our web site or by calling 1-800-453-7461

- *ADHD & LD: Strategies At Your Fingertips,* by Sandra Rief
- *Brain Compatible Classroom,* by Pat Wolfe
- *Character Matters: In Classrooms, at School, at Home,* by Edward DeRoche
- *Classroom Management: A Guide for Elementary Teachers,* by Kenneth Shore, Psy.D.
- *CCSS & ELL (Common Core State Standards & English Language Learners,* by Estee Lopez, Ed.D.
- *CCSS & UDL,* by Joseph Casbarro, Ph.D.
- *Common Core: Step-by-Step Approach—ELA,* by Toby Karten
- *Common Core: Step-by-Step Approach—Math,* by Toby Karten
- *Common Core Standards: ELA—Unique Practices for Inclusive Classrooms,* by Toby Karten
- *Common Core Standards: Math—Unique Practices for Inclusive Classrooms,* by Toby Karten
- *Curriculum Based Measurement,* by John & Michelle Hosp
- *Data Literacy for Teachers,* by Nancy Love
- *ELLs: Thinking Skills & the CCSS,* by Estee Lopez, Ed.D.
- *Executive Function: Practical Applications,* by Sandra Rief

- *Formative Assessment (Elementary),* by Nancy Frey & Douglas Fisher
- *IEPs and the CCSS: Specially Designed Instructional Strategies*, by Toby Karten
- *Multiple Intelligences: Pathways to Success,* by Thomas Hoerr
- *RTI (Response To Intervention),* by Joseph Casbarro, Ph.D.
- *RTI & DI,* by Helene M. Hanson
- *RTI & Classroom Behaviors,* by Jim Wright
- *RTI & ELLs (English Language Learners),* by Seth Aldrich
- *RTI & Math: The Elementary Essentials,* by Karen A. Kemp
- *RTI & Reading: The Elementary Essentials,* by Karen A. Kemp
- *RTI & Socio-Economically Disadvantaged Students,* by Angel Barrett
- *School Climate: Building Safe, Supportive, and Engaging Classrooms and Schools,* by Johnathan Cohen & Maurice Elias
- *Skillful Inquiry/Data Team,* by Nancy Love
- *Social, Emotional and Character Development: For Teachers, For Students, For Parents,* by Ed Dunkelblau, Ph.D.

About the Author

Jim Wright is a well-known trainer and consultant to schools and organizations on a broad range of topics relating to school improvement. A certified school psychologist, he was a school administrator in central New York State for over 17 years.

Wright's areas of expertise are Response To Intervention (RTI), the Common Core State Standards (CCSS), and academic/behavioral interventions and assessments for struggling students. He has worked with a variety of schools in New York and other parts of the country, helping them both to map out steps for improving their educational practices and to motivate their staff to support those positive changes.

Wright is the creator of Intervention Central (www.intervention central.org), a popular website with free intervention and assessment resources for educators in grades K-12. He is the author of the books, *RTI Toolkit: A Practical Guide for Schools* and *RTI Success in Secondary Schools: A Toolkit for Middle and High Schools*, as well as *RTI Data Collection Forms & Organizer (Elementary & secondary versions)* and the laminated reference guide, *RTI & Classroom Behaviors,* all published by National Professional Resources, Inc./Dude Publishing.

He is also the featured presenter on the video, *The Power of RTI: Classroom Management Strategies.*